Women Writing War

Women Writing War
Ireland 1880–1922

edited by

TINA O'TOOLE,

GILLIAN McINTOSH

and

MUIREANN O'CINNÉIDE

UNIVERSITY COLLEGE DUBLIN PRESS

PREAS CHOLÁISTE OLLSCOILE
BHAILE ÁTHA CLIATH

First published 2016
by University College Dublin Press
UCD Humanities Institute, Room H103
Belfield
Dublin 4
Ireland
www.ucdpress.ie

ISBN 978-1-910820-11-7

Cataloguing in publication data available from the British Library

Typeset in UK in Plantin and Fournier by Ryan Shiels
Text design by Lyn Davies
Printed on acid-free paper in England by
Antony Rowe, Chippenham, Wilts.

This publication was grant-aided by the NUI Galway Grant-in-Aid-of-Publication
and by the National University of Ireland's Grant towards Scholarly Publications.

For Patricia Coughlan

Contents

Acknowledgements

This collection is the result of a collaborative research project between colleagues at the University of Limerick, NUI Galway, and Queen's University Belfast, and a wider transnational group of scholars in the field. The editors would like to thank Drs Breda Gray and Niamh Reilly, convenors of the UL-NUIG Gender ARC, who facilitated and funded the initial research workday in 2011 and our 2012 conference, 'Women, War and Letters', held at UL. We would also like to acknowledge the enthusiastic support of Professor Meg Harper and Dr Yvonne O'Keeffe in organising both events, and the vital participation of everyone who presented papers and took part in the research conversation. The development of this collection has benefited hugely from that generous exchange of ideas.

Our contributors to this collection have been a joy to work with; we are privileged to have had the benefit of your scholarship and professionalism in working on this book.

We thank the National University of Ireland and NUI Galway for grants in aid of publication. We acknowledge too the ready support of UCD Press, particularly Noelle Moran, Damien Lynam, and everyone who has worked on the book.

We acknowledge the permission of Penguin Ireland to include a short extract from Lia Mill's novel, *Fallen* (2014); we thank Lia and Brendan Barrington for this.

In obtaining permissions to reproduce photographs and other visuals, the editors would like to acknowledge the help, in particular, of Mairéad McMullan (Feis na nGleann committee), Ruth Hegarty (Royal Irish Academy) and Lucy McDiarmid (Westmont College), whose encouragement and intrepid sleuthing were invaluable when it came to tracing copyright holders. We express our warm thanks to Eitne O'Brien McKeown and Órla McKeown for their permission to use their family photograph of the wonderful Annie Cooney as one of our cover images.

Preface

Feminist scholarship has been one of the most noteworthy features of the Decade of Commemorations. There is a hunger to know more and, thankfully, a new generation of researchers with the skills and the ambition to uncover new material. *Women Writing War* is a very welcome addition, crossing the disciplines of literature and history, using innovative methodologies to shed new light on the familiar while also providing us with new material and new heroines. We encounter radicals, revolutionaries and queer activists, as well as women who remained attached to the domestic sphere.

Using little known or completely unknown texts, the contributors to this volume have not only brought to light many unjustly forgotten women, they have also demonstrated how much can be gleaned from intelligent, ideologically aware analysis of literary sources. In so doing, they provide us, collectively, with a multi-layered, intersectional portrayal of women who sought to make a difference to the society in which they lived. Through their various experiences as women living in turbulent times, we gain new ways of understanding those times.

There are many riches in this material. In the present period, with male heroism in the First World War much lauded, the poetry of Winifred Letts is a welcome corrective. She used her experience of nursing war-wounded in England to write poems that explore themes of grief and loss. The 'Deserter', challenging the heroic image of war, deserves much wider recognition. Peggie Kelly, a Cumann na mBan activist who wrote under the pseudonym 'Garrett O'Driscoll' should be republished with an acknowledgement of her importance in the literary canon of Irish political struggle.

A number of 'New Women' are explored in contributions touching on aspects of Irish women's political involvement from the late nineteenth century. Ulster is included, in a fascinating account of Glens of Antrim women from Protestant ascendancy backgrounds who were as important to the cultural revival as the better-known Francis Joseph Bigger in Belfast. In many attempts at retrieval and restoration, however, the paucity of material remains a source of frustration. For example, although Casement's letters survive, preserved by the recipients, few of the women's letters to him remain in existence. This makes the art of careful reading of material even more necessary, and contributors to this volume have succeeded admirably in this achievement.

Many contributors concern themselves with various aspects of women's participation in this period of revolutionary struggle. Agnes O'Farrelly, often criticised for her speech at the inaugural meeting of Cumann na mBan, is restored as a fully rounded historical figure. Eva Gore-Booth, commonly contrasted with her sister, Constance Markievicz, as a pacifist who rejected the actions of the republican combatants, is revealed as a much more ambiguous and subversive figure. While women activists did not write directly about sexuality, astute attention to the small details of their witness statements reveals much about how the body was viewed, particularly in the pressures and forced intimacies of war conditions.

Perceptions of what is normal or conventional are questioned in these contributions. From the Land Wars, the Boer Wars, the Cultural Revival to the Easter Rising and subsequent War of Independence, women were involved in a variety of ways. They challenged institutions and conventions and worked to make a better world. In this volume we experience the destabilising of boundaries while we are led to reconsider what we already know, learning more along the way. As we develop what is becoming a 'critical mass' of gender-focused material, no one can say that women were not involved in every aspect of Ireland's revolutionary past. From the evidence, not only were they there, but their conception of revolution was all-encompassing, full of generosity and compassion. *Women Writing War* is a thought-provoking, often exhilarating volume that succeeds in correcting the commonplace while also considerably extending our knowledge.

MARGARET WARD

Contributors to this Volume

JODY ALLEN RANDOLPH teaches Irish drama for the University of California, Berkeley and is currently an Adjunct Associate Professor at University College Dublin. Her recent publications include *A Poet's Dublin*, co-edited with Paula Meehan (2014), *Eavan Boland* (2013), and *Close to the Next Moment* (2010). Her *Critical Companion* on Eavan Boland was published by Carcanet Press in 2007 and W. W. Norton in 2008. She has edited or co-edited special issues on Derek Mahon (*Irish University Review* 1994), Michael Longley (*Colby Quarterly* 2003), Paula Meehan (*An Sionnach* 2009), and Eavan Boland (*PN Review* 2014). With Maureen Murphy and Briona Nic Dhiarmida, she is at work on a critical companion on Nuala Ní Dhomhnaill.

LUCY COLLINS is a lecturer in English literature at University College Dublin, Ireland. Educated at Trinity College Dublin and Harvard University, where she spent a year as a Fulbright Scholar, she teaches and researches in the area of modern poetry and poetics. She has published widely on modern and contemporary Irish and British poetry. Recent publications include *Poetry by Women in Ireland: A Critical Anthology 1870–1970* (2014) and an edition of the poems of Sheila Wingfield (2013). She co-edited a volume, *The Irish Poet and the Natural World: An Anthology of Verse in English from the Tudors to the Romantics* which appeared in March 2014.

HEIDI HANSSON is Professor of English literature at Umeå University, Sweden. Her main research interest is women's literature, and she has previously published in the fields of postmodern romance, nineteenth-century women's cross-gendered writing, Irish women's literature and northern studies. Among her works on Irish topics are a full-length examination of the nineteenth-century writer Emily Lawless, *Emily Lawless 1845–1913: Writing the Interspace* (2007), the edited collection *New Contexts: Re-Framing Nineteenth-Century Irish Women's Prose* (2008) and *Fictions of the Irish Land War* (2014), edited together with Professor James H. Murphy.

LUCY MCDIARMID is Marie Frazee-Baldassarre Professor of English at Montclair State University. The recipient of fellowships from the Guggenheim Foundation, the Cullman Center for Scholars and Writers at the New York Public Library, and the National Endowment for the Humanities, she is the author or editor of seven books. Her scholarly interest in cultural politics, especially colourful and suggestive episodes, is exemplified by *The Irish Art of Controversy* as well as by *Poets and the Peacock Dinner: The Literary History of a Meal*. She is also a former president of the American Conference for Irish Studies. Her most recent book *At Home in the Revolution: What Women Said and Did in 1916*, was published by the Royal Irish Academy in 2015.

GILLIAN McINTOSH is a social and cultural historian, with an eclectic interest in the history of the north of Ireland. She has published widely on rituals, symbolism, urban life, the arts and broadcasting. Her publications include *The Force of Culture: Unionist Identities in Twentieth Century Ireland* (1999), *Belfast City Hall: One Hundred Years* (2006), and *Irish Women at War* (2010; co-edited with Diane Urquhart). In addition to chapters in edited collections, she has journal essays in *Irish Historical Studies, Jewish Culture and History, Urban History, New Hibernia Review* and most recently an article on Tyrone Guthrie at the BBC in Northern Ireland in the 1920s which appeared in the 2015 *Éire-Ireland* special issue on broadcasting in Ireland.

LIA MILLS is a novelist, short story writer, and essayist. Her first novel *Another Alice* (1996) was nominated for the *Irish Times* Irish Fiction Prize. Her second novel *Nothing Simple* (2005) was shortlisted for the Irish Book Awards Irish Novel of the Year. Her memoir *In Your Face* (2007) was named as a favourite book of 2007 by several critics and writers. Her latest novel *Fallen* (2014) is set in Dublin during the First World War and the Easter Rising and was the Dublin: One City One Book choice for 2016.

RÍONA NIC CONGÁIL is a lecturer in the Irish Department of St Patrick's College, Drumcondra (DCU), Ireland. Her academic interests include Irish-language literature, women's history and children's studies. Her first monograph, *Úna Ní Fhaircheallaigh agus an Fhís Útóipeach Ghaelach*, was published in 2010 and received an Oireachtas Award and the ACIS Prize for Research Book of the Year in the Irish Language. She has edited two collections of essays on Irish-language children's literature and culture, published in 2012 and 2013. She has recently been awarded an IRC ELEVATE International Career Development Fellowship to the University of York, UK.

MUIREANN O'CINNÉIDE is a lecturer in English at NUI Galway, Ireland where she is programme director for the MA in Culture and Colonialism. She is the author of *Aristocratic Women and the Literary Nation, 1832–1868* (2008) with Palgrave Macmillan, and has edited two volumes (2013–14) in the Pickering and Chatto *Selected Works of Margaret Oliphant* series. She is currently working and publishing on empire, women's travel writing and imperial conflict narratives.

MAUREEN O'CONNOR is lecturer in English at University College Cork, Ireland. She is the author of *The Female and the Species: The Animal in Irish Women's Writing* (2010); editor of *Back to the Future of Irish Studies: Festschrift for Tadhg Foley* (2010); and co-editor with Kathryn Laing and Sinéad Mooney of *Edna O'Brien: New Critical Perspectives* (2006), with Lisa Colletta of *Wild Colonial Girl: Essays on Edna O'Brien* (2006), and with Tadhg Foley of *Ireland and India: Colonies, Culture, and Empire* (2006).

TINA O'TOOLE is a lecturer in English at the University of Limerick, Ireland. Her publications include *The Irish New Woman* (2013), *Irish Literature: Feminist Perspectives* (2008; co-edited with Patricia Coughlan), *Documenting Irish Feminisms* (2005; co-authored with Linda Connolly), and *The Dictionary of Munster Women Writers* (2005). Her journal publications include a special issue of *Éire-Ireland* 2012 on 'Irish Migrancies' (co-edited with Piaras Mac Éinrí), and essays in *Modernism/Modernity, New Hibernia Review,* and *Irish University Review,* among others.

DIANE URQUHART is a reader in modern Irish history at the Institute of Irish Studies of the University of Liverpool, UK. She has published widely on women, political activism and legislative reform. She is the author of *The Ladies of Londonderry: Women and Political Patronage, 1800–1959* (2008) and *Women in Ulster Politics, 1890–1940: A History Not Yet Told* (2007). She is the editor of *The Papers of the Ulster Women's Unionist Council and Executive Committee, 1911–40* (2001) and co-editor of *Irish Women at War: The Twentieth Century* (2010); *Irish Women's History* (2004); *The Irish Women's History Reader* (2000) and *Coming into the Light: The Work, Politics and Religion of Women in Ulster, 1840–1940* (1994). Diane is currently completing a history of Irish divorce.

MARGARET WARD is a feminist historian. Her book *Unmanageable Revolutionaries: Women and Irish Nationalism* was first published in 1983 and it has been an influential study of the role of women in political movements in Ireland. Other works include biographies of Maud Gonne and Irish suffragist Hanna Sheehy-Skeffington. In 2014 she was awarded an honorary Doctor of Laws by Ulster University for her contribution to advancing women's equality. Margaret is currently Visiting Fellow in History at Queen's University Belfast and is editing the political writings of Hanna Sheehy-Skeffington (forthcoming) as a contribution to the centenary celebration of women's enfranchisement in 1918.

List of Illustrations

Every effort has been made to trace and obtain the permission of copyright holders of images used in this book. If there are any omissions, UCD Press will be pleased to insert the appropriate acknowledgement in any subsequent printing or edition.

Introduction

Tina O'Toole, Gillian McIntosh and Muireann O'Cinnéide

This volume investigates the ways in which women's writing in and about Ireland conceptualises conflict in the period 1880–1922. Its main focus is on literary and cultural rather than primarily historical readings of the period. In Ireland, ancient and modern conflicts have a visible presence in the culture, remembered in song and story, and referenced in continuing endeavours to resolve deep-rooted political divides. Despite this, with some notable exceptions, literary expressions of war have been somewhat neglected in Irish scholarship. Moreover, the absence of women's literary work in the scholarship available is indicative of a more general tendency to ignore historical instances of Irish women's political activism and engagement in military arenas. Such occlusion creates the misconception that women were not writing about or involved in revolutionary activism in Ireland, or that Irish women's lives were untouched by international wars in the period. The chapters in this volume provide clear evidence to the contrary, uncovering the work of a range of women who were active cultural producers and agents, deeply invested in the political and military struggles of their day. These women grapple with the experiential representation of conflicts from the Land Wars to the Boer Wars, from the First World War to the Easter Rising, the War of Independence and the Civil War. Furthermore, by engaging with recent theoretical expansion of the relationships between women and conflict, the volume explores ways in which conflict narratives have been read – and productively re-read – as deeply gendered.

As we write, centenary commemorations of the 1916 Easter Rising are under way across the island in the form of official state-run events and activities organised by local communities, museums, arts bodies, libraries, and educational institutions on a range of different platforms. This moment is part of the Decade of Centenaries, a series of commemorations remembering key historic events in the 1912–22 period, such as the signing of the Solemn League and Covenant, the Dublin Strike and Lockout, the First World War, as well as the 1916 Rising, War of Independence, and Civil War. These anniversaries provide us all with the opportunity to take stock, to assess received ideas about the period, and to explore new evidence recently uncovered. For instance, the digitisation of the Bureau of Military History witness statements (launched in 2012), provides searchable access to diverse perspectives on the 1916 Rising; these are only now making their way into published accounts of the period. New critical approaches are providing scholars with opportunities to re-evaluate the alterity of that revolutionary period; this is apparent, for instance, in recent interventions like the The Casement Project (funded by the national Arts Council), which 'dances with the queer body of British peer, Irish rebel and international humanitarian, Roger Casement' (see fearghus.net/projects/the-casement-project/).

On the whole, however, state-sponsored commemorative events often tend to simplify the past and thereby reinforce particular myths of origin, and conceptions of national adherence or identity. Such events can still become highly visible sites of ongoing contestation, as Gearóid Ó Tuathaigh notes of Northern Ireland (Ó Tuathaigh 143). Yet even as the legacies of past and ongoing conflicts explicitly shape commemorative discourse in both states on the island, the contested relationships between gender, nation, and the politics of memory can often prove all too easy to disregard. This became particularly apparent, for instance, during recent debates about the Abbey Theatre's 'Waking the Nation' 2016 commemorative programme.[1] In a year-long schedule of events supported by substantial state funding, the commemorative programme announced only one woman playwright.[2] Following the programme launch, a vibrant social media campaign, started by set designer and arts manager Lian Bell (using the hashtag #Waking TheFeminists), criticised the theatre's management and board; as a result, the commemorative programme attracted adverse national and international media coverage. A grassroots organisation sprang up, comprising arts practitioners in Ireland and abroad, who took the exclusion of women from this centenary programme as a starting point and who went on to use the opportunity to highlight a general invisibility of women's writings, experiences, and bodies on the Irish stage. Ultimately, a widely publicised (and oversubscribed) gathering hosted by the Abbey's director, Fiach Mac Conghail, was held in the theatre and agreement was reached that a more inclusive programme be (re)drafted for the second half of 2016.

Arguably, the publicity generated by #WakingTheFeminists at the end of 2015, by drawing attention to women's part in the founding of the Abbey Theatre and in the Literary Revival, underscored women's active participation in the revolutionary period. At a point when a considerable number of community groups and national organisations were preparing their own centenary programmes for 2016, such widespread public outcry about the Abbey programme resulted in a noticeable effort to recover and promote women's stories at the heart of the Decade of Centenaries' narrative. Crucially, the reintroduction of women's voices in Irish commemorative programmes in 2016 provides a wider-reaching opportunity to *change* the war story, and to reassess ideological constructions through which the political struggles of the period have been conceptualised, whether nationally or transnationally.

Such an extraordinary memory lapse about equal representation is not just an Irish problem of course; women's experience and active participation in armed struggle are consistently ignored or rendered invisible. Cooke and Woollacott describe 'the historical constructedness of the war story that must eliminate the feminine to survive' (Cooke and Woollacott ix). Lucy Collins's chapter in this volume challenges this construction, legitimating the capacity of women writers to bear witness to war and its devastating consequences. Her research uncovers the war work and published writing of a participant in the First World War Winifred Letts. Achieving early recognition as a Revival playwright, Letts is today best known for her war poetry, which drew on her experiences as a Red Cross nurse. Contextualising her work in relation to those high profile 'soldier poets' whose direct exposure to combat during the First World War freighted their literary work with moral authority, Collins shows how Letts's poetry often strikes an ambivalent note, which both troubles and sustains heroic war efforts. This brings to mind Cynthia Enloe's discussion of the interrelationship between conflict, complicity, and citizenship in women's involvement in war.[3]

That subsequent patrilineal plotting fixed women in place in twentieth-century Irish culture is especially ironic given the opening up of gendered spaces in Irish society at the turn of the twentieth century, not to mention the interrogation of fixed ideas about militarisms and masculinities in the writing of the period. Lucy McDiarmid's work brings these issues home by foregrounding women's bodily experiences of the 1916 Rising in Dublin. Irish militant nationalists and feminists populate this chapter, which draws on eyewitness accounts from women involved in the 1916 conflict at every level. By attending to the details of their lives in their own words, McDiarmid's work demonstrates how these women caught up in conflict zones operate at the level of the body. She lays bare their strategies for countering violence and sexual harassment, while offering shelter and solidarity to their comrades, and to other women, in situations of conflict and lawlessness. Ultimately, McDiarmid's analysis of these stories reveals the extent to which the human body has tended to be silenced or decentred in mainstream narratives of war.

Across this volume we can see the recurring motif of the female body made physically vulnerable by the distinctively contained spatial dynamics of localised warfare, whether it be the potential exposure to crowd violence of figures such as Anna Parnell or Anne Blunt on public platforms during the agitation meetings of the Land Wars, or the women of Cumann na mBan facing the bodily threats posed by street violence, home invasion or imprisonment during the 1916 Rising, the War of Independence and the

Civil War. In repositioning women's bodies within Irish conflict history as exposed to potential violence, it is important that we do not de-historicise these bodies, or deny the potential bodily complexities offered by gender identities or by distinctive modes of sexual and romantic experience. Ana Carden-Coyne, arguing that the First World War brought the body as wounded and pained to the fore of cultural responses to conflict, sees it as creating a demand 'that written language and visual representation bridge the gap between the sufferer and the witness' (Carden-Coyne, *Politics of Wounds* 17). While the cultural iconography of the era focused predominantly on the wounded male body, these discourses opened up spaces for the representation of women's empathetic sensory pain: 'the politics of wounds', Carden-Coyne notes, 'is a personal and social inter-dynamic' (Carden-Coyne, *Politics of Wounds* 18). Reviving long-disregarded narratives of women's direct participation in and experience of conflict should not lead us to dismiss the physiological and epistemic damage inflicted through more ideological or distanced experiential participations in warfare.

Bringing to light another trove of hidden narratives, Jody Allen Randolph's essay enlivens the wartime experiences and publications of Peggie (Margaret) Kelly. A teenage member of Cumann na mBan, Peggie was active in military circles in the period following the 1916 Rising, during which time she maintained an active writing life. Her novel *Noreen*, set during the Rising, won a prestigious 1924 Tailteann Games prize for fiction. However, the capacity to conceal her guerrilla activities and melt away into the night had a detrimental effect on her lasting reputation as a writer and activist; Peggie Kelly left few traces. But for the accident of biography, the family connection to Eavan Boland, and the assiduous work of Allen Randolph, her story would remain hidden, like that of so many other Irish women of this period.

While Winifred Letts's name is sometimes remembered today in anthologies of war poetry, those women described in McDiarmid's and Allen Randolph's chapters here have been 'hidden from history', to use Sheila Rowbotham's term. Those few Irish women warriors who *are* remembered today have assumed iconographic, quasi-mythological status, think of Constance Markievicz and Maud Gonne for instance, rendered exceptional by virtue of their class or associations with prominent men. Annette Weber describes this tendency to portray such women as 'temporary transgressors' which means that fixed binaries in our construction of the past are not disrupted (Weber 7). This flies in the face of clear evidence detailing women's active engagement during the Irish revolutionary period; Margaret Ward's groundbreaking study, *Unmanageable Revolutionaries* was published in 1983, and subsequent research by Sinéad McCoole, Senia Pašeta, Lucy McDiarmid, and Roy Foster, for instance, augments our picture of women's involvement in the national struggle. Moreover, focusing on romantic warrior figures like the 'Rebel Countess' detracts from the, arguably, more important work carried out in the late nineteenth and twentieth centuries by women writers working to change ideological and cultural structures and thereby ensure that the work of revolution was sustainable.

The work of radical women writers and Irish-language activists are revealed in a number of the chapters here. For instance, the subject of Ríona Nic Congáil's contribution, Irish-language scholar and nationalist activist, Úna Ní Fhaircheallaigh (Agnes O'Farrelly) (1874–1951), commanded a central position in the political and intellectual life of early twentieth-century Ireland. A founding member of Cumann na mBan and a leading figure of the Gaelic League, Ní Fhaircheallaigh was appointed lecturer in Irish at UCD in 1908, she was part of a newly emerging generation of Irish intellectuals in twentieth-century Ireland. Likewise, in her chapter on the 'New Woman' writers of the period, Tina O'Toole argues for the influence of writers working through literary coteries and language associations in the creation of a cultural nationalist impetus at the turn of the twentieth century. Focusing on a coterie located in the Glens of Antrim, O'Toole shows how the work of northern Protestant writers and educators including Rose Young, Ada McNeill, Margaret Dobbs, Margaret Hutton, Alice Milligan, and later, Alice Stopford Green and Gertrude Bannister, created a vibrant context for the nationalist movement in the north-east of Ireland. Their close ties to and ongoing exchange of letters with Roger Casement, lent a transnational aspect to their activism. These influences came to the fore during their key intervention, the 1904 Feis na nGleann (Glens Festival) which celebrated key elements in the emerging nationalist movement of the day, including arts and crafts initiatives, Irish-language activism, a promotion of local industries, and the involvement of the co-operative movement.

While this discussion of women's war writing has so far focused on the twentieth century, the broad scope of this volume, which takes 1880 as its starting point, facilitates a longer and more internationalised view of women writers' engagement with conflict. Late nineteenth-century Irish feminist discourse and solidarity emerged from what may seem an unlikely place, an agrarian social movement, and the first two chapters in this book offer alternate perspectives on that movement, the Land War. The Ladies' Land League was the first Irish nationalist organisation to be managed at all levels by women, placing women on the political platform and at the centre of public discourse. Diane Urquhart's chapter on the rhetoric of the Ladies' Land League's British campaign between 1881–2, shows how the British press was crucial in shaping the perceptions of this conflict, for both a domestic and an American audience. Central to this story of women's activism is of course Anna Parnell; her distaste for England and the English is striking in this chapter, it certainly did not diminish over time. Ultimately, she was optimistic neither about female enfranchisement nor for Ireland's future in the hands of men: 'There is no reason,' she wrote, 'to suppose the men in possession of the stage in 1917, will be any better than those who possess it in 1893.'

The next chapter by Muireann O'Cinnéide provides a close reading of another woman whose story intersects with that of the Land War: traveller, writer and Arabian horse breeder, Lady Anne Blunt. Her violent experience at a banned Land League meeting in 1887 in Co. Galway provides a prism through which issues of national and transnational, cultural, political and legal narratives are explored and exposed. Underpinning this chapter is Anne Blunt's own fascinating and complex biography, not least as the granddaughter of Lord Byron, daughter of the mathematician Ada King and, of course, as the wife of the poet and anti-imperialist Wilfrid Scawen Blunt. As a couple the Blunts' experiences as travellers, especially in Egypt, and their connection to Augusta Gregory, provide an added layer of marital complexity to the intricate anti-colonial discourses which surrounded this Galway fracas. Overarching O'Cinnéide's detailed narrative and reflections on anti-colonial conjunctions and discourses in Ireland and Egypt is an exploration of the way in which Anne Blunt herself became a contested space which many sought to interpret.

Heidi Hansson's chapter, on Emily Lawless's *A Garden Diary, 1899–1900* and the Boer War, examines another contested space, exploring the ways in which Lawless's diary-cum-gardening guide mediates and domesticates the Second Boer War (1899–1902). The apparent incongruity of connecting such a genre to South African colonial conflict lessens when we consider Constance Markievicz's use of horticultural metaphor as nationalist commentary in her gardening column in *Bean na hÉireann*. For the unionist Lawless, her gardening diary allows her to model unionism as a diverse imperial kinship, with England as a benign if casual mother. Her text, however, ultimately emphasises the limitations of the subjective diary form for authoritative engagement with conflict issues, and implicitly restricts the discursive public authority to be claimed from texts seemingly in the private domain.

Hansson's exploration of the Lawless diary, in the context of the range of materials (published and unpublished) uncovered in this volume, underscores the generic diversity of Irish women's writing in the period 1880–1922.[4] From personal diaries such as Lawless's to the war poetry of Winifred Letts and the nationalist fiction of Peggie Kelly, this volume illuminates the diverse voices of women writers in the period. The subject of Maureen O'Connor's chapter, a play by Eva Gore-Booth, further extends the textual reach of this book into the visual arts. Published in 1916, Eva Gore-Booth's *The Death of Fionavar* was illustrated by her sister, Constance Markievicz, who worked on the play from her cell in Mountjoy Gaol.[5] *The Death of Fionavar* garnered international reviews in 1916; this response and Gore-

Booth's standing in the contemporary literary world suggest a receptiveness to women's literary production in the period. In this authoritative exploration of Gore-Booth's writing, O'Connor delivers a carefully nuanced reading of the author's legendary pacifism, detailing the writer's conviction that making peace required active struggle.

This volume emerged from a series of exchanges between members of a transnational study group on women's war writing, based at the University of Limerick and funded by the UL-NUI Galway Gender ARC. The group's 2012 symposium and exhibition, 'Behind the Lines: Women, War, and Letters', brought international scholars from eight countries to Limerick to hear plenary papers by Professors Lucy McDiarmid and Matthew Campbell, and readings by Honor O Brolcháin (editor of *All in the Blood* (2006), the memoirs of Geraldine Plunkett Dillon) and Lia Mills. During the symposium Lia Mills read from a work-in-progress manuscript that subsequently became *Fallen* (2014), a novel exploring the challenges and divided loyalties of Dubliners living through the 1914–16 period through the eyes of central character Katie Crilly. As with other work in this volume Mills's novel complicates received ideas about the Easter Rising, demonstrating the extent to which women played an active role in the conflict, and concentrating on the mixed feelings of those supporting family members fighting at the Somme while simultaneously having an adherence to the Irish national struggle. Moreover, incorporating Mills's work serves as a reminder of present-day writers actively engaged in meditating on the positioning of women in history, and on the relationship between women, war and writing in twenty-first century Ireland. *Fallen* has since been selected as the Dublin and Belfast One City One Book Festival choice for 2016 and, even as this volume goes to print, the novel is at the centre of myriad commemorative events and readings north and south. We are delighted to conclude this volume with an extract from *Fallen* with a short critical introduction by Lia Mills.

Cork, November 2016

Notes

1   The Abbey is the national theatre of Ireland; founded as the Irish Literary Theatre by W. B. Yeats and Augusta Gregory in 1899, the existing theatre building on Abbey Street was funded thanks to the patronage of Annie Horniman in 1904. The Abbey quickly became a central pillar of the Irish Literary Revival, the cultural nationalist movement imbricated in the struggle for Irish independence. Important plays by J. M. Synge and Seán O'Casey were staged there, and several members of the company including Seán Connolly, who was killed in action, Arthur Shields, Helena Moloney, Peadar Kearney, Barney Murphy, and Ellen Bushell took part in the 1916 Rising.

2   Playwright Ali White was the one exception in an otherwise men-only programme; moreover, her play *Me, Mollser*, is part of a nationwide schools programme rather than a performance on the main Abbey stage. See abbeytheatre.ie/engage/projects/priming-the-canon-me-mollser/.

3   See also Bibbings on masculinity and Cohen on transnationalism in Carden-Coyne, *Gender and Conflict*.

4   While a considerable proportion of the publications discussed in this volume are now out of print, the recent digitisation of some written material, like the witness statements or personal letters for instance, provides new possibilities for scholars and educators. Books and plays from the period too are increasingly becoming available electronically, which not only opens up earlier material to an international audience but has the added benefit of making manuscripts, illustrations, and cursive handwriting clearly legible onscreen.

5   Following the execution of her fellow leaders of the Easter Rising, Markievicz's death sentence was commuted because of her gender.

Works Cited

Bibbings, Lois. 'Men refusing to be violent: manliness and military conscientious objection, 1914 to the present day'. Carden-Coyne, *Gender and Conflict* 41–54.

Carden-Coyne, Ana. *The Politics of Wounds: Military Patients and Medical Power in the First World War*. Oxford: Oxford University Press, 2014.

—, ed. *Gender and Conflict since 1914: Historical and Interdisciplinary Perspectives*. Basingstoke and New York: Palgrave Macmillan, 2012.

Cohen, Laurie R. 'Courage, conflict and activism: transnational feminist peace movements, 1900 to the present day'. Carden-Coyne, *Gender and Conflict* 69–82.

Cooke, Miriam and Angela Woollacott. 'Introduction'. Miriam Cooke and Angela Woollacott, eds. *Gendering War Talk*. Princeton: Princeton University Press, 1993. ix–xiii.

Enloe, Cynthia. *Does Khaki Become You?: The Militarization of Women's Lives*. Boston: South End Press, 1983.

—. *Maneuvers: The International Politics of Militarizing Women's Lives*. Berkeley: University of California Press, 2000.

Foster, Roy. *Vivid Faces: The Revolutionary Generation in Ireland, 1890–1923*. London: Penguin, 2015.

McCoole, Sinéad. *No Ordinary Women: Female Activists in the Revolutionary Years 1900–1923*. Madison: University of Wisconsin Press, 2003.

McDiarmid, Lucy. *At Home in the Revolution: What Women Did and Said in 1916*. Dublin: Royal Irish Academy, 2015.

Ó Tuathaigh, Gearóid. 'Commemoration, public history and the professional historian: an Irish perspective'. *Estudios Irlandeses* 9 (2014): 137–45.

Pašeta, Senia. *Irish Nationalist Women 1900–1918*. Cambridge: Cambridge University Press, 2013.

Rowbotham, Sheila. *Hidden from History: 300 Years of Women's Oppression and the Fight against It*. London: Pluto Press, 1973.

Ward, Margaret. *Unmanageable Revolutionaries: Women and Irish Nationalism.* London: Pluto Press, 1983.

Weber, Annette. 'Feminist peace and conflict theory'. *Encyclopedia on Peace and Conflict Theory.* 2006. Available at: uibk.ac.at/peacestudies/downloads/peacelibrary/feministpeace.pdf (Accessed 31 May 2016).

A 'Crust to Share with You'[1]

The Rhetoric of The Ladies' Land League's

British Campaign, 1881–2

Diane Urquhart

The Irish Land War (1879–82) was a transnational movement. However, the boundaries of this conflict were fluid in more than a geographical sense; its scope not limited to physical combat or one gender.[2] The press, for example, was used by both the Land League and the Ladies' Land League as a propagandist tool.[3] Yet the press was never powerless; in choosing to emphasise specific architects of violence or to minimise reportage of the land campaign, it shaped popular perceptions. And in consequence of the practice of reprinting British press reports in the American newspapers, the import of the former's depiction was considerably heightened.[4] The cross-gender activities of the Land League also offered a new facet to press censure: women's engagement on an unprecedented scale in a movement which defied the law and gender expectations was controversial and initial press curiosity often mutated into revulsion and distain.

DEFENDERS OF THE OPPRESSED

Following the destinations of Irish migrants in Britain, the Ladies' Land League established branches in Manchester, Liverpool, London, Glasgow, Edinburgh, York, Oldham, Newcastle, Stockton, Birmingham, Bradford, Dundee and Lochee.[5] Collectively these comprised the Ladies' National Land League of Great Britain which was under the presidency of Wigan suffragist and London School Board member, Helen Taylor. The London and Liverpool associations, established in February 1881, were the earliest incarnations of the movement in Britain and became the most proactive.[6] Although membership figures are scarce and derive from the organisation rather than a more impartial source, the Oldham branch, initiated in September 1881, claimed 300 members by April 1882 whilst a Dundee meeting of the same month drew an estimated (mostly female) audience of 500. Members' biographical details are also rare although suffragists, like Miss Spender of the Women's Suffrage League, were active in the London branch. Others, like Jessie Craigen, a Scottish trade unionist and former paid worker for the Ladies' National Association, joined as they saw the land campaign as part of a wider programme of social reform.[7] Familial connections, which often drew women into nineteenth-century politics, were also strong. Frances Sullivan, the Irish-American wife of A. M. Sullivan, MP for Meath, was president of the London branch of the ladies' league and Mrs A. M. Bligh, president of the Liverpool branch, was married to a prominent member of the city's male league, with another likely relative Mrs John Bligh also serving as the female organisation's treasurer.

However, establishing a branch of the Ladies' Land League was often cloaked, highlighting the unease caused by coercion. During the establishment of a Manchester branch, for example, an 'ingeniously arranged' poster intonated that a number of MPs had been invited to attend a meeting but not that they would be present. A mixed-sex audience duly gathered where Mrs Burke of the ladies' central executive declared her mission was to raise relief funds, as well as awareness of landlordism and of the work of the women's organisation in England (*Manchester Guardian* 19 Sept. 1881). Anna Parnell, Helen Taylor and Dublin's Marguerite Moore also lectured mixed-sex and all-male assemblies in areas such as Leeds, Blackburn, Salford, Darlington, Jarrow and Huddersfield. A Leeds Land League meeting, for instance, saw an estimated 2,000 pay admission fees ranging from a shilling to three pence to hear Anna Parnell speak (*York Herald* 11 Oct. 1881). Charles Stewart Parnell and other male land leaguers also spoke at women's meetings, which suggests cordiality often overlooked in Land League histories.

The Ladies' Land League's use 'of public speaking as a mobilizing strategy' has been highlighted for Ireland (O'Toole 86), but in Britain, as in America, it could not rely on eviction scenes or heckling land agents at first hand to emote an audience. Although Anna Parnell later questioned the impact of mass meetings, believing them 'overdone in Ireland' and inhibiting 'the explanation or discussion which might further the attainment of a common policy', she regarded eviction assemblies as the 'best kind of meetings' (Parnell 62). Denied this in Britain, the Ladies' Land League had to impart an understanding of the dynamics of the land campaign through platform rhetoric and the press. It also sought collaboration from bodies ranging from the Quakers to Elizabeth Fry's Prison Reform Association although this does not seem to have produced any direct response.

Regardless of the site of meetings, the Ladies' Land League's intent was clear. Issuing a February 1881 manifesto to Irish and English women, it claimed this was prompted by a pre-existing empathy for 'the cause of Ireland':

> The strong desire of Irishwomen living in England and the generous offer of many sympathetic Englishwomen to aid the work of mercy and succour . . . to feel for victims of affliction and oppression, to aid us in alleviating the sorrow and misery which . . . threaten so many of our sex . . . It is essentially woman's mission, and no more pure and noble duty could engage them than . . . lightening the anguish of the prison, or dispelling the darkness of the desolate home. (*Reynold's Newspaper* 27 Feb. 1881)[8]

Such an approach legitimised female involvement by politicising a domain widely held to be their own: the home (Mulligan 168). This became a familiar trope in female land rhetoric. Marguerite Moore, speaking in Birmingham, for example, referred to the desire 'to free their hearths and homes' (*Birmingham Daily Post* 22 Mar. 1882).[9] Closely aligned to this was a moral argument claiming women were 'forced' into politics. This was not because of Land League duping, as the press would later aver, but rather the situation was so pressing that women had to act. They thus presented themselves as defenders of the oppressed tenant farmer and their vulnerable dependents: 'wives and children deprived of their breadwinners' after 'unjust and inhuman' evictions (*The Guardian* 23 June 1881).

In Britain, however, there was a lower level of engagement with women's political role or female enfranchisement than Schneller identifies in America, which can be explained by the less developed British feminist movement (Schneller 12). Direct references to the need for Irish self-government were also uncommon until the latter stages of the British campaign, but female activism was early deemed a patriotic expression: 'Where were the Irishwomen . . . had [they] forgotten their native land so soon[?] . . . In every town in England there should be a branch of the Ladies' National Land League' (*North-Eastern Daily Gazette* 20 Dec. 1881).[10] The themes of British misrule and corruption were also present from the outset. Anna Parnell's initial address in London in March 1881, although she was a relatively inexperienced political speaker having given her first address in February of the previous year, displayed an already characteristic mix of accusatory and mocking language. She claimed that the Royal Irish Constabulary, 'villainous men . . . engaged in the work of extremism and butchery' (*Newcastle Courant* 9 Sept. 1881), fabricated the rationale for Land League arrests. She also ridiculed the policy whereby boycotted tenants could mutilate their own cattle and claim compensation (*Manchester Guardian* 11 Mar. 1881; *Illustrated Police*

News 19 Mar. 1881). In Bradford – the constituency of Forster, the Irish chief secretary from 1880 to 1882 – her speech to a mixed-sex meeting organised under the auspices of the ladies' league, interwove the themes of vulnerability and brutality: Forster's 'war against women and children under the pretext of civilisation and humanity', used a policy of 'buckshot, bayonets, and blood' whilst Gladstone was held responsible for the murder of Ellen McDonough, a child killed in the Ballina evictions, and the arrest of a child for whistling the Fenian tune, 'Harvey Duff' (*Leeds Mercury* 15 Nov. 1881).[11]

Anna Parnell became a regular lecturer in Britain from March 1881, aiming to 'address as many meetings in England as possible . . . as it is the only way I can see open to me to put before the people of this country a portion of the real facts of the case about Ireland' (*Huddersfield Daily Chronicle* 21 Oct. 1881). She thus became the focus of press attention often to the detriment of her British colleagues. Her addresses were covered verbatim but, for instance, when sharing a platform with Helen Taylor, it was only noted that the latter gave an address but its content remained wholly un-recorded (*Manchester Times* 28 Jan. 1882). The British press also interviewed Anna Parnell which was a relatively new approach that originated in 1870s America. Interviewed in Holyhead in late 1881, she highlighted the needs of the prisoners and their families: their distress was 'the most powerful form of propaganda'. With 'unprovoked attacks of the military and constabulary' and increasing arrests, she contended that the government was looking for an excuse to impose martial law in Ireland. Forster, a 'stupid man', was again the target for her tirade and although she credited Gladstone with 'a sufficient head', he too would later be condemned (*Huddersfield Daily Chronicle* 21 Oct. 1881).

Anna Parnell never tamed her anti-Englishness for British audiences, but her rhetoric intensified after a disappointing land act of August 1881 and the widespread arrest of land leaguers, including Charles Parnell, in October 1881. The timing of the fieriest Land League language thus varied between its male and female wings. The men's imprisonment led many towards negotiation whilst the ladies' league emphasised the injustices of British rule and the realities of the Land War as it entered its most bellicose phase. This also revealed a drift in policy. Anna Parnell was particularly muted on the significance of the land courts established by the 1881 land act, and backed the no-rent manifesto as policy rather than political manoeuvre (*Manchester Guardian* 22 Dec. 1881). Ever disparaging of the Liberal leadership, she increasingly lamented Ireland's fate, citing Bright's motto of 'Force is no remedy' as an ironic reminder of the political paradox posed by the Liberal coercion of the land movement (*Leeds Mercury* 15 Nov. 1881).[12]

If any restraining force remained, it was eroded by the Royal Irish Constabulary's decision that the edict supressing the Land League also applied to women in December 1881. This created the spectre of female arrest and imprisonment. The British press reprinted the resultant Ladies' Land League manifesto to its Irish and British branch secretaries which was akin to a rallying call: 'To the women of Ireland! Courage! The Ladies' Land League is still undaunted, cool and defiant. We await the arrival of the enemy . . . To the breach, to the breach!' They called for unity of action whereby if one woman was arrested, another, and 'even the very children', should take her place.[13] The Liverpool branch was the first in Britain to react, holding an 'indignation meeting' following the imprisonment of Hannah Reynolds. Addressing this meeting Anna Parnell was defiant: supressing the organisation would lead only to a 'multiplying [of] their efforts'. An accompanying declaration from the Liverpool ladies' league was similarly rebellious: 'Irish people of Liverpool . . . seize the opportunity to show your detestation of the cowardly and brutal coercion gaolers of your countrywomen' (*Liverpool Mercury* 31 Dec. 1881).

Platform addresses became more distinctly political from January 1882. Directing her words solely to the Irish electorate in England, Anna Parnell asked: 'before they voted for any English Liberal . . . let them ask whether he would support a vote of want of confidence in the Government' (*The Guardian* 24 Jan. 1882). She now castigated 'old Judas' Gladstone alongside 'old hypocrite Bright . . . and that bloodthirsty villain Chamberlain' (*Manchester Guardian* 22 Dec. 1881). Failing to provide shelter for the evicted was emotively framed as conceding to Gladstone who 'wanted to do away with the wooden shed. If he did he would repair the way for another dying by thousands, called an Irish famine. And then . . . the English people would send over a few thousand pounds and say "Look how generous we are"' (*The Guardian* 24 Jan. 1882). Women's relief work thus had a new impetus; it 'removed the necessity of dying quickly . . . and that altered the entire political economy of Ireland' (*Manchester Guardian* 22 Dec. 1881). Her address of the same month to Jarrow's Mechanics' Institute also demanded a restoration of Ireland's right to self-government (Schneller 206). Helen Taylor evoked similar sentiments, optimistically depicting a victorious scene where power passed from the 'bands of robbers and oppressors who called themselves landlords' to tenants. Taylor now placed Gladstone at the head of the 'illegal conspiracy of landlords . . . trying to drive the people of Ireland out of their native land as the Turks drove the people of Crete from that island' (*The Guardian* 24 Jan. 1882).[14] But such censure was now at variance with the ongoing negotiations between Charles Parnell and the Liberal administration.

Although Anna felt hyperbole served little purpose,[15] she was not adverse to scaremongering. At a January 1882 Manchester meeting, her resolution, highlighting the importance of women's relief work, was 'loudly cheered' but was, by this stage of the campaign, standard fare. However, she predicted this 'would probably be her last speech because the silent system was now being extensively applied in Ireland . . . to what was supposed to be the loquacious sex. Those present did not know how fast the arrests of women, and mostly young girls, were going on in Ireland', a dearth of knowledge caused by the manipulation of the English press who:

> ceased to mention . . . [women], being afraid of . . . getting into the Continental papers. But although those arrested were kept secret from the world, they were on going and would increase. They were arrested on suspicion, but they were not arrests under the famous Coercion Act. A new system of imprisonment without trial had been invented exclusively for the benefit of her sex. (*The Guardian* 24 Jan. 1882)[16]

The propaganda value of female land leaguers being prosecuted under the 1361 statutes of Edward III deployed against women of ill fame was therefore not lost. To Anna Parnell this 'female edition' of the coercion act was 'much worse than the male . . . A new system of imprisonment without trial has been invented exclusively for women' (*Manchester Times* 28 Jan. 1882).[17] She also narrated specific cases, in a clear example of the move to more news reportage which Schneller has identified in the American campaign, highlighting the partial application of the law and women's consequent vulnerability, describing 'a girl . . . in danger of being rendered insane by the prison treatment' (*The Guardian* 24 Jan. 1882).[18] Marguerite Moore also used her imminent trial in March 1882 to highlight the injustices of coercion, calling on Irish voters in Birmingham to 'avenge her at the ballot box' and exaggerating that for every woman arrested there were 'at least one thousand' ready to take her place (*Birmingham Daily Post* 22 Mar. 1882).[19]

The difference between the more conciliatory land leaguers and the belligerence of the Ladies' Land League, and more particularly of Anna Parnell, is best epitomised by her letter to the London *Times* on 9 May 1882. Her reference to Forster's past 'butchering of men and women' and criminalisation of providing shelter for the evicted meant that 'the assassin's arm is not idle'.[20] This much vexed her brother whose denouncement of the Phoenix Park murders appeared in the same edition. Here Anna also engaged with her own process of radicalisation: 'Up to the present time her idea never went farther than withholding the rents from the landlords until they had been taught to recognise the rights of the Irish people as human beings', but she was now committed to a no rent policy. This was not without effect: the ladies' league was censured by Catholic clerics in both Ireland and America and there are examples of local priests trying to stem the spread of the Ladies' Land League in Britain. In Liverpool, for example, it was alleged that a number of clerics threatened to expel children from Catholic schools if 'they' joined the league, although it was not specified whether this applied to the children's or ladies' leagues, or both. A more sympathetic Liverpool priest was also threatened with removal (*Liverpool Mercury* 28 Mar. 1881). The ladies' league now faced heightened scrutiny from the authorities: Royal Irish Constabulary members were reportedly in the audience and among the platform party at a packed Liverpool assembly to hear Anna Parnell (*Liverpool Mercury* 14 Nov. 1881) whilst Marguerite Moore, speaking in Dundee, only had the meeting announced on the previous day (*Dundee Courier* 22 Dec. 1881) to deter a police presence. In Greenock Anna Parnell was denied access to the town hall platform due to her 'unbecoming language', with her recent comments on Gladstone as a 'wretched, hypocritical, bloodthirsty miscreant' being the likely cause,[21] while Forster advised his constituents to ignore her pronouncements (*The Times* 13 May 1882). Charles Parnell also lost patience which, conjoined with female disillusion with the Kilmainham treaty, brokered between the male leaders of the Land League and the Liberal administration, paved the way for the Irish Ladies' Land League's August 1882 disbandment.[22]

THE BACKLASH

Some sections of the press who might be expected to sympathise with the Ladies' Land League were never on side. Motivated by class and racial considerations and despising the illegality of the movement, the feminist *Englishwoman's Review* presented Land League women as under male authority and thus denied them agency (Ward 71–92).[23] By comparison, the mainstream British press underwent a distinct change, moving from printing verbatim speeches without passing judgement, to front page opinion pieces castigating the female land movement.

The satirical British press lampooned the Ladies' Land League as un-hinged and violent as early as June 1881. A barbed cartoon, 'In Bad Company' in English comic, *Funny Folks*, for example, showed a furious and armed Anna Parnell. Although this depiction has been described as akin to a 'Spenserian savage Irish woman' with Anna barefoot 'in a home spun outfit' (Schneller 219),[24] she is rather a characterisation of 'Marianne', the symbol of the French revolution who was subsequently adopted by militant republicans. This image also acquired more anarchical overtones following the 1871 Paris Commune, especially the violence of Louise Michel who was transported to Nouvelle Calédonie for her actions. Wearing a Phrygian liberty cap, with a sinister Charles Parnell whispering from the sidelines, *Funny Folks* depicted Anna attacking 'Erin', the feminine allegory of Ireland.[25]

Figure 1.1: Cartoon depicting Anna Parnell, 'In Bad Company'. *Funny Folks* 18 June 1881.

This early derision of the women's organisation was not solely visual. Female resistance to the December 1881 raid on the *United Irishman*'s Dublin office was declared 'very funny' (*Ipswich Journal* 27 Dec. 1881) and *Punch* parodied Archbishop Croke's defence of the Ladies' Land League, punning on his Cashel and Emly/'Emily' diocese as his rationale for defending women. It also satirised more genteel fundraising efforts: 'From bullets and Boycotting to balls and concerts the transition is undeniably a change for the better' in consequence of the 'humanising influence on Irish politics exerted by the lovely members of the Ladies' Land League' (*Hull Packet* reprinted 3 Feb. 1882).

A mainstream press backlash, however, emerged following the imprisonment of Parnell and other land leaguers in October 1881. Within weeks the *Dundee Courier* mused on the 'not very pleasing ... attitude that the Ladies' Land League have taken up'. Again, female exploitation by men was foregrounded: women being encouraged 'in a rather cowardly way' to defy bailiffs and process servers to arrest or physically restrain them at evictions with the aim of embarrassing those in authority (*Dundee Courier* 28 Oct. 1881). Such a construct not only denied female agency but also offered a rationale for their actions: they too were the victims of the Land League.

That the Land War caused higher-class casualties, impoverishing widows and unmarried women who were dependent on rents, led the press to muse on whether these women of a 'different class' should oppose the 'shrieking sisters' of the Land League, overlooking the fact that most of its members were drawn from the upper and middle classes as is reflected in their use of the term 'Ladies' in the organisation's name (*Dundee Courier* 3 Dec. 1881).[26] A sense of latent aggression in 'Infuriated females . . . misguided women [and] viragoes' which could be unleashed if they moved from 'using their tongue and using weapons of a more forcible kind' subsequently emerged (*Dundee Courier* 28 Oct. 1881). The Liverpool ladies' league's expression of sympathy on the arrest of Parnell also led to a suggestion that the organisation was 'a cowardly attempt to drive an unarmed people into revolt' (*Bristol Mercury* 17 Oct. 1881). This polemic continued: the female land leaguers' call to boycott the Irish exhibition if an English official or the queen were invited to open it was speedily bedded under the headline of 'Irish nonsense' (*Sheffield and Rotherham Independent* 12 Oct. 1881).

Liverpool was home to the largest Irish migrant community and one of the most active branches of the ladies' league in Britain, but this did not preclude local press reproach: 'this petticoat league [of] . . . infatuated women who are trying to do so much mischief . . . is only a cover [for] . . . a defiant sisterhood who have presumed to play the role of agitators' (*Liverpool Mercury* 4 Jan. 1882).[27] Land leaguers like Joseph Biggar and Richard Lalor were also criticised for defending a body which, by its deeds and especially its words, now ranked 'among Ireland's worst enemies . . . ranting and agitating under the mistaken idea that they were healing wounds and filling hungry mouths' (*Lloyd's Weekly Newspaper* 25 Dec. 1881).[28]

Anna Parnell was singled out for particular reproach as a woman 'active to excess' with her alleged politicisation of children being cast as a moral case in point (*Dundee Courier* 28 Oct. 1881). Depictions of her 'unrestricted fury' towards the government, hinted to an irrationality which was often claimed of political women (*Manchester Guardian* 25 Oct. 1881). Her 'style of the Amazon and the spirit of the Spartan woman, who used to exhibit outward symptoms of joy when their husbands were slain in battle' also intimated an appetite for violence (*Huddersfield Daily Chronicle* 29 Dec. 1881).[29] Her address as the principal speaker to an assembly of 'rough unsophisticated . . . Irishmen' in Huddersfield in late 1881 was further denounced as a 'fabricated . . . narration of fiction and the utterance of abuse . . . spouting sedition'. A lack of coherence and knowledge of the workings of government was also alleged, but it is hard to align this with the verbatim report of this speech given two days earlier. Her genteel appearance and English accent were further contrasted to her vitriol and held as 'the chief secret' for the organisation's repute: 'In the use of a venomous culminating tongue Miss Anna is really too utterly utter' (*Huddersfield Chronicle* 24 Dec. 1881).[30] She unsurprisingly retaliated at meetings in Liverpool and Manchester, responding to 'certain charges made against her by several English papers' and claiming press partiality (*Liverpool Mercury* 31 Dec. 1881).[31] Yet, her organisation was also not without some defenders in the British press. The *Birmingham Daily Post* was, for example, critical of the fourteenth-century statutes used to detain female land leaguers (18 Apr. 1882).

Although there was considerable coverage of the ladies' league, the claim that this amounted to constant front page coverage is exaggerated (Côté and Hearne 276).[32] The ladies' league sometimes made headline news in Britain, but this was mostly post-October 1881 when the press began its denouncement of the women's movement. The *Newcastle Courant*, for example, gave front page coverage to the criminalisation of the Ladies' Land League on 23 December 1881, criticising government procrastination in previously dealing with its 'seditious meetings in defiance of the law . . . [it was] clear from the first that this combination in petticoats would have to be put down . . . To imprison women in the UK for . . . political offences would be a novel and regrettable proceeding, but the female political agitator is a new character amongst us' and merited a change of custom. Their recent rhetoric was also deemed, with justification, 'as even more violent than those which consigned their male friends to prison'. The same story made the front page of the *Huddersfield Chronicle*: 'the opposite sex . . . play with politics and assume the airs of lords of creation.' Although this paper was pro-suffrage, it did not support women's political action. Indeed, defeminising women, it averred that membership of the ladies' league was 'debasing':

> It blunts the moral susceptibilities of womanhood; it weakens the natural modesty of the fair sex, and cultivates that false pride and overwearing [sic] vanity by which Satan operated with success upon the Mother of the human race.

Like several other newspapers, it did not absolve the government from responsibility; its toleration of the organisation when it was in infancy allowed it to grow 'formidable . . . [and] as influential and even indispensable branch of the revolutionary army as the suppressed Land League ever was'. Its fundraising from Irish migrants was now 'a very powerful weapon . . . against the Government', negating the need to pay rent and encouraging resistance to landlord power. Imprisonment was again suggested as the only fitting response to 'ladies . . . doing their best to restore their country to barbarism under the specious pretext of trying to gain her independence' (29 Dec. 1881).

The next front page coverage of the Ladies' Land League had Anna Parnell as its focus following her apprehension of Lord Lieutenant Spencer in Dublin in mid-1882. She was now described as a 'notorious . . . offender . . . a woman of great force' (*Dundee Courier* 16 June 1882). Subsequently writing to the *London Evening Telegraph*, Anna claimed she shamed Spencer and issued another rallying call for collective action: if prevented from building shelters for the evicted, another location should be found: 'if one man is arrested . . . let another take his place, and thus to leave no shadow of decent cover for a continuation of this outrage on humanity' (16 June 1882).[33]

Unsurprisingly, there was little lament in the British press at the Ladies' Land League's demise. Nevertheless, the aftertaste of its words and actions lingered: at least one British newspaper recalled the 'female patriots who mismanaged the affairs of the Ladies' Land League' in late 1882 (*Sheffield and Rotherham Independent* 9 Dec. 1882).[34]

CONCLUSION

Those sympathetic to the Land War in Britain were denied the immediacy of standing 'as a shield between the oppressors and the oppressed' (*Freeman's Journal* 11 Aug. 1882).[35] Yet, for Michael Davitt English sympathy aroused by the arrest of lady land leaguers delivered 'the finishing blow' to persuade Gladstone not to coerce but conciliate in the form of the 1882 Kilmainham treaty (Cashman 234). There is little evidence of this sentiment in the British press, but the Ladies' Land League repeatedly explained the injustices of the land system and the government, often by means of violent language and victim testimonials. They were, however, working towards a more grandiose solution than the treaty afforded. Anna Parnell's disillusion at the Kilmainham compromise and distrust of Gladstone's 'good intentions' were not unique.[36] To Jessie Craigen, Charles Parnell 'sold himself to the ministry . . . having turned traitor to the national cause' making her 'great sacrifices for the Irish cause . . . to fight for the liberty of the people not to put political tricksters into power' seem futile.[37] Yet some women, like Helen Taylor, fought on: she addressed Manchester's Land Restorative League in 1887.[38]

Although Anna Parnell's estrangement from Charles for his part in the Land War is inflated, as is evidenced in print by her introduction to Jennie Wyse Power's poignantly entitled collection of Parnell's speeches, *Words of the Dead Chief* published in 1892, she played no further part in the campaign for land reform. However, the notion that Ireland could only be supressed by English corruption, 'artificially caused starvation and weakness' and Gladstonian opportunism re-emerged forcibly in her 1907 *Tale of a Great Sham*. Here she alleged English press collusion with the government led them to underplay the distress of the Irish tenantry, and to present 'one version of the facts more agreeable than the true one'. Her distaste for England, the country which was now her home, also remained: 'When I heard English people talking about Ireland, I used to wonder whether the stupidity they displayed was real or only assumed . . . Whatever else may be false about them, their brainlessness is perfectly genuine.' However, her determination of the Land War years was replaced by despondent resignation regarding women's political power: 'If the men . . . have made up their minds it shall not be done, the women cannot bring it about.' She foresaw neither female enfranchisement nor was optimistic for Ireland's fate: 'There is no reason to suppose the men in possession of the stage in 1917, will be any better than those who possess it in 1893' (Parnell 37, 42, 59, 173–4 and 179).[39]

Anna Parnell was often the focus of press interest and censure. The early perception of her as an extremist is epitomised by her effigy (alongside one of the Pope) being burnt in Eltham in Greenwich on 5 November 1880. Katharine O'Shea recalled the procession stopping outside her home and Parnell remarking: 'Poor Anna! Her pride in being burnt, as a menace to England, would be so drowned in the horror at her company, that it would put the fire out' (O'Shea 176).[40] Thus even before the creation of the Ladies' Land League in Ireland or Britain, its staunch rhetoric and female arrests, women's politicking provoked public protest and a distain which later emerged in much of the mainstream press. Although this did not cause the organisation in Britain or elsewhere to curb its language or defiance, it was never its design to establish a permanent association of women. Thus, when Irish nationalism entered a new constitutional phase, with home rule rather than land reform as its primary object, it did so without women. As the *United Ireland* newspaper declared, in the successor of the Land League, the Irish National League, 'the ladies will not take part' (*United Ireland* 5 Aug. 1882).

Notes

1   Murphy, Louisiana. *Dunmore, or the Days of the Land League: An Irish Dramatic Episode.* Dublin: M. H. Gill and Sons, 1888. Act II: 35. *Dunmore* was originally devised as a musical play, see Hansson 121–4.

2   At its peak the Ladies' Land League had between 400–500 Irish branches with additional branches in Britain, America, Canada, Australia and New Zealand.

3   The Irish National Land League, established in 1879, was led by Michael Davitt and Charles Stewart Parnell. The Ladies' National Land League began as a philanthropic organisation in America in 1880, led by two of Parnell's sisters, Anna and Fanny. The Irish Ladies' Land

[3 *cont.*] League was established in 1881, charging annual membership fees of five shillings, less than half of the Land League fees of 12 shillings.

4   The *Chicago Daily News*, for example, reprinted articles on the land campaign wired from the London *Times*.

5   The *United Ireland* newspaper followed a similar path when its editor William O'Brien was imprisoned. Hannah Lynch, the Dublin-born secretary of the London branch of the ladies' league, arranged for its publication in London, Liverpool, Glasgow, Manchester and then Paris.

6   The first British branch was formed in Liverpool. In addition to office bearers, it had a council of 12, held single and mixed-sex meetings, children's history classes and had a Children's Land League. It raised £300 from February–December 1881. With the likelihood of the Ladies' Land League's Dublin offices being raided, a second office was established in Liverpool with duplicated books. Helen Taylor established a Prisoners' Aid Society under the auspices of the London branch.

7   Craigen and Taylor attended Irish evictions. The Ladies' National Association campaigned for the repeal of the Contagious Diseases Acts. An Irish Ladies' National Association was also active.

8   This was a London-based publication.

9   Michael Davitt concurred: 'The fight was to save the homes of Ireland – the sacred, domestic domain of woman's moral supremacy' (Davitt 299).

10   This was a Middleborough-based publication.

11   Thanks to Andrew Maguire for drawing this article to my attention. Anna's 'buckshot' imagery was present in her first speech in Claremorris, Co. Mayo in February 1881. This was covered in the British press, revealing an early interest in the novelty of women's political activism. See, for example, the *Cheshire Observer* 19 Feb. 1881. Anna Parnell also referred to Ellen McDonough's death whilst speaking in Liverpool: 'if they could not take the part of this poor girl . . . they were people without that public spirit which was necessary to success in all countries' (*Liverpool Mercury* 14 Nov. 1881).

12   See also Craigen 32.

13   This was, for example, reprinted in the *Nottinghamshire Guardian* 30 Dec. 1881.

14   In Liverpool Anna Parnell detailed Irish deaths caused by police firing shots into crowds but claimed that was 'no match for several thousands' (*Liverpool Mercury* 14 Nov. 1881). See also the *Manchester Times* 28 Jan. 1882.

15   Charles Stewart Parnell concurred (O'Toole 79).

16   Speaking in Dundee, she also relished the prospect of imprisonment for women: 'they would go gaily to their prison, because . . . the clang of the prison door . . . rang the knell of the buckshot Government' (*Dundee Courier* 22 Dec. 1881).

17   Thirteen women were subsequently imprisoned.

18   The exclusively male composition of juries and the payment of witnesses by the crown were also noted.

19   Moore was tried on 29 March 1882, spending a month in Tullamore prison, Offaly where she wrote prison letters which were subsequently read at female Land League meetings in Britain.

20 Writing to Helen Taylor on 3 July 1882, Anna referred to a change in the Irish people 'that will not let reprisals be all on one side' (Mill–Taylor/18/81, London School of Economics Special Collections [hereafter LSE]).

21 The Irish press did not cite Anna Parnell's comments on Gladstone verbatim, referring to her as a 'prepossessing young lady attired in black' (Groves 193).

22 Branches were to decide their own fate and most ceased their efforts. The Liverpool branch continued to work for some months, sending £100 to Charles Parnell in October 1882.

23 Sections of the American press, like the *New York Herald*, also opposed the Ladies' Land League and the emergence of political women *per se*.

24 For a similar interpretation see de Nie.

25 Louise Michel's violence shocked both French and British commentators. I am grateful to Esther Papworth and Kate Marsh for sharing their knowledge of 'Marianne'. The London branch also appealed to Victor Hugo, the French Romantic novelist and poet whose return to his home country in 1870 symbolised republican triumph, to help the Irish people and thus continue the French tradition of supporting the oppressed. Although there is no record of Hugo's response, such rhetoric located the Land War in a broader historical tradition.

26 The *Englishwoman's Review* made similar comments. See Ward 71–92. On lower-class participation, see Te Brake 63–80.

27 The *Liverpool Mercury* was also critical of government laxity, but believed the law must be applied equally to men and women.

28 This London-based publication also lamented Helen Taylor's involvement in the ladies' league.

29 Hannah Reynolds, the first female Land League prisoner, was also described as a 'brisk Amazon' (*Dundee Courier* 3 Dec. 1881).

30 It also suggested that female imprisonment may be necessary.

31 See also *Manchester Times* 28 Jan. 1882; *Manchester Guardian* 22 Dec. 1881; and Craigen 57.

32 This is also disputed for America (Schneller 31).

33 This letter was reprinted, for example, in the *Manchester Guardian* and *Boston Pilot*.

34 There was some press rehabilitation for Anna Parnell at the time of her death in 1911: she was described as 'one of the two splendid sisters who did so much to make Parnell what he was. Anna Parnell was the fiercest rebel' (*Manchester Guardian* 23 Sept. 1911).

35 This was a direct reference to the work of the ladies' league.

36 Anna Parnell to Helen Taylor, 3 July 1882 (Mill–Taylor/18/81, LSE).

37 Jessie Craigen to Helen Taylor, 19 August 1882 (Mill–Taylor/18/71, LSE). Craigen returned to work for the Ladies' National Association.

38 Anna Parnell campaigned for Taylor's candidacy in North Camberwell in 1885, 33 years before the parliamentary enfranchisement of women.

39 Anna Parnell cited the Boer War as an example of English stupidity. Living under an assumed name in Brockley and then Ilfacombe, she was described as 'nearly always alone . . . noticeable for her sad and abstracted air' (*The Guardian* 25 Sept. 1911). Anna Parnell intimated that Helen Taylor was 'the only English politician, and indeed . . . only English person, who looked on the Irish question entirely from the Irish point of view' (Anna Parnell to Helen Taylor, 5 Nov. 1882 (Mill–Taylor/18/82, LSE)).

40   Katharine O'Shea displayed little sympathy for the ladies' league and less for Anna Parnell, deeming her extremism 'abnormal' (O'Shea 261).

Works Cited

Cashman, Michael. *Life of Michael Davitt*. Boston: Murphy and McCarthy, 1883.

Côté, Jane M. and Dana Hearne. 'Anna Parnell'. Mary Cullen and Maria Luddy, eds. *Women, Power and Consciousness in Nineteenth-Century Ireland*. Dublin: Attic Press, 1995. 263–93.

Craigen, Jessie. *Report on a Visit to Ireland in the Summer of 1881*. Dublin: R. D. Webb and Son, 1882. 1–63.

Davitt, Michael. *The Fall of Feudalism in Ireland*. London and New York: Harper and Brothers, 1904.

de Nie, Michael. *The Eternal Paddy*. Madison: University of Wisconsin Press, 2004.

Groves, Patricia. *Petticoat Rebellion: The Anna Parnell Story*. Cork: Mercier Press, 2009.

Hansson, Heidi. 'More than an Irish problem: authority and universality in Land-War writing'. Heidi Hansson and James H. Murphy, eds. *Fictions of the Irish Land War*. Oxford: Peter Lang, 2014. 107–26.

Mulligan, Adrian N. '"By a thousand ingenious feminist devices": the Ladies' Land League and the development of Irish nationalism'. *Historical Geography* 37 (2009): 159–77.

Murphy, Louisiana. *Dunmore, or, the Days of the Land League: An Irish Dramatic Episode*. Dublin: M. H. Gill and Sons, 1888.

O'Shea, Katharine. *Charles Stewart Parnell*. London: Cassell and Company, 1973 edn, first published 1914.

O'Toole, Tina. *The Irish New Woman*. Houndsmills: Palgrave Macmillan, 2013.

Parnell, Anna. *The Tale of a Great Sham*. Dana Hearne, ed. Dublin: Arlen House, 1986.

Schneller, Beverley. *Anna Parnell's Political Journalism*. Dublin and Bethesda: Academica Press, 2001.

Te Brake, Janet K. 'Irish peasant women in revolt: the Land League years'. *Irish Historical Studies* 28:109 (May 1992): 63–80.

Ward, Margaret. 'Gendering the union: imperial feminism and the Ladies' Land League'. *Women's History Review* 19:1 (2001): 71–92.

Wyse Power, Jennie. *Words of the Dead Chief*. Dublin: University College Dublin Press, 2009 edn, first published 1892.

2

Anne Blunt, 'Arabi Pasha' and the Irish Land Wars, 1880–8

Muireann O'Cinnéide

On the 23 October 1887, the granddaughter of Lord Byron stood on a crowded platform in Woodford, Co. Galway, and listened to her husband, an Englishman passionately committed to anti-imperialist causes, address a public anti-eviction meeting. As the local magistrate arrived with police to break up the gathering, a series of altercations broke out, during which Lady Anne Blunt was hurled from the platform and flung among the crowd. Over the next few months, the details of exactly what happened, to whom, and why, were to become the subject of much courtroom and newspaper dispute. Anne Blunt took the witness stand, testifying on behalf of her husband – but it was her experience at the banned meeting that become central both to Irish nationalist formulations of the event and to the state's counter-representations. Accounts of Anne Blunt's experiences and testimony in Irish newspapers open up a set of legal, political and cultural narratives, in which her assaulted body becomes a rhetorically contested space, subject to the claiming or chastising of the men who seek to interpret the cultural implications of its physical presence. Nor is the imaginative interpretation of her experience confined to male voices alone. Augusta Gregory's ongoing inscription and co-option of Anne Blunt's marital identity subjects it to a curious aesthetic contestation. The Irish experiences of the Blunts facilitated anti-imperial discourses which brought nationalist movements in Egypt and Ireland into conjunction. Such globalised conjunctions, however, could also be turned back upon the couple themselves, with their cultural fluidity and territorial mobility used to locate them as irretrievably alien to the national ideologies and geographies for and from which they speak. To be in Ireland and to suffer in Ireland for Irish causes does not, in the end, make Anne Blunt an Irish woman, yet her disputed co-option into Irish nationalist discourse profoundly disrupts any secure identification of herself with England, Egypt, or even with her own marriage. It also opens up fresh understandings of the gendered dynamics underlying the public demonstrations of the Land Wars and their aftermath, and the added value that could accrue in Irish public discourse to women's bodies marked out as anomalous by virtue (or by vice) of social status, national affiliation, literary heritage or cultural hybridity.

A number of events had brought Lady Anne Blunt to this moment in Irish – and English – colonial history. In marrying Wilfrid Scawen Blunt, she could be seen as demonstrating similarly poor marital judgment as her grandmother, Lady Byron. The poet, scholar and anti-imperialist was a man whose tumultuous political activities were matched by ongoing extramarital affairs that caused his wife considerable pain.[1] The couple eventually separated in 1906. Nevertheless, they shared a mutual love of travel, Arabian horses and the East. The Blunts became close supporters of the Egyptian nationalist Ahmed 'Urabi, known to the British as Arabi or Arabi Pasha, whose revolutionary career was cut short in 1882 by the British occupation of Egypt.[2] Wilfrid Blunt's *Secret History of the English Occupation of Egypt* (1907) depicts his enthusiasm for Arabian causes as intrinsically connected with his wife's literary heritage:

> my wife, Lady Anne Blunt, who accompanied me on all these travels, was the granddaughter of *our great national poet*, Lord Byron, *and so was in the inheritor, in some sort, of sympathies in the cause of freedom in the East*, which were not without their effect upon our subsequent action. It seemed to us, in presence of the events of 1881–2, that to champion the cause of Arabian liberty would be as worthy an endeavour as had been that for which Byron had died in 1827. (Wilfrid Blunt, *Secret History* 5–6, my italics)[3]

He therefore assigns his wife an equal partnership in their ideological aspirations – indeed, she is represented as having partially generated these aspirations. At the same time, she figures as a mediator rather than an originator: a channel through which Byronic nationalist and transnational sympathies can be regenerated in the face of fresh anti-imperial upheaval – and taken up (we may infer) by one of his poetic successors. In this account, Anne Blunt's own travelogues fade into comparative insignificance – and textual absence – compared with the weight of her grandfather's political and artistic legacies, and her husband's poetical and political ambitions.[4]

Moreover, Wilfrid Blunt's championship of Arabian liberty was not a cause shared exclusively with his wife. Augusta Gregory, travelling in Egypt with her husband Sir William Gregory, met the Blunts in the winter of 1881 and became passionately involved with Wilfrid Blunt, the two bonding over their shared support for 'Urabi. Their affair fostered two very different literary productions by Augusta Gregory: her article in the London *Times*,

'Arabi and his household' (*The Times* 23 Sept. 1882), and a series of sonnets later printed by Wilfrid Blunt (by agreement) in his own 1892 volume *The Love-Lyrics and Songs of Proteus*, under the characteristically secretive subheading 'A Woman's Sonnets'. Gregory's challenge to popular misconceptions of Ahmed 'Urabi in 'Arabi and his household' centres upon the epistemological intimacies of domestic space: her defence of him is founded upon her knowledge of his wife and mother. A visit to the women's quarters in Eastern countries – the harem or zenana scene – is a recurring trope in nineteenth-century European women's travel writing, showcasing as it does their access to this most fantasised and least accessible of spaces to male explorers (Grewal; Yeazell). Gregory's social status and connections, however, transfer this gendered epistemology into the pages of *The Times*, and thus to a much more public forum of authority. Gender, in Gregory's astute rendering, allows her to transcend the narrow limitations of national loyalties implicitly constraining masculine discourse. Her access to 'Urabi's female household allows her to inscribe him within a recognisable and sympathetic framework of identification to British readers as 'a Liberal Victorian *pater familias* . . . an English family man' (McDiarmid 73). At the same time, Gregory can claim to be articulating an admiration held in common with her male compatriots yet unutterable by them: a 'lady may say what she likes, but a man is called unpatriotic who ventures to say a word that is good of the man England is determined to crush' (Gregory 4).[5] Yet the article ends on an odd, unsettling note: the putative sexual threat to settled Eastern households from European women, invoked through 'Urabi's mother's objections to his plans to release slaves.

Buried within Gregory's account is an alternative set of hidden domestic and marital connections: 'I went, with Lady Anne Blunt, to see his wife' (Gregory 4). The article's plea for English empathy towards an Egyptian nationalist hero therefore operates through a complex gendered nexus of identifications: Gregory ostensibly aligns herself with 'Urabi's wife and mother, yet in so doing, as McDiarmid argues, uses political engagement as a mode through which to claim both a network of masculine publication *and* a form of intimacy with Wilfrid Blunt himself – an intimacy which transitions from the article through the sonnets into 'no longer an intimacy between lovers but between writers' (McDiarmid 77). Such an intimacy both excludes and co-opts Blunt's wife, who remains strangely outside, yet crucial to, this pattern of identifications.[6] Gregory's encounter with 'Urabi's wife and mother is mediated by Anne Blunt – 'speaking in Arabic, which Lady Anne interpreted to me' (Gregory 4). As with Wilfrid Blunt's *Secret History*, Anne Blunt features as the channel to and mediator of Arabian experience, whose presence and identity facilitates the primary author's claiming of epistemological authority and empathetic credibility. Andrea Bobotis argues that

Gregory, by 'imagining Irishness through a Middle Eastern setting', opens a maternalised space for the inclusion of Anglo-Irish women in nationalist politics and a counter to English stereotypes of Irish brutality (Bobotis 2). However, the fusion of the political, the literary and the erotic that characterised Augusta Gregory's and Wilfrid Blunt's relationship could not transfer seamlessly into the complicated national and marital dynamics generated by the appearance of the English Anne Blunt beside her husband upon a protest platform on an Irish landed estate, or the violence directed towards them by the police of a colonial Irish state.

'Ireland had slipped into Egypt's place in his mind', writes Elizabeth Longford of Wilfrid Blunt's immersion in Irish politics (Longford 228). Indeed, he made an explicit comparison between 'Urabi and the Irish Land League campaigner Michael Davitt (4 Apr. 1886, qtd Longford 228). The Blunts had spent January to March 1887 in Egypt, before returning to England where Wilfrid Blunt publicly campaigned against Arthur Balfour's 1887 Crimes (Ireland) Act. This 'Coercion Act', which banned 'unlawful assembly' among other things, was part of the British government's attempt to quell renewed agrarian protest movements in Ireland in the bitter aftermath of the initial Land War (1879–82). The Plan of Campaign, launched in 1886, assisted tenants to band together to bargain on rents in response to severe agricultural depression and escalating resentment against land owners – especially those such as the absentee marquess of Clanricarde, owner of the Portumna estate around Woodford. Representing the Home Rule Union he had helped to found, Wilfrid Blunt returned to Ireland in October 1887, this time accompanied by his wife. Arrested at the Woodford meeting under Balfour's Act, he was sentenced to two months imprisonment in Galway and Kilmainham jails. As such, he became an object of Irish nationalist celebration, and English outrage, with the local Anglo-Irish gentry positioned uncomfortably between the bonds of familial and social intimacy, the demands of law and property, and the national and political embarrassment inherent in an upper-class Englishman being attacked and arrested by Irish police. As one Irish nationalist paper expounded indignantly: 'Mr Blunt is now treated as a common felon in Galway jail, where, dressed in convict clothes, he is passing the hours away picking oakum' (*Nation* 14 Jan. 1888). For all its patriotic fervour, a sense of social outrage underscores the *Nation*'s response: the shocking element in these events is the demotion of an English gentleman to the status of a 'common felon'. Of course, we can also read the *Nation* as astutely targeting the situation's potential for state embarrassment: the imprisonment of an upper-class Englishman (as Blunt himself was clearly aware (McDiarmid 80–2)), contains considerably more inherent publicity value than that of an Irish politician – or, indeed, any common felon. A further complicating factor was that of the nearby

Coole Park: Sir William and Lady Gregory were in Italy at the time, but rallied their considerable local influence in his behalf (Wilfrid Blunt, *Land War in Ireland* 387).

In *The Land War in Ireland* (1912), Blunt gives a rather different account of his prison experience than that of the *Nation*. Where it depicts him as 'dressed in convict clothes', he represents himself sartorially defending his beliefs and his disputed status as a political prisoner, clashing gallantly with the prison governor over his desire to retain his coat (Wilfrid Blunt, *Land War in Ireland* 380–7). 'Galway gaol, as I remember it,' he observes, 'was a roomy old-fashioned place, built, I should imagine, about a hundred years ago – at any rate before the time of scientific prison planning – and as such not without its attraction to an imaginative mind' (Wilfrid Blunt, *Land War in Ireland* 373). We see here Blunt's self-conscious positioning of himself in a poetic tradition most famously represented by the Cavalier poet Lovelace, in which physical imprisonment is transformed into imaginative freedom by the power of the poetic imagination. Later, he muses on his experiences picking oakum: 'the aspect of the pile of finely-shredded hemp, as it grew with the progress of my work, [was] hardly less attractive than that of a woman's golden hair, so that the adding to it was a daily pleasure rather than a pain' (Wilfrid Blunt, *Land War in Ireland* 378). Such an eroticisation of hard labour is only too characteristic of the sexualised workings of Blunt's political imagination – while also being an imaginative luxury available to an upper-class Englishman who, while suffering several privations, was not driven too hard by the anxious prison authorities (Mitchell 75–84). Blunt's aesthetic reveries are, therefore, inseparable from questions of class and social status.

These questions are also, though, inseparable from the sentimental marital framework through which his political protest was publically mediated – by supporters and opponents alike. In the aftermath of her husband's arrest, Anne Blunt took on the responsibilities for receiving and disseminating messages of support on his behalf (MS 53959 24 Oct. 1887; *Freeman's Journal* 24 Oct. 1887). Indeed, Lisa Lacy suggests that one such message to *The Times* might have been her first real move into 'public political activity' (Lacy, 'Lady Anne Blunt' 229, 513n). For all the excitement accompanying Wilfrid Blunt's arrest and imprisonment, greater sensational potential lay in the presence of his wife at the meeting. In Ireland and abroad, the Ladies' Land League and associated organisations had foregrounded women's participation in radical agrarian and political action; a buffeted female body was still shocking to public opinion, but not unprecedented in the Irish Land Wars.[7] This particular body, however, was that of an Englishwoman, an English *Lady*, and a woman possessing a unique cultural status – one which campaigners were eager to put to good use. The *Freeman's Journal* presents her as the epitome of vulnerable marital loyalty: 'Lady Anne Blunt clung to her husband

and endeavoured to shield him from the brutality of his assailants' (23 Oct. 1887). Expressing horror at the sight of 'those delicate ladies dashed off the platform by the police' (the group included the English MP James Rowlands and his wife), the *Freeman's Journal* closes with an urgent update that suggests where the real excitement of the story lies:

> Since I wired the foregoing I have learned that Lady Anne Blunt was severely hurt in the melee. She was caught by the throat and cast furiously on the ground from the platform. Hours afterwards she complained of severe pain, the effects of the violence inflicted on her.

A subsequent article quotes William O'Brien, MP and one of the leaders of the Irish National League, expressing 'my humble admiration of the brave Englishman *and of his still braver English wife* who suffered in your cause here yesterday' (*Freeman's Journal* 24 Oct. 1887, my italics). Clearly, sex and nationality both add value to physical and emotional suffering endured on behalf of the Irish cause, with Anne Blunt's marital and political affiliations figuring as seamlessly intertwined.

This modelling of wifely devotion also, however, enables representatives of the state to invoke chivalric discourses in vindication of their actions and to undermine the political glamour attained by Wilfrid Blunt. At the investigatory hearing, the arresting magistrate John Byrne seems anxious to represent himself as calm and impartial *except* for her welfare: 'I was perfectly cool until alarmed about the safety of a lady whom I afterwards heard was Lady Anne Blunt – I was afraid she might be roughly handled' (*Freeman's Journal* 25 Oct. 1887). Willingly admitting that he 'may have pushed Mr Blunt', Byrne is insistent that 'I never put a hand upon her . . . I swear I did not put her off [the platform] .' Confirming the prison sentence on appeal in January 1888, the Portumna county court judge T. R. Henn disapprovingly notes Wilfrid Blunt's willingness to proceed 'at very great risk to limb, and perhaps even to life and at such danger to the lady whom he was bound to shield, and who we know was determined to accompany him on the platform, and did accompany him' (*Irish Times* 14 Jan. 1888). The involvement of the Ladies' Land League in public protest often produced similar criticisms aimed at the men of the Land League;[8] the supposed physical vulnerability of the female body becomes simultaneously a tool of protest and a means through which to obliterate women's individual agency. ('*Damn* Henn', was Anne Blunt's own private response to the judge's rebuke (qtd Longford 255)).

Likewise, Wilfrid Blunt's imprisonment becomes as much the story of a marriage as of a martyrdom. In novels of the 1880s featuring the Land Wars, 'sexual and political relations remain hopelessly entangled' (Kelleher 88);

such narrative entanglements were therefore established for supposedly factual reportage to draw upon. The *Nation* centres its most affecting imagery upon the division of spouses: 'Lady Anne Blunt, his devoted wife, was brutally refused permission to see her husband' (14 Jan. 1888). The imagery of violence – 'brutally' – creates an implicit correlation between the bodily harm previously done to her, and the psychic harm of marital separation, with the loving wife as brutalised victim of a mode of government-authorised violence implicitly aimed as rupturing marital bonds as much as political communions. Writing in 1921, Augusta Gregory paints an affecting picture in which 'Lady Anne, devoted and heroic, Byron's granddaughter, Ada's daughter, lingered near the gaol until work on his behalf called her to England' (Gregory, 'Preface' xiii). As with 'Arabi and his household', though, Anne Blunt again is positioned as an unknowing mediator in her husband's and Gregory's politicised erotics: McDiarmid traces the extent to which Blunt's imprisonment provided Augusta Gregory with ongoing literary inspiration, and even a poetic self-figuring as the devoted lover waiting outside the prison gates (McDiarmid 80–8). Indeed, Gregory's reference to Anne Blunt's departure (to canvass for her husband in Deptford, where he was standing as an anti-Coercion candidate) could be read as opening up this imaginative space for her own projections.

Gregory's invocation of Anne Blunt's literary heritage can be seen as simultaneously celebratory and reductive, establishing her prestigious ancestry at the cost of her individual autonomy. This pattern is to be found in earlier and much less interpersonally complicated responses to the Woodford imprisonment: Anne Blunt's distinctive cultural status facilitates a complex internationalisation of her husband's Irish experiences. In an address of thanks at a London dinner to Wilfrid Blunt in December 1887, the Irish nationalist MP John Dillon calls particular attention to the presence at the dinner of Blunt's wife. (Dillon, also a leader of the Irish National League, had himself been arrested in the land cause at Portumna in December 1886). Rather than emphasising marital loyalty, Dillon is eager to depict her as an active and engaged partisan of the Irish cause in her own right. Her presence at Woodford therefore figures in his representation as an active expression of individual political agency, rather than the passive expression of marital devotion implicit in many newspapers' initial accounts. It becomes clear, however, that this elevation of Anne Blunt's anti-colonial loyalties serves as a means through which to lay claim to her ancestry as much as to herself:

> To her it was natural to be a friend of liberty – to her it was natural to be a friend to Ireland. Her grandfather's first and last words in the House of Lords were spoken

for Irish freedom . . . Proud they were to see Byron's granddaughter there tonight, sympathising with the same cause, which was the cause of human liberty whether in Greece, Italy or Ireland. (*Nation* 17 Dec. 1887)[9]

This formulation echoes Wilfrid Blunt's rhetorical co-option of his wife's literary heritage to 'the cause of Arabian liberty', a cause which reappears in the events surrounding his imprisonment. Despite his initial associations between Irish and Egyptian radicals, *The Land War in Ireland* represents the couple as 'far away from all Eastern associations, and in a purely local quarrel in the extreme west of Christian Europe' (Wilfrid Blunt, *Land War in Ireland* 368). Yet he does so in recalling Anne's use of Arabic to speak with him privately on their way under escort to Galway jail. Nor was this the only legacy of their Eastern travels that shaped their Irish experiences. In the words of the *Nation*:

> Arabi Pasha has written a characteristically dauntless letter to Lady Anne Blunt, in which Tory barbarities in Ireland are reprobated and condemned. The brave and lion-hearted Egyptian who heroically stood up for his own land has the courage and chivalry to send us his sympathies and best wishes from his exile prison-home in Ceylon . . . (14 Jan. 1888)

With the intervention into these debates of Ahmed 'Urabi, Anne Blunt again features both as active participant in, and mediator of, the nationalist discourses of those around her. Joseph Lennon argues that 'Celtic-Oriental comparisons allowed Irish writers to rhetorically assert both their proximity to the metropole, or center of Empire, and their proximity to the periphery' (Lennon xxvi). 'Urabi's intervention suggests, not only that these affiliations could work both ways, but also that they could be most powerfully accessed through a sentimental appeal to gender politics: the *Nation* quotes him as saying 'I do not understand how it is competent to the police to attack women and children.' For the *Nation* the message is clear: 'Arabi, the Egyptian Nationalist, has a claim on the gratitude of every Irish Nationalist worthy of the name' (14 Jan. 1888).

This vision of a unified transnational anti-imperialism did not, however, go unchallenged – even by Wilfrid Blunt himself. As early as 1886, he was commenting bitterly of Augusta Gregory that:

> It is curious that she, who could see so clearly in Egypt, when it was a case between the Circassian Pashas and the Arab fellahin, should be blind now that the case is between English landlords and Irish tenants in Galway. But property blinds all eyes, and it is easier for a camel to pass through the eye of a needle than for an Irish

landlord to enter into the kingdom of Home Rule. (Diary 10 June 1886, Wilfrid Blunt, *Land War in Ireland* 146)

Yet the very ease with which the Blunts seemed to synthesise cultural identities could be turned against them, and their own eyes oversaw plenty of property with which they might be blinded. The unionist Irish Loyal and Patriotic Union circulated a pamphlet attacking Anne Blunt as a heartless landowner evicting women and children from her English estates even as she campaigns against landlords in Ireland (*Leinster Express* 24 Mar. 1888). This can be seen as a clear attempt to counter nationalist representations of Anne Blunt by turning her social status against her, replacing the image of her assaulted body with that of even more vulnerable figures. Ranging further afield, Sir Edward Sullivan observes in a November 1887 letter to the London *Morning Post* that 'Mr Blunt, landowner in Sussex, denounces Lord Clanricarde, landowner in Galway . . . Lord C has property in Ireland, and lives chiefly in London. Mr Blunt has property in Sussex, and lives chiefly in the desert' (qtd *Kerry Evening Post* 26 Nov. 1887). Ironically, then, the Blunts' Eastern sympathies become a way through which to dispossess them from Irishness and Irish causes – and in turn to try to fracture the transnational fusion between anti-imperial nationalisms that the couple represents.

The final part of this chapter turns to the voice of Anne Blunt herself – or rather, its mediated appearance in newspaper accounts of Wilfrid Blunt's legal proceedings in February 1888 against his arresting magistrate John Byrne. These accounts excitedly showcase her testimony – a testimony that, it becomes increasingly clear, turns on her presence on the platform at Woodford, and whether it is to be read as an act of wifely loyalty, a declaration of political enthusiasm, or a calculated publicity stunt by her flamboyant husband. Whatever combination of personal convictions, inherited allegiances and marital solidarity shaped Anne Blunt's political thinking, her journal entries for the period reveal her as deeply moved by the suffering she witnesses on the estates, and as an enthusiastic supporter of the Irish tenant movements (Anne Blunt MS 53959–61 1887–8). Underlying her anti-imperialist sympathies, though, is a conviction that the route to political change lies in educating the English people as to the injustices of their colonised subjects: 'If people in England knew what I told them, they would sympathise' (Anne Blunt MS 53961 21 Dec. 1887). This conviction may indicate a subtle difference between the Blunts' anti-imperial outlooks. It also suggests a public significance to the act of bearing witness to suffering. The gendered frameworks of legal testimony, however, produce for Anne Blunt a more indeterminate mode of epistemological agency.

In her version of events as represented in the *Irish Times*, Anne Blunt repeatedly underlines the scrupulous accuracy of her testimony: 'I don't remember the words' (4 Feb. 1888).[10] She depicts John Byrne as violently attacking, not just her husband, but the bonds of marriage itself: '[he] made what I would call a rush at us, and myself and my husband were separated by force. I had to hold my husband under the arms in this way.' Whereas her journal frames this crucial moment in terms of emotional response – 'thanks be to God, I was able to hold firm and down we went together' (Anne Blunt MS 53959 25 Oct 1887) – her public testimony focuses on specific actions, including her call to the police that they would kill her husband if they continued. Events are recounted with a matter-of-factness that still subtly invokes the proximity of her body to violence: 'A baton passed close to my face. It did not hit me.' In her journal, she casts her experience of actual physical assault as the product of John Byrne's malice: 'It seemed to me that this man Byrne had a special animus in attacking Wilfrid and me too for that matter, for at one moment I was almost garrotted by the hands of a person who seized me round the neck from behind and dug his fingers into my throat (Anne Blunt MS 53959 25 Oct. 1887). In her courtroom testimony, however, such emotive (and unprovable) connections are set aside for an emphasis only on her direct, verifiable experience: 'I was seized by the throat by someone from behind. Two fingers were dug into my throat, and my head was violently pulled back.' Wilfrid Blunt's 1912 memoir has no such scruples, though his wife is assigned a considerably minimised, and rather less impressive role: 'Anne had during the whole affair *obstinately* clung to me, and he [Byrne], seizing her from behind by the throat, hurt her considerably' (Wilfrid Blunt, *Land War in Ireland* 354, my italics). He does acknowledge that 'no little courage was displayed by my wife and Mrs Rowlands on the occasion', but depicts this as a gendered anomaly 'at a time when women took little part in political scrambles, or exposed themselves to being rough-handled by the representatives of imperial law and order' (Wilfrid Blunt, *Land War in Ireland* 357). For all his multiple personal connections with politically engaged women, there is limited space in Wilfrid Blunt's narrative of anti-imperial martyrdom for his wife's agency, and none for the public protest experiences of Irishwomen involved in the Land Wars.

Under cross-examination by John Atkinson, QC, counsel for Byrne, Anne Blunt remains carefully precise as to the extent of her awareness. To the question of whether her husband had attended other public meetings, she replies: 'I cannot answer for what he did when I was not with him. *I have no personal knowledge*' (my italics), a cagily, cleverly legalistic comment which, in light of the couple's private history, might carry more irony to the informed reader than necessarily intended. Pressed on this, she asks: 'Do you mean to cross-examine him about it?', before closing up the implicit marital distancing with a renewed emphasis on loyalty and togetherness: 'I very often have accompanied him [to public meetings] – constantly.' The contested presence of women's bodies on public platforms becomes central to the cross-examination: 'Did you go to this meeting to embarrass the police – knowing the police were going to suppress the meeting – by the presence of ladies?' Her wry reply – 'It never occurred to me that the police would be embarrassed by my presence. I don't think they were' – renders the chivalric discourse previously peddled by the state faintly ludicrous, as evinced by the courtroom laughter (according to the newspaper) that it produced. Atkinson seeks to represent her as a canny, knowing witness: 'You are careful to make the point of law.' In return, Anne Blunt maintains her scrupulous delineation of her epistemological boundaries: 'I don't know whether it is a point of law, but they mentioned that it was because of the proclamation that the meeting was illegal.'

As the cross-examination proceeds, her testimony takes on a curious affect of self-erasure, constructing her presence at Woodford as that of a disengaged observer: 'I didn't anticipate anything . . . I was not told. I heard him say it . . . I waited to see what would happen . . . I waited to see.' This implicit, escalating constriction of testimonial authority – a reiterated bearing witness to what she has not witnessed – suggests the limitations for women of invoking their public presence as in itself a form of political intervention. It also, though, hints at another putative mode of experiential agency: Anne Blunt as the traveller and travel writer. Having already recorded sharp observations on previous encounters (Anne Blunt MS 53959 Oct. 1887; Longford 249), she had, as her testimony notes in passing, 'brought a book [to the meeting] to make sketches'. Such a rhetorically detached observational mode is not altogether compatible with any of the conflicting representations anxious to place her as loyal (and/or misguided) wife, or as enthusiastic (and/or hypocritical) champion of Irish liberties. It may, however, inform the peculiarly hybrid agency that emerges from her testimony's tantalising invocation of incomplete action. Whereas her journal entry represents her as both falling and then being hurled from the platform (MS 53959 25 Oct. 1887), she tells the court that 'I was pushed, *but I half jumped, was half pushed . . . I did not fall down.* I had a book in my hand which I could not hold, and I gave it to someone else' (my italics). The constraints of legal testimony, therefore, provide a framework for the systematic occlusion of emotional and personal subjectivity, yet also shadow out an experiential agency which both lays claim to and recoils from participation in public discourses.

In conclusion, it must be noted that all this testimony, however faithfully reported, still does not give us the authentic voice of Lady Anne Blunt: it is, after all, inevitably mediated by the interventions and selections of the lawyers, the judge, the journalists and the newspapers. As such, it in fact remains all too compatible with the uncertainties surrounding the authorship and authority of her travelogues, her journals and her letters.[11] Whether authorial or national, Anne Blunt's identity seems to remain perpetually up for dispute. Even after her husband's release, her cultural identity continues to be the topic of intrigued speculation, a speculation apparently inseparable from her literary heritage and the various national, racial and political affiliations with which she was associated. The *Irish Examiner* of 7 November 1890 reports that:

> A Scotchman, writing home from Cairo, says that Lady Anne Blunt, the grand-daughter of Lord Byron, has, with her husband, Mr Wilfrid Blunt, and a daughter, adopted the life and customs of the Arabs. They have permanently pitched their tents on the borders of the Egyptian desert, and eat, drink, and dress like natives to the manner born.

As a woman attacked on a political platform, as an Englishwoman embroiled in Irish affairs, as Lord Byron's granddaughter, and as Wilfrid Scawen Blunt's wife, Lady Anne Blunt offers contemporary commentators a distinctive focal point for transnational correlations between anti-imperial struggles. The physical vulnerability implied by her femininity; her apparent transcending of narrowly Anglo-centric loyalties; the Romantic political aesthetics of her grandfather's life and writing; and the ambiguous terms of her emotional and intellectual partnership in her husband's causes – all these conspire to keep her central to, yet perpetually eluded and elided by, the conflicts of her day.

Notes

1 See Longford and Winstone.

2 For further context, see Longford 167–92, Berdine, and Cole.

3 George Gordon, Lord Byron famously died in Greece in 1824 while supporting the Greek struggle for independence from the Ottoman Empire.

4 See especially Anne Blunt's *Bedouin Tribes* (1879), to which her husband contributed some anthropological material, and *A Pilgrimage to Nejd* (1881).

5 Gregory's account is framed by a brief prelude, presumably by Thomas Chennery the editor: 'We have been favoured by Lady Gregory . . .'

6 Anne Blunt is thought to have been initially unaware of his affair with Gregory, and her later discovery of it precipitated a crisis in their marriage (McDiarmid 63–6).

7 See O'Toole, especially Ch. 3. Women in Scotland at the time were also involved, sometimes violently, in protesting evictions (Gleadle Ch.8).

8 See Urquhart 17–18 in this volume.

9 Dillon had previously read out Byron's 'The Irish Avatar' after a dinner with the Blunts (Anne Blunt MS 53959 18 Oct. 1887).

10 This discussion of Anne Blunt's testimony is based on the *Irish Times* report as one of the most comprehensive. Reports in other newspapers corroborate (or at least reiterate) most of the key features of her evidence as discussed here.

11   For discussions of the distinctive difficulties posed by both the Blunts' papers see Longford, McDiarmid, and Archer and Fleming.

Works Cited

Archer, Rosemary and James Fleming. 'Introduction'. *Lady Anne Blunt: Journals and Correspondence 1878–1917*. Cheltenham: Heriot, 1986. 11–15.

'The banquet to Mr Wilfred [sic] Blunt'. *Nation* 17 Dec. 1887: 1.

Blunt, Anne. *Bedouin Tribes of the Euphrates*, 2 vols. London: John Murray, 1879.

—. *A Pilgrimage to Nejd, the Cradle of the Arab Race*, 2 vols. London: John Murray, 1881.

Blunt, Lady Anne. 'Journal'. 1887–8. MS 53959–61, Wentworth Bequest. British Library.

Blunt, Wilfrid Scawen. *The Land War in Ireland: Being a Personal Narrative of Events*. London: Stephen Swift & Co., 1912.

—. *The Love-Lyrics and Songs of Proteus*. London: William Morris, 1892.

—. *Secret History of the English Occupation of Egypt: Being a Personal Narrative of Events*. New York: Knopf, 1922 edn, first published 1907.

Berdine, Michael D. *The Accidental Tourist, Wilfrid Scawen Blunt, and the British Invasion of Egypt in 1882*. New York: Routledge, 2005.

Bobotis, Andrea. 'From Egypt to Ireland: Lady Augusta Gregory and cross-cultural nationalisms in Victorian Ireland'. *Romanticism and Victorianism on the Net* 48 (Nov. 2007): 1–27. Available at: id.erudit.org/iderudit/017439ar DOI: 10.7202/017439ar.

'The charge against Mr Blunt'. *Freeman's Journal* 25 Oct. 1887: 6.

Cole, Juan R. I. *Colonialism and Revolution in the Middle East: Social and Cultural Origins of Egypt's Urabi Movement*. Princeton: Princeton University Press, 1992.

Freeman's Journal 24 Oct. 1887: 5.

Gleadle, Kathyn. *British Women in the Nineteenth-Century*. Houndsmills: Palgrave Macmillan, 2001.

Gregory, Augusta (Lady Gregory). 'Arabi and his household'. *The Times* 23 Oct. 1882: 4.

—. 'Preface', 1921. Wilfrid Scawen Blunt. *My Diaries: Being a Personal Narrative of Events, 1888–1914*, vol. 1. London: Forgotten Books, 2013 edn, first published 1922. vii–xiv.

Grewal, Inderpal. *Home and Harem: Nation, Gender, and Empire and the Cultures of Travel*. Durham: Duke University Press, 1996.

Irish Examiner 7 Nov. 1890: 2.

Kelleher, Margaret. 'Prose writing and drama in English, 1830–1890: from Catholic emancipation to the fall of Parnell'. Margaret Kelleher and Philip O'Leary, eds. *The Cambridge History of Irish Literature*, 2 vols. Cambridge: Cambridge University Press, 2006. I: 449–99.

Lacy, Lisa. 'Lady Anne Blunt and the English Idea of Liberty: in Arabia, Egypt, and the Empire'. Ph.D. dissertation, University of Texas at Austin, 2012. Available at: hdl.handle.net/ 2152/ETD-UT-2012-05-5046.

—. *Lady Anne Blunt in the Middle East: Travel, Politics and the Idea of Empire*. London and New York: I. B. Tauris, 2015.

Leinster Express 24 Mar. 1888: 5.

Lennon, Joseph. *Irish Orientalism: A Literary and Intellectual History*. Syracuse: Syracuse University Press, 2004.

Longford, Elizabeth. *A Pilgrimage of Passion: The Life of Wilfrid Scawen Blunt*. London: Wiedenfeld and Nicolson, 1979.

McDiarmid, Lucy. *Poets and the Peacock Dinner: The Literary History of a Meal*. Oxford: Oxford University Press, 2014.

Mitchell, James. 'The imprisonment of Wilfrid Scawen Blunt in Galway: cause and consequence'. *Journal of the Galway Archaeological and Historical Society* 46 (1994): 65–110. Available at: jstor.org/stable/25535636.

'Mr Blunt and Lord Clanricarde'. *Kerry Evening Post* 26 Nov. 1887: 4.

'Mr Blunt's action against Mr Byrne'. *Irish Times* 4 Feb. 1888: 6.

'Mr Blunt's appeal'. *Irish Times* 14 Jan. 1888: 3

O'Toole, Tina. *The Irish New Woman*. Houndsmills: Palgrave Macmillan, 2013.

'The proclaimed meeting at Woodford'. *Freeman's Journal* 23 Oct. 1887: 5.

'What the nation says'. *Nation* 14 Jan. 1888: 1.

Winstone, H. V. F. *Lady Anne Blunt: A Biography*. London: Barzan Publishing, 2003.

Yeazell, Ruth. *Harems of the Mind: Passages of Western Art and Literature*. New Haven and London: Yale University Press, 2000.

3

Battles in the Garden

Emily Lawless's *A Garden Diary,*

1899–1900 and the Boer War

Heidi Hansson

The personal and pastoral title of Emily Lawless's *A Garden Diary, 1899–1900* (1901) obscures the fact that an important strand in the text is the description of how war is experienced by a bystander. Alongside the gardening sections, gendered and domesticated war writing offers insights into the subhistory of the Second Boer War (1899–1902) as a mediated event. Integrating everyday conversations about the war and emotional reactions to victories and defeats in a domestic context could be understood as a way of feminising the masculine genre of war reportage, and the text certainly has this effect to a great extent. At the same time, Lawless explicitly voices as her opinion that war writing belongs to the masculine domain. While establishing a domestic discursive register for the Boer War sections in *A Garden Diary*, she undercuts its ideological importance by framing her text as private, and by implication unimportant in the public, national space of war writing.

A Garden Diary is dedicated to 'the garden's chief owner, and the gardener's friend', and describes a year in Hazelhatch, the cottage that Lawless shared with Lady Sarah Spencer in Gomshall, Surrey from 1898 to her death in 1913. Before being brought together in a book, portions of the text had appeared in the journals *The Pilot* and *The Garden*, the latter an influential magazine launched by the Irish gardener William Robinson. In keeping with the practical tone of these publications, *A Garden Diary* contains observations of the growing habits of certain plants, recounts the problems of transplanting and describes garden design. In the *Sheffield Daily Telegraph* the book is described as 'chiefly devoted to gardening matters, especially to landscape gardening and the natural history that belongs to gardens' (2 May 1901) which suggests that it was received as a kind of handbook. The text is however much more than a gardening manual. Since garden writing naturally follows the course of the year, it is close to the diary form and easily takes on characteristics of self-writing. Establishing herself as a subjective presence in the text, Lawless joins a tradition of women writers at the end of the nineteenth century who used the garden journal to intersperse philosophical arguments, personal reflections and comments on current affairs among the horticultural tips (Bellanca 20; Hansson 60–1). The form suits her digressive style: 'one starts intending to fill a page with one subject, but before one has got very far one discovers that in reality one is filling it up with quite another!' she writes (Lawless 11). The result is a hybrid text described in the publication notice in *The Times* as 'discursive and reflective' and 'a quaint kind of literature' (31 Aug. 1901).

The two main themes in *A Garden Diary* are gardening matters and personal reactions to the war news. By relating the situation in South Africa to developments in her garden, Lawless forges an affective link that gives the Boer War local and private relevance. The juxtaposition of the war and the garden is incongruous, almost shocking, but captures how the conflict pene-trated into people's homes as one of the world's first media wars (Gooch xix). Correspondents on site were able to convey the news from the front to readers at home within a day or less. The popular press attracted new categories of newspaper buyers, and many journalists used fictional strategies to incite emotional responses and invite readers to be imaginative participants in the battles. The new style of reporting created a sense of recognition and involvement that made the war everybody's affair. Lawless provides the rarely acknowledged perspective of the committed news reader, presenting the war from the point of view of a media consumer. As a work that revolves around the domestic reception of the Boer War, *A Garden Diary* is thus situated in a media landscape as well as a national imaginary space and the actuality of the garden. In this, the text demonstrates and contributes to a general domestication of battle news that had the ultimate aim of ensuring public support for the war.

In simple terms, the Boer War was a struggle over natural resources between opponents of European origin in land that belonged to neither of them. Hostilities lasted from 11 October 1899 to 31 May 1902 and began with a Boer offensive leading up to the 'Black Week' between 10 and 15 December 1899 when the British lost three major battles in five days. The defeats led to a surge in army recruitment but domestic opinion was divided and the military effort was not universally supported. A major component in the war was the conflict that built up in the course of the nineteenth century between British settlers who were resolved to remain European and Boers who had begun to develop a more hybrid sense of identity (Smith 436). The identity question resonated with nationalist movements across Europe, and from an

Irish perspective, the division into friends and enemies was far from straight-forward. The pro-Boer Transvaal Committee, usually regarded as a precursor to Sinn Féin, was formed in the early winter of 1899, with influential figures like James Connolly, Maud Gonne and Arthur Griffith among the founders (McCracken 50–7). For Irish nationalists, the war offered an opportunity to oppose the British, as exemplified by the volunteer force led by the Irish-American Colonel John Blake and Maud Gonne's later husband Major John MacBride fighting on the Boer side. Others managed to reconcile apparently contradictory commitments, like Emily Lawless's cousin, Bernard Fitzpatrick, Lord Castletown, who was a member of the Gaelic League and a proponent of Pan-Celticism, but also a dedicated unionist who commanded troops on the British side. The references to the Boer War in *A Garden Diary* do not acknowledge the fraught situation with Irish participants fighting on opposite sides, and as a unionist, Lawless identifies with the British. Even so, she uses the conflict to articulate a more nuanced view of nationhood where England under military pressure loses its role as Ireland's primary enemy, which might be interpreted as a covert comment on the problematic Irish position.

As it emerges in *A Garden Diary*, Lawless's unionism seems to be emotionally rather than politically driven and based on a sense of common heritage or origin. Imagining the situation at the front, she pictures the soldiers as her kinsmen:

> One is amongst them. One is standing in the midst of them. One can see, literally all but see, that tattered, sunburnt, rather dilapidated-looking host – friends, cousins, kinsfolk; countrymen and fellow-subjects at all events. How odd you all look, dear friends, and yet how familiar! Big English frames, shrewd Scotch faces, tender, devil-may-care Irish hearts. Surely one knows you? Surely you are very near to us, disguise yourselves as you may? The setting may be new, the remoteness consider-able, but neither setting nor remoteness can hinder one from feeling at home in the midst of you! (Lawless 75)

After her move to England, Lawless's commitment to developments in Ireland decreased, and her emotional involvement in the war can be partly understood as a rejection of the polarised definitions of Irishness circulated at the time. Her description of the army as made up of soldiers from various parts of the United Kingdom expresses a heterogeneous sense of nationality as well as her unionist position. The boundaries between English and Irish are blurred and the meaning of national belonging re-evaluated, at least in a limited sense.

The first diary entry that explicitly deals with the war is from Christmas Day 1899, when the news about the Black Week provides occasion for Lawless to re-examine her childish perception of England as 'the Great Bully, the Supreme Tyrant, red with the blood of Ireland and Irish heroes' (Lawless 68):

> What an odd convention it is, when one thinks of it, that habit of embodying a country in an individual! Considered seriously the whole contention is absurd. To talk of a nation as a person is to talk sheer nonsense. If one handles the idea a little it tumbles to pieces in one's fingers. The fiction of unity resolves itself into a mere vortex of atoms, all moving in different ways, and moreover with a different general drift in each successive generation. (Lawless 68)

When England can no longer be represented as the personification of an idea, it becomes disunited and more difficult to cast as the enemy (Lawless 68). The reference to unity has a particular resonance at a time when definitions of authentic Irishness were being constructed. Like many of her contemporaries, Lawless romanticised the Irish West, but felt excluded by the discourse of Celticism and resisted nationalist efforts that promoted a homogeneous version of identity. Recreating Ireland in her Surrey garden as a number of separate plots rather than a symbolic landscape, she emphasises diversity:

> My particular vein of sentiment has lately taken the form of linking together sundry small spots here with others far away, upon the other side of St. George's boisterous channel. Thus I have a Burren corner, a West Galway corner, a Kerry corner, a Kildare corner, even a green memento or two of the great lost forest of Ossory, of which only a few shadowy remnants survive to a remote, but happily not an indifferent generation. (Lawless 125)

The representation of the Irish landscape as incoherent and mobile becomes a metaphorical justification of her unionist politics. If Ireland can be transplanted to England, even in this minor way, absolute differences between the countries cannot be maintained and national belonging must be conceived as multiple and unstable. In relation to the South African conflict, this nuanced view of nationality is possible partly because the Boer War is largely depoliticised in the text. National pride is present as a consideration, but it is primarily the human dimension that is foregrounded.

   While the title of *A Garden Diary* suppresses the theme of war in the text, it also frames the conflict as a domesticated event. The hierarchy between different topics is initially unstable, and in the first entry alluding to the hostilities on 27 October 1899, the developments in South Africa are of secondary importance to private matters: 'Who dare forecast even his nearest future? These last four weeks have been so charged with anxiety not only, or even chiefly, war anxieties that I have not made so much as a single entry in this diary' (Lawless 62). But a few weeks into the new year Lawless's attitude has changed, and the war has become her main interest. Moving seamlessly between descriptions of plants and reactions to war news, she places the war in a local and private, as opposed to a global and public, context.

The constant return to the domestic space, as represented by household duties and gardening, corresponds to the idea that the main purpose of war is to defend the tranquil heart of the nation. But in the case of the Boer War, ordinary life in England was hardly under immediate threat and occasionally the entries in *A Garden Diary* establish a distance to the conflict. The sense that warfare is at the same time central to and completely removed from everyday reality is conveyed when a long, rather abstract discussion about civilian involvement during wartime, where Lawless directly addresses the reader, is superseded in importance by the pretended demands of mealtime: 'Yet hark! what sound is that? Surely it is not the luncheon bell? How exceedingly inconvenient! Well, our invasion must be postponed for the moment' (Lawless 144). Enclosing her discussion of warfare within the mundane, Lawless creates an anticlimactic structure that undermines her public authority and ensures that the 'discursive space' (Buck 438) of the text remains private.

The development that probably affected the home audience the most in the early stages of the war was the besiegement of the garrison towns Mafeking, Kimberley and Ladysmith. The news about the deprivations of the civilians and military personnel inspired compassion and distress, and Lawless is passionately engaged in the fate of Ladysmith in particular, despite the fact that she has no personal attachment to anybody in the town. Developments in the garden become a way to measure military progress, as when she estimates the time until the besieged town will be forced to surrender:

> Three weeks! It is not a very long time. Only a few more crocuses and scillas will be out in our little Dutch garden; only a few more oaks and chestnuts cut in the copse, yet within that time the fate of Ladysmith must be decided. (Lawless 108)

The coincidence that the garden in question is 'Dutch' is probably unintentionally ironic. The importance of the comment is that the suffering of the people under siege can be imagined and followed through the spring growth of the plants outside Hazelhatch, so that the war zone in a sense moves into the garden. Military timeframes are envisaged in terms of budding flowers and trees, and conversely, garden and household time is temporarily arrested until an acceptable solution has been achieved for those shut inside the garrison town. Commenting on the relief of Ladysmith by British forces under Sir Redvers Buller on 28 February 1900, Lawless concludes:

All is right, all is well, and we may go back to our own little concerns; our house-keepings, and our marketings, our weedings, and our seed-sowing, with lighter; let us hope, perhaps also, with a trifle gratefuller hearts? (Lawless 119)

The release of the beleaguered people is figured as an implicit condition for the possibility of new growth and the return of normal procedures. In a similar manner, the relief of Mafeking on 17 May after 217 days of siege is conflated with a change in the weather and placed in the context of the thriving spring garden:

It is the nineteenth of May. S. S. [Lady Sarah Spencer] has returned, and the east wind which has long been vexing our souls has departed for the moment, and a soft caressing zephyr blows seductively. The garden, comforted by recent showers, is smiling one broad smile from the red steps at the top of it to the new pergola at the bottom. And now this morning comes the news of the Relief of Mafeking. Joy for the victors; joy for the nation; joy for everything and everybody. (Lawless 194)

The connection between military success and the elements makes the victory seem natural and gives it transcendental significance. Nature's bounty becomes a mirror of national pride and a symbolic release of anxiety.

The telegraph and the popular press guaranteed that updated reports were readily available and Lawless changes the duties of her garden boy from digging and weeding to procuring the latest newspapers (Lawless 102–3). Following the reports increasingly becomes an obsession that has to be curtailed, and in February 1900 she resolves '[n]ot to devote an indefinite number of hours to the reading of war news' (Lawless 92). It is a resolution she soon breaks, because of the affective involvement created by the reports:

Has it often happened I wonder in the history of a country that this sort of external and public news – the news of the street and of the newspaper – becomes to each individual his own absolutely private news; news that for the moment seems to supersede even the acutest personal grief; news that makes the tears start, the pulses throb, the heart, at apprehension of what may be going to happen, literally stand still from fear? (102)

The *Daily Mail* was established in 1896 and it is probably no coincidence that it is the only newspaper explicitly mentioned in the text (Lawless 76). It heralded the advent of the popular press and when the war broke out, a number of new publications appeared as a direct result of the hunger for news from South Africa (Gooch xx). Popular newspapers and illustrated weeklies provided an alternative to the more sober reports in newspapers like *The Times* and circulated stirring war images suitable for household consumption rather than political analyses or truthful accounts of battlefield conditions (Judd and Surridge 10). The marketing strategies of the popular press shaped a journalistic style based on drama and emotion and like the poems and adventure novels published at the time, the articles nourished a desire for heroism and military triumphs that objective information could not satisfy. Steve Attridge suggests that there might have been 'a tension in the public mind between what it wanted the army to be, and to do, and an awareness that it was patently failing to succeed' (Attridge 45). Depictions of heroic deeds and fearless soldiers could alleviate such doubts, and as a Tory 'halfpenny paper' the *Daily Mail* was one of the most important distribution channels for war stories (Blackburn 225). That some readers preferred reassurance to information is evident in Lawless's account of a conversation with her gardener after the unfavourable reports about Black Week. The location of the exchange underscores the sense in the text that the war penetrates into all domestic activities:

> 'This is bad news, Cuttle,' I said, as we met outside the greenhouse.
> 'Well ma'am, they do try to make it out to be baddish, but I wouldn't believe it, if I was you.'
> 'But it is in all the papers, Cuttle.'
> 'Very likely it is ma'am, but what of that? I don't hold with none of those papers. They must be a-stuffing themselves out with something.'
> 'But I'm afraid the generals admit it themselves.'
> 'Excuse me ma'am, but that's just where you're making a great mistake. We don't know nothing about what the generals admit. All we know is that the papers say they admit it, which is a very different story. Mark my words, you'll find that it'll turn out to be some of their muddlings. Just you mark my words for it, that's how it is.' (Lawless 66)

Although Cuttle 'reads his paper diligently' (Lawless 65) he displays an awareness of the constructedness of newspaper reports and refuses to accept any information that challenges his confidence in British superiority. Without the promise of an ultimate British victory, the reports have no value within a framework that is meaningful for him, and instead of accepting the possibility of British setbacks, he counterposes his own authority – 'mark my words' – against the printed accounts.

Relayed through the conversation with Cuttle, Lawless acknowledges that the newspapers are commercial products whose survival in the market relies on proffering new and sensational material, whether the news is good or bad. Contrary to the gardener's opinion the papers were, however, more likely to publish complimentary than critical articles. War correspondents were expected to provide eyewitness accounts which meant that they had to be close to the army to either see for themselves what happened during the battle or piece together a report based on interviews (Badsey 190). In either case, they had to have a good relationship with the troops. To gain access to the telegraph in the field, they had to submit to military censorship which restricted the scope of what they could write (Badsey 189). Actual facts of the campaign could not be suppressed, but they could be presented in the best possible light. If the conversation with Cuttle reveals Lawless's awareness of the newsworthiness of catastrophe and therefore predilection of correspondents to report disasters, her exchange with her acquaintance Mr R. P. displays her recognition that news accounts may also occasionally be over-positive:

'They have had a baddish time, you must remember. Stormberg and all that! quite enough to give anyone the jumps, I should say. Of course it has been kept out of the papers. In the papers the Tommies always figure as heroes. Is Anemone Blanda in flower with you yet?' – this with a sudden rise of animation. (Lawless 105)

Although both Cuttle and Mr R. P. question the authority of the newspapers, Cuttle remains inside whereas Mr R. P. is shown to place himself outside the imagined patriotic community who believe in the Tommies' heroic behaviour. Referring to the British army in South Africa in the third person, he keeps the war at a distance. It is this distance, rather than his questioning of the truthfulness of the accounts, that upsets Lawless, since for her, the conflict has become an integral part of everyday life. Thus, Mr R. P.'s animation is reserved for the state of the flowers in the Hazelhatch garden, whereas Lawless's order of priorities has been reversed:

I adore my garden, and yield to no one in my estimation of its supreme importance as a topic; still there are moments when even horticulture must learn to bow its head; when the reputation of one's Flag rises to a higher place in one's estimation than even the reputation of one's flower-beds. 'Anemone Blanda!' I repeated several times to myself in the course of the afternoon, and each time with a stronger feeling of exasperation. '*Anemone Blanda*, indeed!' (Lawless 107)

Ironically, of course, the very nature of the text requires the superimposition of Anemone Blanda over British imperial defeat, but Lawless's stated position is that domestic matters cannot be allowed to overshadow the conflict. Garden pride has to await better news.

The easy access to updated news reports meant that the war became everybody's business, and in the descriptions in *A Garden Diary*, the shared concern for British military personnel and civilians in South Africa is shown to cut across class and gender boundaries. Lawless's account of Cuttle's claims to military expertise is one example, and another is the description of how Lawless and Lady Sarah Spencer learned about the relief of Kimberley from a park attendant:

> We had gone to see a friend; she left me to take a turn in the Park; in a few minutes she returned breathlessly; she had met a park-keeper and he had told her the news. Five minutes more we were both in the park; had caught the same inspired park-keeper, and had fallen upon him simultaneously. 'Is it true? How do you know? Who told you?' (Lawless 110)

The relief of Mafeking three months later caused street celebrations across England during the so called Mafeking Night 18 May 1900 when working-class and middle-class people were united in patriotic enthusiasm. The revels were inspired by newspaper headlines and signs outside the telegraph offices and were certainly not as spontaneous as was suggested at the time. According to Paula M. Krebs, they 'say less about British support for im-perialism than they do about the power of the press to tease the British public into a frenzy of anticipation and then to release that tension in a rush of carefully-directed enthusiasm' (Krebs 2). As unofficial expressions of relief, the street parties illuminate how public interest is excited by the war as human drama rather than as politics. The sieges and subsequent releases of Kimberley, Ladysmith and Mafeking gain symbolic value not least because newspaper reports of life in the blockaded towns highlight the civilian side of the conflict and demonstrate the higher purpose of war to preserve peaceful domesticity. This focus on the human dimension legitimates women's interest in war news, and when Lawless learns about the relief of Ladysmith her hunger for more information overthrows gender norms and social conventions:

> I sprang into a carriage, all but shaking hands as I did so with an absolutely unknown old gentleman, who was its only other occupant. Everyone knows the shrinking, the more than maidenly dread of the solitary travelling he, for the unknown travelling she, however harmless the latter may look. On this occasion public interest overcame even that terror. As a river bursts through its banks, so my old gentleman burst into a torrent of repressed information. (Lawless 118)

The relief of Ladysmith could boost domestic morale not only in its capacity as a military triumph but perhaps more importantly as a human story with a happy ending. The human interest quality of the news meant that it could cross from the public to the private arena, which allows Lawless to share her elation and makes her an appropriate audience for her fellow traveller.

As the conversations with Cuttle, the park keeper and the gentleman on the train indicate, there is little sense in the text of conflicted loyalties, and even Mr R. P., who signals his detachment from the forces in South Africa through his use of third person references, is described as guilty of no more than a mistaken sense of priority. Support for the British is taken for granted, and Lawless neither questions the necessity of the war nor Britain's imperial aspirations. In contrast to Mr R. P.'s distancing pronouns, her choice of the inclusive first person pronoun demonstrates her personal commitment to the British cause:

> It is still going on, this war of *ours*, and seems likely moreover, to do so for a considerable time longer. Botha, De Wet, Delarey, with half a dozen more guerrilla leaders, are swarming about, active as ants, and at least as dangerous as hornets. *We* have got Pretoria, but *we* have emphatically not got *our* new colonies, though both, I see, are now officially annexed. That *we* shall get them some day or other, and that the last of England's big daughters will in the course, say of the coming century become as friendly and tolerant of her as are the other two, a good many people seem to expect. Possibly. The very moderate view she takes of the motherly function will certainly be a help in that direction. In these days grown-up daughters are not expected fortunately to be deferential especially, perhaps, to their mothers. (Lawless 232–3, my italics)

To some extent, Lawless's expressions of loyalty can be seen as the logical effect of her unionist beliefs, but she represents the colonial relationship as mainly a matter of formality, with England as a not particularly controlling and even rather indifferent parent. Her engagement in the war is rhetorically based not primarily on any expression of patriotism or duty, but on the human dimension foregrounded through the narrativisation in the newspapers. With newspaper correspondents reporting directly from the field, the papers created a sense of immediacy that made readers feel that they were actually on the scene, at least as observers. The war could be contained in the ready-made framework of the adventure story, and presented as a human, emotional rather than an impersonal, political matter. Hence, many articles from the war zone are characterised by literariness and aestheticism. At least as Lawless sees it, such features bring the experience closer to the reader:

> 'BULLETS – The air was a sieve of them. – They beat upon the boulders like a million hammers. They tore the turf like a harrow!'
> These three lines came out of a recent number of the *Daily Mail*, and they describe Elandslaagte. Is it, I wonder, because Literature is so much more familiar to me than War that I seem to require the aid of the one in order to bring home to me the reality of the other? These three lines are certainly literature, literature of the impressionist kind, which, if not the best in the abstract, is at any rate the best for such a purpose. Trying to put oneself into the position of such a bystander as the

writer of them, I am able to fancy that if the bullets came thick enough they really might seem to tear the turf like a harrow. (Lawless 76–7)

The Battle of Elandslaagte took place on 21 October 1899 and ended in British victory. The article recreating the atmosphere of the encounter was written by George Warrington Steevens, one of the most famous war correspondents of the time whose trademark was image-rich and vivid reporting (Stearn 210). Like most of the reports by English correspondents, his articles were mainly intended to bolster patriotism at home. Steevens's style is not exceptional although he was probably better than most at conveying the sensory realities of the battlefield. He died during the siege of Ladysmith, which gave his reports additional pathos in retrospect. Many commentators highlight the similarity between his articles and short stories, as in the obituary in *Literature* where he is described as having 'brought to journalism the talents, and sympathies, and touch hitherto regarded as belonging more properly to the writer of fiction' (qtd Blackburn 190).

The account of the Battle of Elandslaagte that Lawless quotes from in her text thus exhibits all the signs of fiction. Steevens uses simile and metaphor and employs figurative verbs that give the impression of bustling activity: the trains and trucks not only puff along (Steevens 44) but bristle 'with the rifles of infantry' (Steevens 43) and vomit 'khaki into the meadow' (Steevens 47). The Boer military post is given a Lilliputian fairy tale atmosphere as 'the little blue-roofed village and the little red tree-girt station' (Steevens 44). Onomatopoetic words convey the battle noises, the shells coming through the air with a 'hissing shriek' (Steevens 43) or a 'faint whirr' (Steevens 48) and landing behind the British lines with the sound of '[p]lump: plump' (Steevens 43). The fictional devices create a sense of immediacy and on-the-scene experience. When the battle properly begins, the sentence is interrupted as by an enemy attack: 'The hill was crowned, was turned – but where were the Bo ' (Steevens 47). The end of the piece is breathless, giving a sense of the soldiers' weariness and fear: 'Another ridge – God! Would this cursed hill never end? It was sown with bleeding and dead behind; it was edged with stinging fire before. God! Would it never end? Oh, and get to the end of it!' (Steevens 54). Steevens's fictionalisation communicates the emotional power of the battle, and mediates a larger truth where the battlefield events become meaningful within a familiar plot structure. His text engages the home audience by offering a vicarious experience of the sounds, sights, smells and sensations of battle. Like Lawless, he takes part in shaping a discursive register where the war is brought within the sphere of knowledge of the non-combatants. Although the image of the bullets working the soil like a harrow that caught Lawless's attention (Steevens 76) is agricultural rather than horticultural, it corresponds to the domestication of the war in *A Garden Diary*. A similar metaphor is the description of enemy fire as a 'hellish hail of bullets' (Steevens 61), first literalised by Lawless in a description of an 'exceptionally imposing hailstorm' (Lawless 77) in Sussex, and then brought back to the experience of war:

> Through such a furious hail – only appropriately black – the famous Bagarrah cavalry rode to their deaths last September year. Through such a hail, as thick, as fierce, as brutally indifferent, who that one knows, that one cares for, may not be riding or walking to-day? (Lawless 77)

Referring to Steevens's article as 'Literature' (Lawless 76), Lawless shows her awareness of its fictional dimensions, but she sees no conflict between news reporting and a literary style. Nevertheless, while the effect of the piece relies on fictional conventions, its authority remains a matter of the newspaper context where it originally appeared. Quotation marks establish that the passage is external to Lawless's text and reinforce the difference between the private domain of the diary and the public domain of war reporting. It is not that Lawless regards newspaper publication as a guarantee of truth. On the contrary, she mocks the prematurely published reports of British victims of the Boxer rebellion in China the summer of 1900 and is clearly aware of the sales value of sensation:

> The newspapers certainly do nothing to minimise it; perhaps they would say that it was hardly their province to do so! Such headings, however, as 'The Chinese Cawnpore!' 'Last shots reserved for the women!' 'White children carried on spears!' seem to be rather more than it is their absolute duty to offer to their readers! (Lawless 208)

When it is reported that those presumed dead are actually alive, her caustic comment is that 'were I the responsible head of a daily newspaper I should prefer to immure myself from society for the next few days!' (Lawless 217). The difference between the Boxer rebellion headlines and the passage from Steevens's article lies in the kind of feelings they are intended to evoke and the way they position the reader. The China headlines are designed to arouse indignation and disgust, whereas the article about the Boer War focuses on sensory and emotional aspects to produce the illusion of participation. For Lawless, the aestheticisation of war in Steevens's article becomes an imaginative truth that does not rely on literal truth, while the headlines about the Chinese situation lose their power if the events they describe are revealed to be untrue.

It could be expected that Lawless's preference for fictionalised reporting should legitimise the alternative war discourse in *A Garden Diary*, but this is actually not the case. Instead, she ends by rejecting diary accounts in general as 'subjective forms of literature' with 'little validity' (Lawless 242). After describing the domestic, private intrusions of the war for most of the year covered in the diary, she appears to arrive at the conclusion that the personal, egotistical perspective of the diarist is inappropriate for the subject:

> There are moreover seasons when such outpourings seem even less appropriate than others, and this year – September to September – appears, looking back, to be one of these. It has been a black, a despairingly black, twelve months for thousands; how black, how despairing, few of those thousands would have credited when it began. (Lawless 243)

As a private, subjective text, a diary lacks the necessary authority to treat serious matters, and in Lawless's ostensible opinion, the domestic framing of the Boer War in *A Garden Diary* detracts from the importance of the campaign and diminishes the value of the soldiers' sacrifices. Rather than claiming space for women's writing about war, she seems to reject the feminising effects of a homely context. In finally concluding that the war is a public, and by implication, masculine affair, she apparently counters the domestic discursive register she has established in her text, and as a result takes up the opposite position from the press and military spokesmen whose efforts were geared towards establishing the local significance of a war in South Africa. These manoeuvres produce a tension in the text where what she actually does jars with what she states that she ought to be doing. Although *A Garden Diary* takes part in domesticating the Boer War in practice, Lawless's restriction of the private domain implies that she is at least intellectually out of step with the developments of the new century, when the domestic was no longer a space apart to be defended on a battlefield elsewhere, but increasingly the space of battle itself.

Works Cited

Attridge, Steve. *Nationalism, Imperialism, and Identity in Late Victorian Culture: Civil and Military Worlds*. Gordonsville: Palgrave Macmillan, 2003.

Badsey, Stephen. 'War correspondents in the Boer War'. John Gooch, ed. *The Boer War: Direction, Experience and Image*. London: Frank Cass, 2000. 187–202.

Bellanca, Mary Ellen. *Daybooks of Discovery: Nature Diaries in Britain 1770–1870*. Charlottesville: University of Virginia Press, 2007.

Blackburn, Vernon. 'The last chapter'. G. W. Steevens. *From Capetown to Ladysmith: An Unfinished Record of the South African War*. Vernon Blackburn, ed. New York: Dodd, Mead and Co., 1900. 157–98.

Buck, Claire. 'First World War English elegy and the disavowal of women's sentimental poetics'. *English Literature in Transition* 53:4 (2010): 431–50.

Gooch, John. 'Introduction'. Gooch, ed. *The Boer War: Direction, Experience and Image*. London: Frank Cass, 2000. xi–xxi.

Hansson, Heidi. 'Emily Lawless and botany as a foreign science'. *Journal of Literature and Science* 4:1 (2011): 59–73. Available at: literatureandscience.org/issues/JLS_4_1/JLS_vol_4_no_1_Hansson.pdf.

Judd, Denis and Keith Surridge. *The Boer War*. London: John Murray, 2003 edn, first published 2002.

Krebs, Paula M. *Gender, Race and the Writing of Empire: Public Discourse and the Boer War*. Cambridge: Cambridge University Press, 1999.

Lawless, Emily. *A Garden Diary: September, 1899–September, 1900*. London: Methuen, 1901.

McCracken, Donal P. *Forgotten Protest: Ireland and the Anglo-Boer War*. Belfast: Ulster Historical Foundation, 2003.

'Notes'. *Sheffield Daily Telegraph* 2 May 1901: 3.

'Reviews of books'. *The Times* 31 Aug. 1901: 12 col. B. *The Times Digital Archive*.

Smith, M. van Wyk. 'The Boers and the Anglo-Boer War (1899–1902) in the twentieth-century moral imaginary'. *Victorian Literature and Culture* 31:2 (2003): 429–46. Available at: jstor.org/stable/25058635.

Stearn, Roger T. 'G. W. Steevens and the message of empire'. *Journal of Imperial and Commonwealth History* 17:2 (1989): 210–31.

Steevens, G. W. *From Capetown to Ladysmith: An Unfinished Record of the South African War*. Vernon Blackburn, ed. New York: Dodd, Mead and Co., 1900.

4

Winifred Letts and the Great War

A Poetics of Witness

Lucy Collins

For many years the work of women poets in the First World War was virtually invisible. The earliest anthologies and critical studies defined war poetry in narrow terms, privileging the soldier poet who had direct experience of combat.[1] Such critical discourse itself became an act of commemoration, ensuring the continued significance of shared memories of active service (Campbell 203).[2] Yet the canonised 'war poets', most of them middle-class officers, had only ever spoken for a minority, leaving the way open for more sustained and searching scholarship on the representation of violent conflict (Tylee 5). The work of retrieval has included important studies of women's writing as well as that of witnesses and combatants whose perspectives had previously been elided from the canon.[3] Often these positions are interwoven: the nature of women's involvement in the war was shaped by class issues and their experiences 'differed dramatically between geographical areas, trades, age groups and classes' (Braybon, qtd Gillis 105). These differences draw attention to the complex relationship between individual and collective experiences and how these can be represented in language. Women poets – who often bore witness to war, rather than directly participated in it – offer unique perspectives on the responsibility of the human subject in times of cultural crisis. In this chapter I will explore one poet whose particular background and experience have shaped her representation of the First World War in important ways.

The poet Winifred Letts, born in 1882, was a woman whose engagement with Irish and British cultures during the early decades of the twentieth century reveals a complex attitude towards the issue of war and its poetic representation. Though she spent much of her adulthood in Ireland, Letts maintained close personal ties with England, the place of her birth and early education; indeed she exemplifies the complex network of connections, both political and familial, that existed between the two countries at this time. The Great War was from the start entangled with Irish domestic politics and social development, both in delaying the attainment of Home Rule and shaping aspects of Ireland's economic affairs. Political tensions in Ireland were not eased by the onset of the war, however, but were instead transferred to a wider arena; Irishmen from both sides of the political divide joined the British army as a way to gain advantage for their cause once the conflict had ended.[4] Officially, though, the First World War remained an unacknowledged part of Irish experience; and the role that women poets played in bringing it to the attention of readers offers new perspectives on processes of cultural marginalisation.

Though poetry written by combatants during the First World War would become an enduring part of modern literary history, few Irishmen who enlisted wrote of their experiences. *Earth Voices Whispering*, Gerald Dawe's anthology of Irish war poetry between 1914 and 1945, contains work from just eight such figures, including Francis Ledwidge, Patrick MacGill and Thomas MacGreevy. This literary legacy has been further compromised by the scant acknowledgment of Ireland's involvement in the Great War within narratives of the independent state – a point of contrast with cultural memory in Northern Ireland. The fact that those who lost their lives on the battle-fields of the First World War would inevitably be compared to the revolu-tionaries of 1916 became immediately clear: Tom Kettle, a former Home Rule MP killed at the Somme recognised that 'these men will go down in history as heroes and martyrs, and I will go down – if I go down at all – as a bloody British officer' (qtd Brearton 20).[5] These tensions made the represen-tation of Irish war experience, and later discourse around it, an uneasy matter.

While scholarship on war poetry must take subsequent political events into account, the poetic texts themselves are more often concerned with the immediate questions of representation and recall. Much war poetry tended towards the traditional, both in form and idiom, yet there was also a desire to speak with immediacy – even with haste – of the specifics of experience. Women poets may have been less reluctant than many of their male counter-parts to confront the larger consequences of the war, and personal relationships proved especially important in shaping their understanding of events.[6] Katharine Tynan, whose sons fought in the trenches, is acutely conscious of the sacrifices made by the soldiers, and of the need to affirm principles of honour even after the tide of popular approval had turned.[7] For Eva Gore-Booth, whose pacifism was connected both to her socialist convictions and to her belief in practical action, the vision is one of the human hopelessly enmeshed in violence: 'The guns break forth with their insistent din, / The dews of noon-day leave a crimson stain / On grass, that all men's feet must wander in' (Gore-Booth 22).[8]

Though now largely a forgotten figure, during her lifetime Winifred Letts made a significant contribution to Irish literature. A prolific prose writer, Letts was also one of the few women to have had plays produced in the Abbey Theatre during the Revival period. Her skill in establishing narrative pace and in creating distinctive voices for her characters would help to shape her poetic achievement in a number of ways. Living and working in Dublin gave her early texts their distinctively Irish intonation and subject matter and distanced her from the strident patriotism of much British writing in the first decade of the twentieth century – an emphasis on militarism intended to divert attention away from class and gender inequality at home (Tylee 45).[9] Letts first became known for dialect verse celebrating rural life, as exemplified in her first volume *Songs from Leinster*, published in 1913, and again in *More Songs from Leinster* (1926). These poems are characterised by an appealing wit and energy, as well as considerable metrical skill. Though sometimes classifying her as an 'English poet', most reviewers draw attention to the specific Irish character of Letts's work. *The Times* describes *Songs from Leinster* as 'singing with true insight . . . the thoughts of the simple Irishman or Irishwoman', while the *Spectator* compares her to Moira O'Neill, whose more sentimental *Songs of the Glens of Antrim* was a considerable popular success (Letts, *Songs*). A reviewer from the *Scotsman* registers what we might now see as an apt hybridity, praising the work as 'good English verse, with a natural and affecting brogue that harmonises fresh and sweet cadences of poetry with racy local idiom' (Letts, *Songs*).

Though Letts's mastery of aspects of poetic form is evident at this early stage, her war poems proved to be of more enduring significance and continued to be anthologised, especially in America, until the 1960s. They achieved immediate exposure too, appearing in British publications such as the *Spectator* and the *Westminster Gazette*, as well as in Ireland in the *Dublin Review*.[10] These poems, which constitute some of her most moving and memorable work, can be found in the volume *Hallow-e'en and Poems of the War*, first published in London in 1916. Both the range and the immediacy of her response to the war is significant: these poems reflect the poet's awareness of the far-reaching cultural effects of the conflict, as well as her personal sympathy for the soldiers that she cared for after volunteering as a Red Cross nurse. 'Though they do not come from the battle front', remarked the *Spectator* reviewer, 'several of Miss Letts's poems show direct contact with war in hospital . . . She grieves over the shattered flotsam of battle' (Letts, *Hallow-e'en*). In this respect Letts is sensitive not only to the suffering of the injured men, but also to the feelings of the women bearing witness to the loss, a rare concern among war poets.

Letts is also attentive to the complexity of cultural allegiances and her poems indicate how closely the lives of Irishwomen could become enmeshed in events in Europe. The title of the collection itself is suggestive of this confluence of cultural and historical factors: by 1916 British troops had already experienced such significant encounters as the First Battle of the Marne and the Battle of Ypres, as well as the disastrous Gallipoli campaign, yet the poet chooses not an English, but an Irish, cultural marker to express this traumatic time. Hallowe'en, with its roots in the Celtic festival of Samhain when the border between this world and the next were thought to be permeable, offers Letts a productive symbol for the way in which a culture may come to terms with its most bitter losses. The volume as a whole moves between the worlds of the living and the dead, with poems such as 'Screens' and 'What Reward?' dwelling on the experiences of the injured and dying (Letts, *Hallow-e'en* 21; 23) and others exploring the grief and loss felt by those who wait for their return – the title poem is primarily concerned with this act of homecoming, and there are a number of other poems, including 'Loss' and 'The Dream', that record similar perspectives.[11] It is this dialectic between physical and emotional trauma that lies at the centre of the poet's moral investigation. As a group, these poems record the varying emotions generated by the war – among men and women, soldiers and civilians, English and Irish – and the collection succeeds in simultaneously questioning and affirming heroic accounts of the war. Individual poems use irony to create alternative readings, a strategy that may be linked to Letts's double perspective as a woman with strong links to both Ireland and England; a poet whose range of writing and of experience compels her to problematise easy responses. For her the duality also assumes a striking stylistic manifestation. Already renowned as the writer of *Songs from Leinster* (1913), Letts allows aspects of this richly idiomatic work to find expression again in *Hallow-e'en and Poems of the War* – a testament to her acute ear for sound patterns, especially those of the human voice. If Peter Howarth identifies 'the timelessness of apocalypse or the eternal haunting of the unburied dead' as elements of modernist experimentation born of war experience (Howarth 58), then the measured containment of Letts's work, its use of short lines and full rhyme schemes, conversely indicates her need for formal stability in the face of chaos.[12]

The elegy is an important mode for women poets of the war. Margaret Higonnet identifies mourning and melancholia as key dimensions of their writing and sees the aesthetic choices made by these women as 'inseparable from their richly allusive conversations with poetic predecessors, as well as with contemporary official discourses about the war and with the poetry being published by men such as Brooke, Owen and Rosenberg' (Higonnet 186). In a world in which continuity was always in question, these connections are vitally sustaining for women poets. In the case of Letts a conversation with male war poets is less pronounced than the dialogue with her own earlier work, and in particular with the ethics of care that can be glimpsed in her first volume in such poems as 'Deirdre in the Street'. The dialogic mode is an important formal dimension of Letts's work too and the construction of the speaking voice in her poetry often posits a specific listener, adding to the intimacy of the work. Yet many of the poems are fundamentally concerned with the estrangement of war and with the questions it raises about the relationship between individual and collective understanding. Her work constructs an ethical perspective, marking the need to care for those to whom life brings us close, no matter how fleetingly.

For Letts, landscape is an important dimension in understanding the place of the subject within the theatre of war and the response this circumstance calls forth. Her poems are often situated in space and time, drawing attention to the specificity of the historical moment as well as alluding to the significance of experience as a means to understand events. 'July, 1916' is an interesting case: here the unspoken place is the Somme, where the bloodiest battle of the war began at this time. The poem, however, situates itself 'Here in happy England' in a rural idyll of larks' song and 'the drone of bumble bees' (Letts, *Hallow-e'en* 27). The quiet is both literal and metaphorical: those in England are at a distance from the deafening sounds of artillery and removed from the immediacy of war experience. As a nurse stationed in Manchester, Letts may be reflecting on her own ambiguous relationship to the conflict that she understands not through direct experience, but through the broken bodies of the soldiers she encounters. Her version of England is intensely pastoral, the imagined 'maid' and 'lad' representing a pre-modern state of innocence. Its pattern of alliteration and assonance ('steeped' – 'saving' – 'deep') create a sense of peaceful contentment that is confirmed by the regularity of the verse, its full rhymes and additional beat in the opening and closing lines accentuating the carefree dimension of the scene. The second stanza, turning to France, uses the rhythm and rhyme to mark the relentlessness of the violence:

> But over there, in France, the grass is torn and trodden,
> *Our* pastures grow moon daisies, but *theirs* are strewn with lead.
> The fertile, kindly fields are harassed and blood-sodden,
> The sheaves they bear for harvesting will be our garnered dead.
>
> (Letts, *Hallow-e'en* 27)

Though the contrast between the landscapes is stark, it is lessened by the human history the countries now share; the two places are linked by the knowledge that Englishmen who fought in France are now buried in French soil.[13] Following other women poets of the period, Letts laments the sacrifice made by the young and juxtaposes the simplicity of a name inscribed on a memorial with the potential of these lost lives. By bringing together the beauty of the English landscape and the young 'who left this golden heritage, who put the Summer by', Letts uses the form of the poem to effect an uneasy unity between the experience of the soldiers and the land they seek to defend (Letts, *Hallow-e'en* 27). This forecloses the horror of the battle-fields in France, of which Letts herself has no direct experience, and marks the difficult position of the woman who bears witness to the devastation of war.

While 'July, 1916' resembles the work of other women poets who invoke the cycles of nature to explore the emotions generated by suffering in war, elsewhere in Letts's work the subject position plays an important role in establishing an ethical perspective. While her engagement with the war is influenced by her own experience as a nurse, she does not confine herself to a personal response. As Jane Dowson has suggested, women war poets often adopt a male voice in order to engage more closely with the immediacy of violence (Dowson 41). 'Screens' uses the hospital setting but the speaker is a soldier bearing witness to the death of a fellow combatant. The separation of the living from the dying man marks the singularity of death, even in a context of mass killing and widespread injury and suffering. The observers read the signs of their comrade's impending death: the presence of the screens around his bed effecting his separation from the group but also indicating the impos-sibility of disguising his fate. In choosing this as the title of her poem, Letts reflects upon the process of writing itself as one that has the potential to obscure or reveal the realities of war. The red and white of screen and counter-pane offer an emblematic representation of violent injury but also a partial rendering of the national flag that will be draped over his body in death:

> An ounce or more of Turkish lead,
>> He got his wounds at Suvla Bay;
> They've brought the Union Jack to spread
>> Upon him when he goes away.
>>> (Letts, *Hallow-e'en* 21)

The dying man is concealed not only from his peers but also from readers; his exact identity remains undisclosed, in keeping with the anonymity of large-scale warfare. Kieron Winterson identifies him as an Irish casualty of the Gallipoli campaign (Winterson 24–5), but Letts is deliberately ambiguous on this point, suggesting the displacement of subject and emotion that charac-terises war experience. This man is both part of the group and separate from it, marking a shifting relationship between self and other that is increased in the apparently dispassionate tone of the speaker: 'But – Jove – I'm sorry that he's dead' (Letts, *Hallow-e'en* 22). This carelessness marks the necessity of distance on the part of the soldier who may return to the battlefield to fight again. It also disturbs the rhetoric of heroic comradeship that dominated much of the poetry of the time by showing the necessary drive towards survival that each man must maintain. Here the gulf in human connection is not between combatant and non-combatant but between the living and the dying. In 'What Reward?' too, it is the difference between the fate of the soldiers that is the focus of the poem: '*You* gave your life, boy, / And you gave a limb: / But he who gave his precious wits, / Say, what reward for him?' (Letts, *Hallow-e'en* 23). Here Letts distinguishes between the 'glory' offered to those with physical injuries and the shame of those who suffer mentally from their war experiences. Once again the conscious engagement with suffering, and how that can be understood both by the soldier and the bystander, is an important preoccupation of the poet.

The fate of the individual soldier – how his experience may be understood and remembered – is an important preoccupation for Letts. 'Casualty' begins by naming the victim, John Delaney of the Rifles, while at the same time noting his fundamental anonymity. His conspicuously Irish name again extends the English frame of reference invoked in many of the poems in this volume and signals the diversity of war experience. Here it is the lack of commemoration that highlights the undifferentiated treatment of the war dead, leaving his grave unmarked and the young man not properly mourned: 'No history will hold his humble name, / No sculptured stone will tell / The traveller where he fell' (Letts, *Hallow-e'en* 13). The contract between soldier and citizen is broken: the sacrifice made by the dead man is not fully recognised, Letts suggests, except in the most abstract sense. By naming the soldier she emphasises reality above symbol, so that though this man functions as a metaphor for the suffering of the individual, he transcends that role because the reader is invited to engage directly with his story, as well as to think about the wider implications of his treatment.

'The Deserter' is similar in its approach to how the fate of the individual is understood by those not immediately involved in the theatre of war. It is a powerful poem, both in the directness of its address and in the clarity of its message, yet it too presents certain ironies that shed significant light on the poet's sympathy for the traumatised soldier:

> There was a man, – don't mind his name,
> Whom Fear had dogged by night and day.
> He could not face the German guns
> And so he turned and ran away.
> Just that – he turned and ran away,
> But who can judge him, you or I?
> God makes a man of flesh and blood
> Who yearns to live and not to die.
>
> (Letts, Hallow-e'en 30)

With its short lines and anecdotal mode, this poem is stylistically connected to the established folk dimension of Letts's work. The throwaway rhythm of the opening line is a powerful testament to the obliteration of identity that this poem investigates. If 'Casualty' begins by debunking the fallacy of intimacy – 'John Delaney of the Rifles has been shot. / A man we never knew' – 'The Deserter' does not even attempt to name the man. His anonymity is crucial to the unbridgeable gap between the common perceptions of heroism and cowardice that this work seeks to investigate. The apparent simplicity of the poem is instead the key to its acknowledgement of the most complex of human responses, and to the incapacity of society to deal with them. It also marks the transgressive nature of such a poem, given the shared ethos on which the war machine depends; as Claire Tylee points out, 'The idea of war was intimately connected with many other values of Western culture. To challenge its heroic image was to undermine ideas fundamental to their world and to their conception of history' (Tylee 20). The simple repetition of 'And so he turned and ran away. / Just that – he turned and ran away', emphasises the instinctual imperative, the terrible fear that extends beyond reason. The importance of instinct unmixed with self-conscious or manipulative action is again affirmed through linking the man to child and animal: he 'was scared as any frightened child /. . . / I've seen a hare with eyes as wild' (Letts, *Hallow-e'en* 30). The construction of end rhymes through the repetition of words 'away', 'die', 'wild', 'death', 'grey', 'heart' and 'strife' skilfully restrains the pace of reading to create in the reader the feeling of entrapment experienced by the soldier himself, and the emotions of the two likewise become entangled. The shame that is associated with fear is thus double-edged, in that the tone of the poem leads us to read the shame as a response not to a breaching of the masculine characteristic of bravery, but rather to the moral breakdown of the society that placed these young men in such a traumatic position in the first place. In running away from death, the soldier seals his own fate:

They shot him when the dawn was grey.
Blindfolded, when the dawn was grey,
He stood there in a place apart,
The shots rang out and down he fell.
An English bullet in his heart.
An English bullet in his heart!
But here's the irony of life, –
His mother thinks he fought and fell,
A hero, foremost in the strife.

So she goes proudly; to the strife
Her best, her hero son she gave.
O well for her she does not know
He lies in a deserter's grave.
            (Letts, *Hallow-e'en* 30–1)

His execution, blindfolded 'when dawn was grey' shows the strange futility of covering the eyes no longer capable of seeing any distinguishing features in the world. The syntax of the poem creates an interesting tension between the speed of forward motion – the blind haste with which the judgment is given and the execution carried out – and the doubling back over phrases to emphasise their irony: 'A hero, foremost in the strife / . . . to the strife / Her best, her hero son . . .' Most arresting is the repetition of the phrase 'An English bullet in his heart. / An English bullet in his heart!' – the only line to be repeated in full in an entire poem of echoes and doublings. Straightforwardly, this is an irony (as the poem itself notes) because the young man's mother will assume him to be a victim of enemy fire. For the reader, though, the situation is yet more complex, since a different irony pertains if this soldier is in fact Irish. It is an irony shaped by the escalating threat of violence in Ireland that preceded the outbreak of the European war, and by the fact that in the same year as this volume was published, Irish rebels would themselves be executed for their more deliberate resistance to Britain's national imperatives.

    The complexity of Letts's cultural position is matched by her awareness of the moral ambiguities of war. 'Chaplain to the Forces' depicts the complex position of the army chaplain – present in the arena of war, yet at some distance from the dangers that the ordinary soldier faces.

Ambassador of Christ you go
    Up to the very gates of hell,
    Through fog of powder, storm of shell,
To speak your Master's message: 'Lo,
    The Prince of Peace is with you still,
    His peace be with you. His goodwill.'

It is not small, your priesthood's price,
    To be a man and yet stand by,
    To hold your life whilst others die,
To bless, not share the sacrifice,
    To watch the strife and take no part –
    You with the fire at your heart.
            (Letts, *Hallow-e'en* 11)

The work, though apparently traditional in style, in fact permits two very different readings to coexist: in one of these the passionate commitment of the chaplain to the cause he serves is restricted by his ministry, which prevents him from expressing this commitment through personal sacrifice – a sacrifice that would mimic Christ's own in dying to save the world. But there exists another reading; one that allows the priest's protected status to be viewed with irony. This possibility is raised in the very first stanza of the poem, where the 'fog of powder, storm of shell' is juxtaposed to the priest's assertion: 'The Prince of Peace is with you still'. The irony of asserting peace in the midst of relentless violence is taken further in the second stanza, where Letts's careful handling of syntax emphasises the safety of the chaplain's position. She begins with a double negative – 'It is not small' – yet in doing so allows the suggestion of the 'smallness' of the sacrifice to rest in the reader's mind, an impression deepened by four lines that reflect on the conditional nature of the chaplain's role: 'To be a man and yet stand by, / To hold your life whilst others die . . .' The repetitive structure highlights the contrast between passive and active states: the first two of these lines are balanced, both in rhythm and rhyme; the next two reveal syntax and vowel patterns to be unstable. The analogy with Christ's suffering in the Garden of Gethsemane is especially thought-provoking, as this suffering is caused by knowledge of the physical trauma to come; the cup from which Christ must drink is never proffered to his representative in this poem. Instead the chaplain is equated with the mother of God: 'a sword must pierce your own soul through' paraphrases Simeon's words to the Virgin Mary – 'Yea, a sword shall pierce through thy own soul also' (*King James Bible*, Luke 2:35). The act of bearing witness, which is an important part of the maternal role, seems less appropriate for the exclusively male profession of the clergyman here, yet it links the experience of the priest with that of the writer, in ways that suggest an element of self-reflection on the part of the poet here. The position of women at this moment in history – poised to assume greater personal and political freedoms, though not yet fully in possession of them – is an oblique concern for Letts. Many of her poems emphasise the power of experience in shaping under-standing and in justifying a moral position, and the very difficulties that women encountered in sustaining an active role during the war may bring particular personal force to this investigation. The comparison between the packing case that the priest uses as an altar and the stable in which Christ was born endorses the notion that it is only by the surrender of material comfort that true redemption is possible, yet the chaplain remains somehow remote from observable personal sacrifice. The engagement of this work with religious texts – first in the biblical phrase and then in an echo of Julian of Norwich, the most famous English mystic: 'All shall be well, and all shall be well, and all manner of things shall be well' – reinforces the delicate interweaving of experiential and intellectual responses here.

The presence of these interpretative links and echoic effects contribute in important ways to the emotional impact of the volume as a whole and are expressive of the fragmentary yet continuous experience of war that is reflected on here. The book has, in effect, two title poems: 'Hallow-e'en, 1915' and 'Hallow-e'en, 1914'. The placement of these two poems is indicative of the complex temporal relationship between the texts in this volume. While the first two sections of the book are titled 'Ad Milites' and 'Ad Mortuum', indicating the progression from life to death, the individual poems them-selves are not organised to create a narrative of the war but instead to offer multiple perspectives on the events. There may be a separation, however, between the domestic perspectives that precede Letts's decision to volunteer as a nurse and the more graphic accounts that draw on her experiences in a Manchester hospital.[14] The two opening poems of the volume both dwell on the power of the returning dead and their emotional impact on those waiting at home. At the opening of 'Hallow-e'en, 1915' the speaker calls the men back from the 'alien graves' to the 'open door' of their homes and the love of their grieving women (Letts, *Hallow-e'en* 3). The autumnal beauty of the scene with its church tower, 'purple woodlands' and sleeping dog stands in clear contrast to the 'weary trenches' of the men's recent experience. It reprises too the idyllic imagery of early W. B. Yeats but with fresh significance.[15] If the purple woodland and silver fish are at once suggestive of the Connemara of 'The Lake Isle of Innisfree', the creative death that Yeats's 'pavements grey' implied are here rendered as actual graves. The close of the poem offers a new reading of this haunting however:

> We have no fear of you, silent shadows, who tread
> The leaf-bestrewn paths, the dew-wet lawns. Draw near
> To the glowing fire, the empty chair,—we shall not fear,
> Being but ghosts for the lack of you, ghosts of our well-beloved dead.
>
> (Letts, *Hallow-e'en* 4)

The collective positions that Letts offered are reversed here: it is not the fallen soldiers who are 'ghosts' but rather those at home, bereft of their loved ones. The Irish idiom – more muted in this opening poem but nonetheless evident – also has important ramifications for the representation of war in this volume. Hiberno-English expressions draw attention to Irish involvement in the conflict and to the shaping force that this commitment exerted on families and communities in Ireland. Yet the title poem contains ambiguities: the soldiers are described as 'men of the manor and moated hall and farm', dwellings more clearly associated with an English landscape than an Irish one. Likewise, the poem 'The Spires of Oxford' is located in the unmistakable environment of privileged English student life. Significantly it was this poem that was selected as the title poem for the American edition of the volume, perhaps suggesting that English references would be more readily associated with the war experience than Irish ones. Yet Letts is fully aware that the Englishness that formed such an important part of war rhetoric could mask other, barely discernible, forms of identity. To this extent Letts seeks to situate her examination of the war in specifically English but also in subtly Irish ways.

'Hallow-e'en, 1914' reprises some of these themes, taking the form of a dialogue between a 'stranger' and a waiting woman. The stranger's role is to elicit the woman's story, as well as to prompt reflection on states of intimacy and estrangement. The woman's most personal wishes are imparted to the stranger and this process of making private emotions public is a testament to how the boundaries between the states have been breached by the condition of war. Yet 'Hallow-e'en, 1914', until its final line, offers a hopeful reading belied by 'Hallow-e'en, 1915'; it allows the reader to be drawn back towards the optimism of the early months of the war, though its closing phrase will unite it to its companion poem in which the vision of survival has already been shattered: '"The candles are lighted, the hearthstones are swept, / The fires glow red. / We shall welcome them out of the night – / Our home-coming dead"' (Letts, *Hallow-e'en* 6). In spite of her conservative use of form and technique, Letts plays with the tensions between hope and despair, as well as drawing attention to the processes of concealment and revelation that are a key part of how the war is represented, both in official communications and creative works.

The perspective of Winifred Letts as a woman poet with Irish affiliations sheds new light on the moral ambiguities of violent conflict. By considering the larger significance – culturally and politically – of military operations, Letts pits the ideology of war against its individual acts of conscious suffering. Without denigrating the experiences of the individual soldier, the poet exposes the failures of the war machine, and its annihilation of human individuality. She does this not in obscure or philosophical terms but through the deft manipulation of language and form – an apt response to a world of masculine hierarchies and military might, where human subjectivity is so easily crushed.

Notes

1   Stacy Gillis has commented on the apparent homogeneity of First World War poetry, judging by the material that formed the basis of anthologies and critical works between the 1960s and the 1990s. See Gillis 101–2.

2   James Campbell uses the term 'combat gnosticism' to indicate 'the belief that combat represents a qualitatively separate order of experience that is difficult if not impossible to communicate to any who have not undergone an identical experience' (Campbell 203).

3   Key works on women's writing of the First World War include Nosheen Khan, *Women's Poetry of the First World War* (1988); Claire Tylee, *The Great War and Women's Consciousness: Images of Militarism and Womanhood in Women's Writings 1914–64* (1990) and Sharon Ouditt, *Fighting Forces, Writing Women: Identity and Ideology in the First World War* (1994).

4   'Theoretically, both the Ulster and the Irish National Volunteers enlisted in loyal support of Britain's war aims; in reality, the leaders of both sides volunteered their troops in an attempt to influence British policy' (Brearton 10).

5   Brearton argues that the sheer scale of the deaths during the First World War made the idea of individual sacrifice difficult to understand, in a way that it was not for those who commemorated the 1916 Rising (Brearton 18).

6   Variations in experience, and representation, of war and revolution are displayed in the work of key women poets of the time: Katharine Tynan (1858–1931), Dora Sigerson Shorter (1866–1918), Eva Gore-Booth (1870–1926) and Winifred Letts (1881–1972). In the next generation, Mary Devenport O'Neill (1879–1967) and Sheila Wingfield (1906–92) engage with these events in unique ways. See selections in Collins, ed. *Poetry by Women in Ireland, 1870–1970: A Critical Anthology.*

7   Katharine Tynan wrote five volumes of poetry in the course of the war: *Flower of Peace* (1914), *Flower of Youth* (1915), *The Holy War* (1916), *Late Songs* (1917) and *Herb o' Grace* (1918). These volumes combined devotional and pastoral modes and generally supported a heroic reading of British involvement in the conflict.

8   The poem '1916' is unusual in its interleaving of references to the Easter Rising and the Battle of the Somme.

9   The impact of militarism on printing and publishing in the decades preceding the war is explored by Jane Potter in *Boys in Khaki, Girls in Print.* 9–51.

10   For a nuanced discussion of Letts's shifting political attitudes, and their impact on her publishing history, see Winterson 19–28.

11   There are, in effect, two title poems to the volume: 'Hallow-e'en, 1915' (3) and 'Hallow-e'en, 1914' (5). 'Loss' (38) and 'The Dream' (39) are in the second section of the book – 'Ad Mortuum'.

12   This relative conservatism of form has been judged to fall short of the 'cultural demand for ahistorical, transcendent, and 'difficult' writing'. See Plain 26.

13   Kieron Winterson argues that the deeper juxtaposition of this poem is between 'happy England' and 'unhappy Ireland'. However, it seems likely that Letts is meditating on the complex relationship between nations and territories in more oblique ways. See Winterson 26.

14   Letts's registration card shows she enrolled as a VAD on 21 June 1915. She was posted in Manchester from 25 August 1915 to 30 June 1916. See British Red Cross, available at: tiny.cc/97nkox (Accessed 10 June 2015).

15   The poem carries hints of 'midnight's all a glimmer, and noon a purple glow' as well as the silver trout of 'The Song of Wandering Aengus' (Yeats 60; 76).

Lucy Collins

Works Cited

Braybon, Gail. 'Women and the war'. Stephen Constantine, Maurice W. Kirby, and Mary B. Rose, eds. *The First World War in British History*. London: Arnold, 1995. 145.

Brearton, Fran. *The Great War in Irish Poetry: From W. B. Yeats to Michael Longley*. Oxford: Oxford University Press, 2000.

Campbell, James. 'Combat gnosticism: the ideology of First World War poetry criticism'. *New Literary History* 30:1 (Winter 1999): 203–15.

Collins, Lucy, ed. *Poetry by Women in Ireland 1870–1970: A Critical Anthology*. Liverpool: Liverpool University Press, 2012.

Das, Santanu, ed. *The Cambridge Companion to the Poetry of the First World War*. Cambridge: Cambridge University Press, 2013.

Dawe, Gerald. *Earth Voices Whispering: An Anthology of Irish War Poetry, 1914–45*. Belfast: Blackstaff Press, 2008.

Dowson, Jane. *Women, Modernism and British Poetry: 1910–1939*. Aldershot: Ashgate, 2002.

Gillis, Stacy. '"Many sisters to many brothers': the women poets of the First World War'. Tim Kendall, ed. *The Oxford Handbook of British and Irish War Poetry*. Oxford: Oxford University Press, 2007. 100–13.

Gore-Booth, Eva. *Broken Glory*. Dublin: Maunsel and Co., 1918.

Higonnet, Margaret R. 'Women's poetry of the First World War'. Santanu Das, ed. *The Cambridge Companion to the Poetry of the First World War*. Cambridge: Cambridge University Press, 2013. 185–97.

Howarth, Peter. 'Poetic form and the First World War'. Santanu Das, ed. *The Cambridge Companion to the Poetry of the First World War*. Cambridge: Cambridge University Press, 2013. 51–66.

Khan, Nosheen. *Women's Poetry of the First World War*. New York and London: Harvester Wheatsheaf, 1988.

Letts, W. M. *Hallow-e'en and Poems of the War*. London: Smith, Elder & Co., 1916.

—. *Songs from Leinster*. London: John Murray, 1913.

Ouditt, Sharon. *Fighting Forces, Writing Women: Identity and Ideology in the First World War*. London: Routledge, 1994.

Plain, Gill. 'Great expectations: rehabilitating the recalcitrant war poets'. Vicki Bertram, ed. *Kicking Daffodils: Twentieth-Century Women Poets*. Edinburgh: Edinburgh University Press, 1997. 25–38.

Potter, Jane. *Boys in Khaki, Girls in Print: Women's Literary Responses to the Great War 1914–18*. Oxford: Oxford University Press, 2005.

Tylee, Claire M. *The Great War and Women's Consciousness: Images of Militarism and Womanhood in Women's Writings, 1914–64*. Iowa City: University of Iowa Press, 1990.

Winterson, Kieron. 'Green flags on their bayonets: Winifred Letts and the Great War'. Gillian McIntosh and Diane Urquhart, eds. *Irish Women at War: The Twentieth Century*. Kildare: Irish Academic Press, 2010. 17–34.

Yeats, W. B. *The Poems*. Daniel Albright, ed. London: Dent, 1990.

5

The New Women of the Glens

Writers and Revolutionaries

Tina O'Toole

Transnational kinship networks have become clearly visible across the Irish diaspora over the past 40 years in particular. This chapter demonstrates that such networks pre-date the contemporary period and, moreover, argues that the development of a radical politics in early twentieth-century Ireland depended upon them. From the Great Famine on, Irish culture had been characterised by an intense consciousness in public and private life about the boundaries of belonging to family, community, and nation. Each of these social institutions was gendered in a very specific way, with public and private domains demarcated along gendered lines; these gendered divisions persisted throughout the twentieth century in Ireland. Those who found themselves outside the structures and definitions of their family of origin circumvented this fixed heteronormative and patriarchal structure by creating lateral support networks of their own, alternatives to more hierarchical family structures. Focusing on the women writers and activists who influenced and supported Roger Casement's radical nationalist politics, this work considers the ways in which their chosen kinship group – centred on the Glens of Antrim but operating transnationally across Ireland, Britain, and the wider colonial world – unsettled fixities of family and national affinity in Irish culture.

This research extends recent paradigm shifts opening up late nineteenth- and early twentieth-century Ireland to scrutiny, particularly in relation to the active participation of women as agents and the existence of queer communities and codes.[1] When embarking on a reading of Casement's community, the reader might expect a chapter about the intimate lives of the men in his circle. However, his close affinities to women friends in the same period are equally compelling, not just in relation to Casement's identity and politics, but in the new insights they provide into a vibrant community of interest at work on a range of activist projects in the early twentieth century. In particular, the efforts of several key women in Casement's life at the time of his trials and in the campaign for clemency stand out: Alice Stopford Green, Gertrude Bannister, Ada McNeill, Alice Millligan, and Eva Gore-Booth (the latter came to support him in court although she hadn't known him before the trial), all of whom might be described in the terms of the period as 'New Women' as will be explained. One especially memorable moment in that campaign was the petition made by these stalwart women for a royal pardon, which they insisted on presenting in person to George V at Buckingham Palace.[2] Long before that moment, these women and others like them had been an important influence in the shaping of Casement's Irish nationalist sensibilities. By attending to Casement as a member of a community, a wider kinship group, this chapter questions the tendency to see Irish revolution-aries as exceptional men, existing in isolation from a wider community. Exploring Casement's writing in tandem with that of Alice Stopford Green and other 'New Woman' writers, reveals their influence on his Irish nationalist education and politics, and provides new insights into the gendering of national identities in the period.

While Casement's trials strengthened the ties between his women friends, their central importance in his life and identity formation are evident from his early adulthood onwards. Having lost his parents at an early age, Casement's family of origin dispersed; his connection to paternal relations in Magherintemple left in *loco parentis* following his father's death was distant (for instance, he spent subsequent holiday periods in his school or with the families of schoolfriends). Casement's diary entries in the early years of his African travels detail leave periods, often Christmases, spent miserably in Magherintemple and Ballymena; doubtless the sense of restric-tion and enclosure he experienced 'at home' with members of his father's family contributed to his decision to migrate. This echoes Anne Marie Fortier's description of 'home as not-home' in the narratives of 'lesbian/gay people' who experience 'estrangement in the original home', and whose migration is thus 'a movement away from being estranged' (Fortier 129, 118). Casement went to work for a shipping company at the age of 16, then he followed in his maternal uncle Edward Bannister's footsteps and went to Africa three years later. Thus began a long career in the colonial service culminating in his important humanitarian interventions in the Congo and the Putumayo. Perhaps as a result of his early loss of both a fixed family and rooted home experience, Casement developed and carefully maintained a kinship network of his own, and because of his peripatetic existence, that network was a transnational one.

Having cast off from the Casements of Magherintemple, Casement did not cut himself off entirely from his homeland and its concerns however. Through his sister, Nina, in Portrush, and his close friends in London, Robert Lynd and Sylvia Dryhurst, he became intimate with a network of

Figure 5.1: Agnes O'Farrelly (Úna Ní Fhaircheallaigh) (1874–1951), professor of Irish at UCD, during a 1945 conferral ceremony at Maynooth University. (Courtesy of UCD Archives)

radical writers and nationalist activists in Ireland and Britain at the turn of the century. While this coterie included a significant number of male friends, Francis Joseph Bigger and Bulmer Hobson to name but two, he relied upon several close women friends and family members throughout his life. Chief among Casement's chosen kinship group were his Bannister cousins Gertrude and Elizabeth in Liverpool; he was especially fond of 'Gee' (his pet name for Gertrude) who became a teacher in a girls' school. Two prominent Irish intellectuals also featured in Casement's coterie, Alice Stopford Green, described by Margaret O'Callaghan as 'historian to the revolutionary generation of 1916 in Ireland' (O'Callaghan, 'Alice Stopford Green')[3]; and Irish language scholar Agnes O'Farrelly (Úna Ní Fhaircheallaigh) who later became professor of Irish at UCD, and was a well-known campaigner for women's educational rights and founding member of Cumann na mBan. Moreover, while Casement's associations with Magherintemple were unhappy, his abiding connection to that hinterland was lifelong, and in fact his dying wish was to be buried at Murlough Bay in the Glens of Antrim. His 'New Woman' circle in the Glens included Rose and Charlotte Young, Ada McNeill, Margaret

Dobbs, and Margaret Hutton. Exchanges between these individuals created, among other initiatives, the first Feis na nGleann (Festival of the Glens) held at Waterfoot (Glenariff, Co. Antrim) in 1904. McNeill, Dobbs, and Rose Young, along with Casement and Bigger, were central figures in the original Feis, which became a focal point in the Irish cultural revival.

Casement and his circle, like other young people all over Ireland in those years, began to interrogate traditional political and cultural formations, evaluating traditional structures against new ideas and values then emerging in European culture and politics. Many of Casement's cohort in north Antrim came from Conservative unionist families; the Youngs, for instance, contributed funding to establish the Ulster Volunteer Force. During the political upheavals of the early twentieth century, many of these families were split

Figure 5.2: Portrait of Ada McNeill (1860–1959).
(Courtesy of Feis na nGleann)

Figure 5.3: Portrait of Margaret Dobbs (1871–1962).
(Courtesy of Feis na nGleann)

ideologically on gender lines, the men continuing to support the union with Great Britain, the women joining the Gaelic League, and sometimes openly espousing 'separatist' (i.e. Irish nationalist) tendencies. Such women were no different to their peers whose names are more familiar to us in the narrative of the Irish struggle for independence, like Constance Markievicz and Albinia Broderick for instance, in having Protestant ascendancy backgrounds. In terms of Irish women's nationalist activism, we might trace a line of political influence down to them from the period of the Ladies' Land League, which also had a cross-community membership. Middle-class Protestant families produced their fair share of Irish rebels too, of course, such as Belfast-born Mabel McConnell (later Fitzgerald), who encountered Irish nationalist politics for the first time at Queen's University; she later commented 'I seem to base all my friendships in nationalism; other things are as important, but not nearly as much so' (qtd Foster 16).[4] However, despite diversity in the confessional backgrounds of members of the revolutionary generation, the subsequent partition of the island and sectarian aspect of Free State discourses made northern Protestant contributions to Irish nationalism more difficult to perceive and commemorate. Perhaps the most poignant example of this was the destruction of a large Celtic cross, the memorial stone marking Bigger's grave, by a loyalist bomb in 1980.

The family of Ada McNeill provides a concise example of such divided political loyalties. A member of the McNeill family of Cushendun, she was a first cousin of Ronald McNeill (Lord Cushendun), a unionist and conservative MP who had close ties to Edward Carson and James Craig. Yet Ada was an early member of the Gaelic League, became a fluent Irish speaker, and was an enthusiastic member and secretary of the first Feis na nGleann committee and the committee of Coláiste Uladh, the Irish language school, as well as an ardent republican in later life. In reminiscences of Casement, she wrote: 'I was in a Unionist milieu, and Roger was too, on the Ballycastle side of the mountain. It was not surprising we made friends' (Phoenix et al. 47). Margaret Dobbs, similarly, broke with family tradition in her investment in Gaelic culture; Dobbs's father was the high sheriff of Carrickfergus and Co. Louth, and her brother James was a unionist who took part in the Larne gun-running. By contrast, she became an executive member of Cumann na mBan in 1914 (Dudgeon 219). Such decisive rejections of unionist family traditions in favour of an investment in Gaelic culture, are consistent with contemporary feminist challenges to the family and stultifying bourgeois culture. These could all be described as 'New Women'; they were part of that generation of newly empowered, educated, active and radical women in Ireland – scholars, educators, artists, and writers – who openly professed first-wave feminist ambitions and were engaged in public discourse and social activism of one kind or another.

In the 1890s the 'New Woman' had become a common phenomenon in popular culture, and an exemplar for several generations of young women.[5] Sarah Grand (Frances Bellenden Clarke, 1854–1943), perhaps the best-known 'New Woman' writer, came from Donaghadee (a mere 60 miles from the Glens of Antrim). Grand's landmark essay, 'The new aspect of the woman question' (1894) brought the term 'New Woman' into being. Sally Ledger outlines some of the multiple manifestations of the New Woman figure thus: 'She was, variously, a feminist activist, a social reformer, a popular novelist, a suffragette playwright, a woman poet; she was also a fictional construct, a discursive response to the activities of the 1890s women's movement.'[6] Grand's popular novels were premised on a central female character who, having her consciousness raised by feminist ideas, gains confidence in her ability to voice her rights, and is ultimately willing to fight for them. Writers like Grand sought to revolutionise the prevailing gender order; they issued a challenge to contemporary vested interests in order to advance women's social autonomy, a challenge that was no less radical than that of their sisters in the campaign for women's suffrage. The creation of these fictional feminists made way for their readers – a generation newly literate in the 1890s – to follow in the footsteps of their literary heroines, and so the imbrication of social activism and literary representation is part of this picture. Needless to say, the work of New Woman writers on the page and feminist activists on the streets coincided with a turbulent time of anti-imperial and class agitation in Ireland and internationally.

Today, those empowered young Irish women who played an active part in the struggle for Irish independence are just beginning to be mentioned in the 'official' national narrative. Yet, in light of women's earlier involvement in Land League agitation, and Gillian McIntosh's recent work on women mill-workers in Belfast in the same period,[7] it seems that these women radicals were just the visible sign of happenings beneath the dominant surfaces of Irish culture in the late nineteenth century, subversive energies producing new resistance movements among women of different classes. For a new generation of young Antrim women coming to consciousness at the turn of the century, in a context in which political radicalism gripped the island, the decision to throw in their lot with the national struggle is not so difficult to credit. Simultaneously, of course, a number of other Irish feminist activists and writers such as Isabella Tod, Margaret Byers, and Mary Bulmer Hobson, as well as Edith Somerville and Violet Martin (Somerville and Ross), were unionists; they saw no future for political radicalism in a Home Rule Ireland, and fought its advance as a threat to their feminist agenda.

The vehicle for bringing their nationalist sisters together in the Glens was another kind of cultural revolt in the form of the Gaelic League. As Margaret Mac Curtain and others have observed, the Gaelic League was the first nationalist organisation in Ireland after the Land League to involve women, and offer them a level footing with men. In a 1907 letter to Ní Fhaircheallaigh, Casement makes specific reference to this: '[t]he Gaelic League is largely inspired and partially directed by women' (NLI MS 3172319 Dec. 1907). Crucially, from the perspective of these Glens women, the League was a cross-community organisation involving Catholics and Protestants and thus it became a meeting point for young people who might otherwise never have encountered one another socially. Diarmaid Ó Doibhlin emphasises the effectiveness of Cuideachta Ghaeilge Uladh (the Ulster Gaelic Society) in bringing people from different social classes together, as the educated middle classes went out to learn the language from rural working people (Ó Doibhlin 16). The Irish language was still thriving in the Glens of Antrim right up into the 1890s, as Ó Doibhlin tells us 'particularly in Glenarm and Cary and in Glenariff' (Ó Doibhlin 19); in other words, those women learning Irish in the Glens at the turn of the century encountered spoken Irish in their childhood, and had ready access to communities of native Irish speakers, particularly on Rathlin Island off the north Antrim coast. In tandem with this, the re-energising of the Irish language in what Richard Kirkland terms 'Belfast's red-brick Gaeltacht' continued apace, and the involvement of Casement's friends there has been well documented.

On account of this living tradition, the Glens provided a haven for Irish language enthusiasts such as Margaret Emmeline Dobbs (1871–1962), who moved to Glenariff with her mother in 1898. Along with her friend Ada McNeill, Dobbs became a central figure in the Glens group. Her lifelong study of the Irish language and culture is evident in her many publications, including *Side-Lights on the Táin Age and Other Studies* (1917), numerous editions of Irish language texts, a range of essays on historical and archaeological subjects in local and international philological journals, as well as seven plays.[8] Dobbs's commitment to both Gaelic culture and feminist principles is evident in the introduction to an edition of *The Ban-Shenchus* [sic] in Irish with her own English translations. She describes this as a 'history of women'. Dobbs's own origins were staunchly unionist, there was little Irish language culture or tradition in the family; her interest in the language is said to have originated with a servant (probably a nanny) in her family home in Dublin. Self-taught, she later attended the Irish college at Cloghaneely. Having moved to the Glens in 1898 after her father's death, she taught Irish in the summers on Rathlin Island and at Gortahork; she also funded scholarships to the Gaeltacht. The educative function of her publications is clear, she provides English-language translations and explanations throughout her edition of the *Bansheanchas* for instance, and she delivered lectures to historical societies in the region. Dobbs had the liberty and means to pursue a fairly single-minded commitment to the language movement,

and her home in Portnagolan, Cushendall, was central to all cultural nationalist activities in north Antrim, becoming something of a Glens equivalent of
Bigger's Antrim Road house, Ardrígh. She was a founding member of the
Feis committee in 1904, and became a good friend to Casement; Ó Doibhlin
suggests she was his closest friend (Ó Doibhlin 21).

Ada McNeill (1860–1959) attributed her investment in Irish culture to
Casement. When they became acquainted in Antrim in their early twenties,
he prompted an interest in Irish culture that was entirely new to her, '[w]e
were a horrid cynical transplanted family. In the West Highland homes of
the past we would have been among our own set and neighbours' (Phoenix
et al. 47). During their many tramps through the Glens together she found
herself plunged into an ideological battle. In 1929 she wrote about those
conversations:

> Roger had the history of Ireland at his finger ends . . . We often argued and fought
> out our battles of long ago. I criticised the Irish side – but he always made excuses
> for them . . . I remember rainy grey days in the dark old library [at Churchfield,
> Casement's cousins' home] . . . Roger refuting my gutsy excited arguments with
> quotations upon which he could always lay his fingers. I learned a lot like this – and
> to read for myself. (Phoenix et al. 47)

The crucial point here is the last one, all of these women were learning to
'read for themselves' in those years, to deconstruct the received cultural and
social world they had inherited from their planter families. By the time McNeill
reconnected with Casement in the early twentieth century (his migration to
the Congo ended their close connection for a time) this re-education had
borne fruit; Ada was by then an ardent member of the Gaelic League. She
recalls that her first attempt at a letter 'in the Gaelic' was written to him from
the Aran Islands (Phoenix et al. 49).

It is unfortunate that so few of these letters survive, as is the case with
most of the correspondence from these women to Casement; while his
letters to them have been preserved, scholars have to rely on a one-sided
conversation in order to trace the interconnections. As such, Ada's published
reminiscences are a valuable resource, not least because they provide a unique
insight into the affective impact on this new generation as they embarked on
a new cultural movement:

> A spirit was awakening in Ireland. Even in the sleepy old Glens, people turned out
> to meetings . . . got enthusiastic about reviving old customs. We were no longer
> Ireland of the Gall – the stranger. We tried to revive dancing – Roger took his place
> in the four hand reels. Strode about the roads hatless, encouraging, working up the
> heedless. I was not long ago talking to Stephen Clarke and he drew a picture of

Roger – so full of energy and prompt work. There was a Feis in Cushendall and all our negotiations had failed to get the field we wanted for a hurling match. Another field full of weeds and dockens and thistles had to suffice . . . Immediately Roger went for the scythe in hand and while we were talking and cursing, began to work hard cutting down the weeds and preparing the ground. (Phoenix et al. 49)

Rose Maud Young (1865–1947), another original member of the Feis group was also a lifelong friend of Casement's; on the eve of his execution, Casement sent 'Love to R. Y. and to Charlotte' from the Tower (Sawyer 43). The Youngs, unionist merchants from Ballymena, had been good to him from the time of his schooling, providing him with holiday respite from time to time (there was a distant family connection between them). John Young was the chief sheriff and deputy lieutenant in Antrim but Jeffrey Dudgeon suggests that his first wife, Grace (née Savage), was an Irish

Figure 5.4: Portrait of Rose Young (Róis Ní Ógáin) (1865–1947). (Courtesy of Chris Brooke)

Figure 5.5: Cover of the 1996 reissue of Rose Young's ballad collection, *Duanaire Gaedhilge* (1921). (Courtesy of Diarmaid Ó Doibhlin)

nationalist and that she may have influenced her daughter, Rose's, political outlook and that of the young Casement (Dudgeon 65). As such, Rose Young grew up in a unionist household at Galgorm Castle, but the plaque unveiled there to the memory of Róis Ní Ógáin in 1996 (by her grandniece Lady Brookeborough) describes her as 'scoláire Gaeilge' (Mac Reamoinn). Ní Ógáin's lifelong commitment to the revival of the Irish language is evident, in particular, in her collection of songs in the three-volume *Duanaire Gaedhilge* (1921).[9]

Ó Doibhlin suggests that her Irish language education began with Bishop William Reeves, rector of Ballymena, who discussed his Irish manuscripts collection with her. Having trained as a teacher in England, Ní Ógáin began taking Irish language classes in London while staying with her sister there; along with Ada McNeill, she continued these studies back in Antrim, taking classes in Belfast, and attending summer schools in Donegal. She was among the group present on 28 February 1904 at a public meeting in Cushendall when it was decided to organise the first Feis na nGleann; clearly, such a celebration of the culture was consistent with her individual efforts to document and revive the Irish language. Ó Doibhlin's pioneering work on her diaries (1883–1945) illustrates the diverse ideological interests at play, which is typical of that of many of these women. Ní Ógáin details visits to speak Irish with the old people in the Glens and attendance at the 1905 Oireachtas in Dublin with Douglas Hyde, while dining with leading unionist figures and celebrating Coronation Day 1911 at Galgorm Castle. Her brother George became a key figure in the Orange Order, county grand master of Antrim, and the Unionist MP for Bannside. Dudgeon observes that this 'crossover culture' was typical of the period, giving the example of the Belfast Naturalist Field Club, 'a key meeting ground where Protestants collided with modern attitudes and ancient Gaelic ideals' (Phoenix et al. 66).

The inaugural Feis na nGleann brought those 'modern attitudes' and 'ancient Gaelic ideals' into sharp focus, as well as providing an important meeting point for the principals in this coterie. Margaret Dobbs credits Bigger and his 'young friends' with the idea 'when spending a holiday in Cushendun' (Phoenix et al. 41). That intervention brought an audience of 2,000 people to Glenariff on 30 June 1904, comprising leading figures in the Gaelic League, the GAA, antiquarian societies, as well as writers, actors, musicians, and dancers. Crucially, it provided an encounter between revivalists and the traditional work practices, arts and crafts of the Irish-speaking population in the Glens (as well as the Rathlin islanders, Casement having chartered transport to bring the 'Rachary' people across). Photographs of the Feis depict the opening procession from Cushendall to Waterfoot, which featured banners representing local clans and the nine glens; spectators clearly visible in surviving photographs include Casement, Dobbs, McNeill, and

Bigger. Competitions and displays of traditional dance, music, language and history, as well as a local industries section, were the centrepiece of the Feis (Phoenix et al. 3). A hurling match on the beach was won by Carey Faughs (which club still displays the Shield of Heroes commissioned by Bigger for the event); Casement was one of the umpires at the match.[10] At the end of the day, prizes were awarded and speeches made by Horace Plunkett, pioneer of the co-operative movement in agriculture, with Stephen Gwynn and Eoin MacNeill awarding literary and language prizes. While its place in the local history and that of cultural nationalism is assured, the Feis was also crucial in cementing relationships and thereby facilitating the further exchange of ideas and strategies between its main actors.

Exchanges between members of this coterie focus primarily on the de-Anglicisation of Ireland, to use Hyde's term. Their letters almost always open with a salutation in the Irish language, often written in uncial (Gaelic) rather than Roman hand, and using the *séimhiú* (signified by a superscript dot) rather than 'h' as was the custom in the early twentieth century. Writing to Úna Ní Fhaircheallaigh, Casement begins with 'A Díl Cara' written in this way; in one of the few available letters in Gee's hand she addresses her friend Ada McNeill in Irish, 'A Íde, A Chara'. The Gaelicisation of names is interesting here too, evident in the switch from 'Ada' to 'Íde'. Adopting the Irish-language version of their names or changing their names was consistent with their sense of being engaged in a project to reinvent the culture; Rose Young wrote under the name Róis Ní Ógáin, the Bannister sisters took the Irish names Una and Eilis, Margaret Dobbs became Maighréad, etc. Such name-changing was common, too, among 'New Woman' writers who frequently wrote under pseudonyms, though as a mark of their feminist commitment many chose distinctly female names like 'Sarah Grand', rather than obscuring their identities as with the 'Georges' of an earlier era. In both cases, there is a distinct sense of new identities being assumed and a community of interest being forged by the use of these new names.

Rejecting their given names and the ideological adherence of their families, these Glens women rejected patriarchal authority in other ways too, choosing not to marry and opting for public careers as scholars and writers. This contradicts received ideas of the period, in which Irish patriotism and masculinity are indivisible. As a counterpart to contemporary hypermasculinity during the revolutionary period, cultural nationalism configured a passive femininity, making strong, self-actualised representations of Irish women in public discourse difficult to achieve. Yet, arguably, the kind of community-building efforts and social networking that underpin the revolutionary struggle in that period tend to be much more often associated with women's ways of working. Alice Stopford Green underlines this point in *Women's Place in the World of Letters*: 'In modern thought and literature, in fact, the personal note dominates all others . . . there are many signs that the feminine as opposed to the masculine forces in the modern world are becoming more and more decisive in human affairs' (Stopford Green, *Women's Place* 29).

With the arrival of Alice Green (1847–1929) in Cushendall for the 1904 Feis, this revolutionary group came together in the Glens of Antrim for the first time.[11] A close friend of Casement's, and an influential figure in his radicalisation, Green was the most widely read Irish historian of the period (O'Callaghan, 'Alice Stopford Green' 2013). Her homes in London and on Stephen's Green in Dublin were well-known salons for political radicals; she was good friends with Beatrice Webb for a time, and maintained an extensive correspondence with a number of public intellectuals and social radicals,

including John Francis Taylor (*Manchester Guardian* correspondent for Ireland in the late nineteenth century), as well as Douglas Hyde and Eoin MacNeill (O'Callaghan, 'Alice Stopford Green' 2013). This quote gives us a hint of her personality: 'The aim of conversation is to "shut up" your companion (alias for the time being opponent). If he is feeble, he deserves it, and if he is strong it is a duty we owe it to society to silence him for once' (McDowell 17). Casement was an avid reader, and Green's reputation and clear sense of a mission to correct received ideas about Ireland as an uncivilised place in the period before colonisation, cannot have failed to impress him, not to mention her rejection of Anglicisation:

Figure 5.6: Portrait of Alice Stopford Green (1847–1929). (Courtesy of the National Library of Ireland)

> The child who knew only Irish was given a teacher who knew nothing but English; his history book mentioned Ireland twice only – a place conquered by Henry II and made into an English province by the union . . . the Irish boy was taught to thank God for being 'a happy English child'. (Stopford Green, *Irish Nationality* 248)

In a much-quoted letter to his old headmaster, Casement used similar grounds to compare his schooling unfavourably to Pearse's St Enda's:

Now from my own recollection of the old Diocesan School and from what I know of similar establishments in Ireland, their aim is not so much to fit a boy to live and thrive in his own country, as to equip him for export from it. I was taught nothing about Ireland at Ballymena School. I don't think the word was ever mentioned in a single class of the school . . . As an Irishman, I wish to see this state of things changed . . . Patriotism has been stigmatized and often treated as 'treason', as a 'crime' – or dismissed with superior scorn as 'local'. (qtd Singleton-Gates 42)

The 'local' adherence of his friends in the Glens, of course, was challenging to their unionist families; not to mention the fact that, ultimately, Casement's patriotism would lead to his being executed for treason.

Green and Casement first made contact through Edmund Morel and their mutual interest in the anti-slavery movement; we are told that Casement wrote a 15-page letter of introduction to her in 1904, 'without reflecting but straight from my heart' (McDowell 74). From then on, they became close friends, and Casement wrote many homesick letters to her from his various postings abroad. The two were intellectually and ideologically compatible in various ways; her influence on Casement's emerging Irish nationalist sensibilities is beyond doubt, while his humanitarian efforts and commiment to the anti-slavery movement chimed with Green's liberalism. In other circumstances, they might have made a striking couple, Casement's dark features and charisma were well matched by Green's natural vitality and 'mass of red hair'. Her biographer, R. B. McDowell, describes her as having 'a decided sense of fun. From stories she records in her diary, she must have read *Punch* with gusto and she was quick to perceive and enjoy the incongruities and absurdities of human behaviour' (McDowell 17). They also shared an acute understanding of the close connections between colonial occupation and the exploitation of indigenous labour. Margaret O'Callaghan observes that Casement 'bombarded his acquaintances with her [Green's] writings' (O'Callaghen, 'Casement'), and Dudgeon describes him as having 'taken on the role of a one-man publicity department and distributor' for her 1911 publication *Irish Nationality*. Between them, they ignited the revolutionary group in the Glens and beyond, providing a forceful intellectual foundation to support the Irish nationalist cause.

The range of counter-cultural projects involving this network was sustained by the letters traded between the Glens women and like-minded individuals in Dublin, London and, where Casement is concerned, the Putumayo. Booklists and poems are exchanged and books reviewed in subsequent letters; in one such, Casement praises Margaret Hutton's *The Táin* to Ní Fhaircheallaigh but criticises the Anglicisation of the names in the text (NLI MS 31723 22 Nov.1907). Many of the letters refer to the bilingual project they are invested in, discussing efforts to find teachers for

Irish schools (many candidates had the language skills but no teaching quali-
fications), or the difficulties in finding financial support for local schools in
Gaeltacht areas. While the focus of these exchanges is most often the project
of language revival, there is an abiding interest in philanthropy too, in stimu-
lating local industries (as evidenced by the Feis for instance), alongside an
understanding of the material realities of life in remote regions.

Moving between the Glens, the west of Ireland, and the wider colonial
world in that period enabled Casement to draw keen-eyed comparisons
between typhus outbreaks in Connemara and the Putumayo, and between
Irish poverty and the enslavement of indigenous peoples under colonialism;
his comment about the 'white Indians' of Connemara, which he described
as the 'Irish Putumayo' is a clear example of this, for instance (NLI 13073).[12]
Just as he had earlier committed himself to the re-education of Ada McNeill,
his prodigious letter-writing meant that his 'New Woman' network in the
Glens had access to these ideas, and to his perception of social injustice in
the wider world he moved through; moreover, Casement's achievements in
highlighting human rights abuses in the Congo and the Putumayo encouraged them to believe that, where political will is available, social change is
possible. The Glens women put this awareness to good use, bringing their
own capacity to bear in their efforts to right local wrongs. For instance, in
this (undated) letter Gertrude circulated after Casement's death to raise funds
for the Aran Island schools, she mentions his earlier intervention in a place

> where the children acquire their education under conditions of great hardship . . .
> When Roger Casement visited the islands in 1913 his heart . . . was moved with pity
> for the plight of these poor little ones. He gave a sum of money to be expended in
> providing food (a cup of hot cocoa or milk or bread and jam) for the children in the
> middle of the day so that they might face their school tasks with more energy than
> is possible when children are cold and hungry. (NLI MS 39,120/5)

Their willingness to carry on consciousness raising in his name to achieve
social justice and foster the Irish language shows the extent to which social
change was the central motivating principle of this group.

Inevitably, Casement's trial and execution brought this group of women
closer together, and as their letters to one another show, their later efforts
to commemorate him were the basis for several initiatives, not least their
collective involvement in subsequent iterations of the Glens Feis. In 1928,
Margaret Dobbs was a driving force in the re-establishment of the Feis,
along with Ada McNeill and Gertrude Bannister (who had since moved to
the Glens from England, following her marriage to Sydney Parry); Dobbs
maintained an active involvement in the committee until her death in 1962.

In later life, the extent to which these women constituted a self-reliant community is plainly evident; to give just two examples of this, Ada McNeill took Eilis in when the Bannister sisters became homeless in 1942 following the wiping out of their savings in a stock market crash, and Rose Young shared Margaret Dobbs's home in Cushendall until her death in 1947. Their sense of common cause in the period following Casement's death was doubtless enhanced when, following the foundation of two new states on the island of Ireland, their ideological affinities were radically at odds with the northern majority.

Partition of the island in 1922 meant that this nationalist community was left somewhat stranded in the Glens. Alice Green's earlier introduction to *Woman's Place in the World of Letters* might have been written in tribute to them:

> Of all pilgrims and sojourners in the world, woman remains in fact the most perplexed and the most alien . . . With her dim consciousness of having come from beyond the Law, or at least from regions where there is the adumbration of a new Law, her eyes are turned only to the Future. There she imagines ceaselessly another Life to be revealed which shall utterly efface old codes and systems. In her need and desire she has allied herself with the poor, the slaves, the publicans and sinners, with all who, like herself, were seeking something different from that which they knew. (Stopford Green, *Woman's Place* 23)

Ultimately, this vision of a new law and a time when 'old codes and systems' would be overturned, has proved a considerably longer project than she envisioned. Meanwhile, the names of these women have largely been forgotten, even in connection with the well-known men in their circle, Roger Casement, Bulmer Hobson, F. J. Bigger. A poem by another Antrim writer, John Hewitt, captures the gendered nature of public memory which contributes to this forgetfulness. In 'Fame', the scene is set in a rural community, a group of men gather in a 'joiner's rock-floored shop' at the end of a day's hay-making; the speaker, an outsider to the group, tries to gain a foothold in the company by turning the conversation to something he knows something about, poetry. He mentions work by a local poet and his intervention is immediately rewarded by the enthusiasm of his fellows, who know the poet in question; to the chagrin of the speaker, however, their main interest is in the tales they tell about this man's escapades, and so poetry is quickly out-classed by their yarning. Undaunted, he tries again to turn the conversation to poetry but this time, the men begin comparing notes on local rhymers and *seanachies* such as Henry Pat, whose 'every hit was clear / still, all the parties he was tilting at were dead and gone this many's a year'. The speaker has one final parry, mentioning the name of a renowned Glens poet, Moira O'Neill.[13] This is the response of the Glens men:

> Oh aye, ye mean the young Miss Higginson
> who lived with the M'Neills of Cushendun.
> She was a decent girl. I seen her when
> they had the first big feis here, in the Glen.
> They said that she writ poems now and then.

Notes

1 Discussions of queer kinship emerged in scholarly and activist work chiefly as a means to explore alternatives to heteronormative family structures and claim legitimacy for LGBTQ families. See for instance: Kath Weston, *Families We Choose: Lesbians, Gays, Kinship* (New York: Columbia University Press, 1997); Heather Murray, *Not in This Family: Gays and the Meaning of Kinship in Postwar North America* (Philadelphia: University of Pennsylvania Press, 2010).

2 Gertrude Bannister, Eva Gore-Booth, and Alice Stopford Green, along with Henry Nevinson and Philip Morel, had an audience with King George V on 2 August 1916, the day before Casement's hanging. The king refused a royal pardon on the basis that it was within the home secretary's jurisdiction; while George V did pass on the request to the home secretary, all appeals including this one were denied. See Sonja Tiernan, *Eva Gore-Booth: An Image of Such Politics* (Manchester: Manchester University Press, 2012), 193–4.

3 Margaret O'Callaghan is currently engaged in a full-length study of the historical writings of Alice Stopford Green and her circle.

4 Máire Mhac an tSaoi's anecdote about Mabel Fitzgerald in the post-Civil War period underscores her republican adherence: 'At that time Mrs Fitzgerald's espousal of the republican cause was so intense that she would not let her husband, Desmond, a minister in the Free State government, come home to his own house.' (Máire Mhac an tSaoi, *The Same Age as the State* (Dublin: O'Brien Press 2013), 74).

5 According to Ríona Nic Congáil, Agnes O'Farrelly's first novel, *Grádh agus Crádh* (1901), was a 'New Woman' novel. See Nic Congáil 117, 122–5.

6 See also Tina O'Toole, *The Irish New Woman* (London: Palgrave Macmillan, 2013).

7 Unpublished report for the Irish Temperance League (2012), 'Providing an alternative to the public house: the Irish Temperance League and the creation of the first coffee chain in Belfast in the 1870s.'

8 For further background on Dobbs's sustained commitment to local culture and language education, see interview with Mairead McMullan, local historian and archivist to Feis na nGleann (interviewer: Philip Campbell; from the 2009 BBCNI/TG4 series *Taisce na Tuaithe*). Available at: youtube.com/watch?v=4nY9ZtPN3Uw.

9 This was reissued by Cló Iar-Chonnacht in 2009, titled *Duanaire Gaedhilge Róis Ní Ógáin: A Collection of the Most Popular Songs of the Time*. Diarmaid Ó Doibhlin, ed.

10 This is now seen as a key event in northern GAA history, according to the Boston College GAA Oral History Project (see bc.edu/centers/irish/gaahistory.html); the strong hurling tradition for which Antrim was famous throughout the twentieth century is partly attributed to the annual Feis (the main GAA stadium in Belfast is called Casement Park; the Cushendall GAA club, founded in 1906, is named 'Ruarí Óg's', see ruairiog.com/about-us/history).

11 Gertrude Bannister's involvement would come later, in the aftermath of the revolutionary period and Casement's execution.

12 This is from a note made by Casement on a letter to him about the Putumayo from Charles Roberts, 6 June 1913.

13 Moira O'Neill (Agnes Higginson-Skrine) (1864–1955) was an Irish-Canadian poet who published *Songs of the Glens of Antrim* (1900) and *More Songs of the Glens of Antrim* (1921); she was the mother of writer Molly Keane (Nesta Skrine) (1904–96).

Works Cited

Dudgeon, Jeffrey. *Roger Casement: The Black Diaries*. Belfast: Belfast Press, 2002.

Fortier, Anne Marie. '"Coming home": queer Migrations and multiple evocations of home'. *European Journal of Cultural Studies* 4:4 (2001): 405–24.

Foster, R. F. *Vivid Faces: The Revolutionary Generation in Ireland 1890–1923*. London: Allen Lane, 2014.

Hewitt, John. 'Fame'. *The Bell* 16:4 (Jan. 1951): 13.

Hutton, Margaret. *The Táin: An Irish Epic Told in English Verse*. Dublin: Maunsel, 1907.

Kirkland, Richard. 'The shanachie of Belfast and its red-bricked Gaeltacht: Cathal O'Byrne'. *Bullán* 4:2 (1999–2000): 67–82.

Ledger, Sally. *The New Woman: Fiction and Feminism at the Fin de Siecle*. Manchester: Manchester University Press, 1997.

Mac Reamoinn, Seán. 'An Irishman's diary'. *Irish Times* 20 Mar. 1996.

McDowell, R. B. *Alice Stopford-Green: A Passionate Historian*. Dublin: Allen Figgis, 1967.

Ní C. Dobr., Maighréad (Margaret Dobbs). *Side-Lights on the Táin Age and Other Studies*. Dundalk: William Tempest, 1917.

—. *The Ban-Shenchus*. Paris: Revue Celtique, 1930.

Nic Congáil, Ríona. *Úna Ní Fhaircheallaigh agus an Fhís Útóipeach Ghaelach*. Gaillimh: Arlen House, 2010.

O'Callaghan, Margaret. '"With the eyes of another race, of a people once hunted themselves': Casement, colonialism and a remembered past'. Mary E. Daly, ed. *Roger Casement in Irish and World History*. Dublin: Royal Irish Academy, 2005. 46–63.

—. 'Alice Stopford Green: historian to the revolutionary generation?'. Ruairi Mac Easmainn/Roger Casement (1864–1916): The Glocal Imperative. Conference. Tralee, Co. Kerry. 24–26 Oct. 2013.

Ó Doibhlin, Diarmaid. 'Womenfolk of the Glens of Antrim and the Irish language'. Phoenix, et al. 15–30.

Phoenix, Eamon, Pádraic Ó Cléireacháin, Eileen McAuley and Nuala McSparran, eds. *Feis na nGleann: A Century of Gaelic Culture in the Antrim Glens*. Belfast: Stair Uladh, 2005.

Sawyer, Roger. *Casement: The Flawed Hero*. London: Routledge & Kegan Paul, 1984.

Singleton-Gates, Peter and Mauric Girodias. *The Black Diaries: An Account of Roger Casement's Life and Times*. New York: Grove Press, 1959.

Stopford Green, Alice. *Irish Nationality*. London: Thornton Butterworth, 1929 edn, first published 1911.

—. *Woman's Place in the World of Letters*. London: Macmillan, 1913.

6

Eva Gore-Booth's Queer Art of War

Maureen O'Connor

In 1916 Eva Gore-Booth reissued an excerpt of her 1905 play, *The Triumph of Maeve*, as *The Death of Fionavar*. It was a commemorative publication reviewed around the world and illustrated by Gore-Booth's sister, Constance Markievicz, while in Mountjoy Gaol, where she was facing execution for her part in the Easter Rising, though her death sentence would be later commuted to life in prison. The collaboration between the sisters on this rapidly produced, unique work of art, published in May 1916, just weeks after the Rising in April, memorialised not only the women's intensely close relationship, but the complexities of Eva's perceived pacifism. My reading of the text skews or 'queers' the way in which Eva Gore-Booth's attitude towards the Rising and, possibly the way the Rising itself, is generally understood.[1] Gore-Booth, like many of the participants in the Rising, was opposed to the Great War, often figured by Irish nationalists as the slaughtering of millions in the name of colonialist aggression. Gore-Booth was an active anti-conscription activist, and was especially concerned that conscription was about to be established in Ireland. Declaring a republic, even if the effort failed, could delay such a development. One of the martyrs of the Rising and close friend of Gore-Booth's, James Connolly, articulated the significance of this motivation for the rebellion, timed to disrupt and divert the energies of the British war machine, to *curtail* rather than promote bloodshed, when he declared: 'Starting this, Ireland may yet set a torch to a European conflagration that will not burn out until the last throne and the last capitalist bond and debenture will be shrivelled in the funeral pyre of the last warlord.'[2]

In the popular imagination the Gore-Booth sisters are best known for their posthumous appearance in the W. B. Yeats poem, 'In Memory of Eva Gore-Booth and Con Markievicz'. In Ireland at least, Markievicz is remembered, though not always with appreciation, while Gore-Booth has faded from collective memory, even though Eva, the younger sister, radicalised Constance and in many ways led a less conventional life. Markievicz's exploits may have been more spectacular and public, but Gore-Booth's public and private lives were more defiant of the status quo.[3] While still in Ireland, Gore-Booth was politically active, attending Land League meetings and setting up a female suffrage society in Sligo with her sisters, Constance and Mabel. Both Constance and Eva abandoned lives of privilege in order to be of service in the causes of labour, women, the poor, and the Irish nation. Neither would rank these causes; in fact, they would have seen them as aspects of a single advocacy, that of the universal right to self-determination. Gore-Booth left Ireland, the sylvan glades of Sligo, and the cultured luxury of the family home, Lissadell House, in 1897 for Manchester's industrial slums to share her life with her partner, Esther Roper. The couple met the year before in Italy. Gore-Booth's commitment to social action became a much more central part of her life in Manchester where, with Roper, an already battle-hardened social reformer, Gore-Booth dedicated enormous reserves of time and energy to, predominantly, the cause of working women, whose interests Roper is generally credited with bringing into the previously largely middle-class campaign for women's rights.[4] Gore-Booth was involved in a number of successful campaigns that influenced legislation concerning women in occupations like barmaids, florists, circus performers, and pit mine workers. Both women were involved with the Manchester University Settlement, a programme of educational outreach for workers. There Gore-Booth regularly taught a course on Shakespeare and established a dramatic society for women. It was through the Manchester Education Committee that the couple made their early contact with the Pankhursts, Emmeline and her daughters Christabel and Sylvia. Roper and Gore-Booth would eventually become estranged from the Pankhursts over the issue of the use of physical violence in the pursuit of women's rights, including resisting arrest, assaulting police officers, and breaking windows. Gore-Booth was, in the prosecution of this cause at least, staunchly constitutional. Emmeline and Christabel Pankhurst were also dedicated supporters of the Great War, going so far as to advocate for the suspension of suffrage agitation during the conflict and participating in the 'white feather' movement. As will be discussed, Gore-Booth, like Sylvia Pankhurst, was passionately opposed to conscription and to the war effort in general.

At the same time as she was actively engaged in politics and teaching, Gore-Booth was writing and publishing poetry and plays, as well as articles and pamphlets. She published seven plays and nine collections of critically acclaimed poetry. Her poems appeared in numerous newspapers and journals in Ireland, England, and the United States. She began publishing poetry in the 1890s including some pieces in *The Irish Homestead*. Yeats was an early champion of her literary efforts, despite coming to regret in later years the sisters' politics, their 'conspiring among the ignorant', as 'In Memory of Eva

Gore-Booth and Con Markievicz' describes them. *The Death of Fionavar* is an image of Gore-Booth's politics that complicates, if it does not contradict, the general consensus regarding the nature of her pacifism. The play is dedicated to the martyrs of the Easter Rising: 'To the Memory of the Dead / The Many who died for Freedom and the One who died for Peace', the one being Francis Sheehy-Skeffington (Gore-Booth, *Fionavar* 7). The poem that follows this dedication names some of those who died in the 1916 Rising and acknowledges Markievicz's sacrifice by their side:

> Poets, Utopians, Bravest of the brave,
> > Pearse and MacDonagh, Plunkett and Connolly,
> Dreamers turned fighters, but to find a grave,
> > Glad for the dream's austerity to die.
>
> And my own sister, through wild hours of pain,
> > Whilst murderous bombs were blotting out the stars,
> Little I thought to see you smile again
> > As I did yesterday, through prison bars ...
>
> Oh, bitterest sorrow of that land of tears,
> > Utopia, Ireland of the coming time,
> That thy true citizens through weary years,
> > Can for thy sake but make their grief sublime!
>
> Dreamers turned fighters but to find a grave,
> > Too great for victory, too brave for war,
> Would you had dreamed the gentler dream of Maeve ...
> > Peace be with you, and love for evermore.
> > > (Gore-Booth, *Fionavar* 9)

These are not exactly the words of an 'absolutely uncompromising pacifist' who 'could not countenance the notion of a just war' (Dixon 192), which is how Joy Dixon describes Gore-Booth, who, while she did not see the Great War as just, could recognise justifiable instances of taking up arms. Despite the fairly wan regret expressed in subjunctive mode in the opening poem's penultimate line, trailing off into ellipses, that a gentler dream had not been followed, the overall tone is one of admiration for, if not romanticisation of, those who fought and died for freedom, calling them brave dreamers, utopianists, and true citizens. Markievicz's contribution to the publication is her 'decorations', a word that more accurately describes her artwork than does the word 'illustration'. Drawn with quills made from rooks' feathers found in the prison yard, or so Markievicz claimed, the iconography and patterning of those decorations offer potential clues to interpreting what may seem a contradiction in Gore-Booth's dedication prefacing an ostensibly anti-war play. Gore-Booth did everything slant; even her deviations deviated from expectations. She managed to queer every position she occupied, and she occupied a number of heterodox positions. As she claimed in a 1925 letter, 'One has to turn one's mind upside down and change all the values, before one can understand *real* things at all.'[5]

Joy Dixon's work on feminism and Theosophy in the fin-de-siècle period is indispensable, but like other North American scholars who write about first-wave Irish feminists, especially when the women have passed their adult life in England, Dixon fails to make vital distinctions between Irish and English experience in this extraordinarily fraught time period. The historical differences between the islands of experience of gender, class, confessional affiliation, history, and power remain irreducible. In Dixon's discussion of Gore-Booth's own idiosyncratic deployment of Theosophy, in the course of which the assertion is made regarding the poet's 'uncompromising pacifism', Ireland is never mentioned, nor is Gore-Booth's relationship to Markievicz acknowledged, and this relationship would be especially undermining of Dixon's point. A neat and generalised division between a position of pro-peace and one of pro-militancy does not survive under a reading of the breadth of Gore-Booth's writing, whether in prose, verse, or drama. As Sonja Tiernan notes, Gore-Booth published an account of the 1916 executions in the *Socialist Review*, a pacifist periodical expressly opposed to the Rising, 'but Gore-Booth does not denigrate the armed rebellion anywhere in her article' (Tiernan 195). From her very earliest poems, written more than a decade before the Rising, to the 1917 collection *Broken Glory*, once again dedicated to the Rising's participants and in particular the memory of Roger Casement, there is a consistency of viewpoint in Gore-Booth's attitude towards Irish rebellion, however militarist a form it might need to take. So in 'Clouds', for example, a poem from the 1890s, the speaker complains of Ireland's 'acquiescence' and sees the flashing eyes of Justice exhorting the nation to rise, 'live and hope again', to 'Bear the sword of Freedom foremost in the strife' (Gore-Booth, *Poems* 58–9). This poem appears in her first collection of 1898, which also includes adulatory poems about Joan of Arc and the French Revolution. 'In Praise of Liberty' acknowledges that 'Some call for glory, some for peace':

But peace, or strife, or toil, or rest,
    The stir of life, the silent grave—
I know that Liberty is best,
    And no man sadder than a slave.
        (Gore-Booth, *Poems* 4)

Another poem in the collection, 'A Traitor', continues this theme:

Fair flag of freedom, splendid star of Truth,
 I will follow every where thy beams are shed;
Yea, though they light me to the grave of youth,
 And shine athwart pale faces newly dead.
[. . .]
Trust in the spirit's striving that ascends
 To hard-earned life, far stronger and more free
Than all your long-lost loves, my scornful friends.
 'Tis life, life, life, the battle on the height—

Freedom as the ultimate value, and one worth fighting and killing for – 'The fight for freedom and for brotherhood' (Gore-Booth, *Poems* 60–2) – is a theme found repeatedly in Gore-Booth's poetry. Several poems are appended to her 1904 verse drama *Unseen Kings*, a number of them about Maeve, including 'To Maeve', which describes the warrior queen as a 'hero soul' whose 'golden deeds' have been buried by treacherous and envious men who feared her battle prowess when she was alive (Gore-Booth, *Unseen Kings* 60–2). The epigraph for 'Lament of the Daughters of Ireland' is from Sophocles: 'In women, too, dwells the spirit of battle.' The poem recalls the glorious hour when the sun shone on Maeve, decked in 'the might of her battle array'. A lament for the days when women were on the battlefield, the poem identifies Irish women as 'children of the sword', reduced to sitting dully around the distaff, gaining nothing but 'peace for our souls' reward, / And the sword slips out of the grasp of hands grown white and feeble and fair'. Women have, for the sake of peace, abjured 'The swift delight of the sword, the joy that is fiercer than pain' (Gore-Booth, *Unseen Kings* 66–9).

Gore-Booth's martial imagery and rhetoric intensify in both poetry and prose after the Rising, which indicates a reaction to the rebellion and its aftermath that was not one of revulsion or even disillusion. Her imagery also becomes less conventional in other ways, as I will indicate. When the Rising ended with Pearse's surrender, a rumour circulated that Markievicz had been shot in the skirmishing. Gore-Booth recalled her strange relief at the news: 'I had almost wished the discredited story had been true, so much worse does it seem to be executed coldly and deliberately at a certain hour by the clock than to be killed in the hurry and excitement of battle' (qtd Roper 45). This observation is included in a speech reported by Roper that Gore-Booth delivered in London a few days after the couple had been in Dublin on 11 May 1916, to visit Markievicz, having heard of her reprieve. The speech is filled with scathing denunciations of the history of English rule in Ireland, including the sights that greeted the women as they 'steamed into Dublin Bay that May morning':

> A great mass of khaki-clad soldiers crowding round the gangway shook the glamour of the scene and brought queer memories of past generations.
>
> Soldiers of all times, of the same nationality and on the same quest . . . An endless procession of soldiers, with every kind of weapon, always on the same errand, always going, as they are going now, to conquer and hold down Ireland. (qtd Roper 42–3)

Gore-Booth's 1917 collection of poems, *Broken Glory*, 'In Memory of August 3rd, 1916', the day of Casement's execution, features work about rebels and rebellion, mythical, historical, and contemporary. 'Government' refers to the 'rulers of the earth' as 'savage and blind' and represents Casement, Socrates, Jesus Christ and Joan of Arc as 'God's splendid rebels' who 'die on God's dear battle plain', all engaged in the same eternal, sanctified struggle (Gore-Booth, *Complete* 507–8). Many poems in the collection close with an image of renewal. 'Government' concludes: 'The world's true will / Has brought, in this dark hour of pain and strife, / A violet to life.' 'Easter Week' ends by saying of the 'noble dead' that 'Their strange heroic questioning of Fate / Ribbon with gold the rags of this our life', while the same heroes are remembered in 'Heroic Death, 1916' not with fading flowers, but 'the deathless wreath—a crown of thorns' (Gore-Booth, *Complete* 508–9). In each case sacrifice brings beauty into the world, something meaningful arises from the desolate wreckage of bodies and landscapes, and this kind of mythic cyclical structure of destruction and renewal is central to Gore-Booth's aesthetics and politics.

The collection is dedicated to Casement, whom Gore-Booth never met, but to whom she felt an intense personal connection, after they seemed to recognise each other from across the courtroom when she attended his trial for high treason on 17 May 1916.[6] Gore-Booth attended every day of the trial after this and lobbied energetically against Casement's execution. Casement's cousin, Gertrude Parry, who carried messages between Casement and Gore-Booth, described their unorthodox relationship, conducted at a mediated distance in the last days of his life, as 'A mutual attraction. A little half affair' (qtd James 224), a doubly 'queer' attraction between a gay man and a lesbian. Among the conventional paeans to the rebel dead included in the collection dedicated to Casement's memory are more perverse poems that possibly queer the rising, including the poem 'To C. A.' (Clare Annesley):

> You seem to be a woman of the world,
> Gorgeous in silky robes of blue and green,

Hair in soft shining coils, white throat bepearled.
It is not true, you are what you have been.

I know you for the Umbrian monk you are,
Brother of Francis and the sun and rain.
(Gore-Booth, *Complete* 516–7)

Theorists have offered many queer readings of the kinds of passionate, emotionally homoerotic, if not physically sexual, relationships that would have been experienced in same sex environments such as nunneries and monasteries,[7] so imagining Clare Annesley was not only a man in a former life but also a monk is suggestive. In 'The Little Girl's Riddle', a child wonders if she was a rebel, a student, a fighter, an old king or a priestess in a past life, and another poem of passion, written for Constance, merges rebellion with images of female sexuality and a wild, forbidden night-time encounter:

Comrades
The peaceful night that round me flows,
    Breaks through your iron prison doors,
Free through the world your spirit goes,
    Forbidden hands are clasping yours.

The wind is our confederate,
    The night has left her doors ajar,
We meet beyond earth's barrèd gate,
    Where all the world's wild Rebels are.
(Gore-Booth, *Complete* 511)

The sisters' intimacy was profound. While Markievicz was imprisoned they set aside a time every day to think only of each other in the hope of establishing a telepathic connection.

The intensity of this relationship is one element that complicates a reading of *The Death of Fionavar*. A review of it in *The Irish Homestead* saw the collaboration as contributing to the project's coherence: 'The drawings share in the spirit that breathes in the verse and gives unity to the book' (Gore-Booth, *Complete* 20). However, a review, in the *New York Times Magazine* (10 Sept. 1916), the Sunday supplement, notes an ironic juxtaposition in its title: 'Irish rebel illustrates non-resistance play: Countess Markievicz, in jail for life for her part in Dublin uprising, makes mystic drawings for sister's poetic drama'. The review, mostly a puff piece about the glamorous, exotic countess, turns to the text in its last sentences:

The play is, it may be said, a plea for peace, a glorification of non-resistance, a Goethe-like defense of thought against action. There is something ironical about the fact that this most passionately pacific work should be made by so convinced and practical a direct actionist as Countess Markievicz, the woman with the sword, who with her little band of fighting men helped hold the streets of Dublin for days and nights against the British machine guns.

The *Manchester Guardian*'s review argued that 'the little volume may serve the cause of peace in Ireland and help convince English people that the Irish movement was not in essence revolutionary' (qtd Tiernan 182). And so the ostensible tension or contradiction between the collaborators identified by the *New York Times*, if reduced to an amusing irony, is ignored entirely by the *Manchester Guardian*. Gore-Booth's strenuous and well-publicised anti-conscription campaign and her vocal opposition to the war categorised her as, simply, a pacifist, and therefore uninterested in revolution. In a 1924 letter, however, she asserted that 'There is *no passive* alternative to violence' (Gore-Booth, *Complete* 96, italics in original). The fairly straightforward distinction that Gore-Booth recognises is between militarism in an imperial and in a colonial context.[8] Gore-Booth was active in the anti-war effort in England and in Ireland, but, as Tiernan points out, in her Irish campaign Gore-Booth never used the word 'peace'. It is everywhere in her poems about the nation, however, though in interesting, unexpected permutations. Gore-Booth's own introduction to the play, entitled 'An Interpretation', provides some more clues to the puzzle:

> As I have been accused of taking liberties with an ancient myth, I would say in defence that all myths have many meanings, perhaps as many as the minds of those who know them: and it is in the nature of things that where there is a variation of meaning there is also a variation of form. The truth of this will be seen by studying the various forms of the old Greek myths, such as the stories of Proserpine or Psyche, and comparing their deep and mystical eastern versions with the common-place love-stories familiar to the Latin mind. (Gore-Booth, *Fionavar* 11)

Her syncretism is evident here, her gesture of integration of past and present, east and west, but also her investment in multiplicity and fluidity. There is no single overarching narrative or way of determining meaning or transcendent value.

At this point a brief summary of the play may be necessary. At the beginning of the full-length play, *The Triumph of Maeve*, the magnificent warrior queen, already tiring of war, is sitting with her court, surrounded by female warriors, on November Eve, when Nera, a harper who has spent a year in 'Tirnanogue' appears, his hair bedecked with spring flowers. He explains the out-of-season blooms by saying, 'I have seen roses growing at Samhain / In the enchanted gardens of the Sidhe' (Gore-Booth, *Triumph of Maeve* 32). He makes a crown of primroses for Maeve who weaves some into her hair, and he is bearing an enchanted harp, which we find out he has stolen from a faery. The tale he tells inspires Maeve to attempt to storm the land of the sidhe: she declares, 'The gardens of the Sidhe must be more fair / Than any land I conquered in old days' (Gore-Booth, *Triumph of Maeve* 33). However, at the entrance to Tirnanogue she falls into an enchanted sleep after drinking from a fountain, and is visited by the spirit of Deirdre, a figure Maeve has often evoked. Deirdre is the subject of another of Gore-Booth's plays, *The Buried Life of Deirdre* (1908), which much more radically than *The Triumph of Maeve* takes liberties with an ancient myth: Deirdre is the reincarnation of a king who lived a thousand years earlier whose bloodthirsty deeds must be expiated through Deirdre's fate. In *The Triumph of Maeve*, Deirdre brings her millennial wisdom to Maeve, which the author glosses as 'force is a futile and useless gesture against the soul', but her somewhat cryptic message does not seem to interest the queen (Gore-Booth, *Fionavar* 12). However, another prophetic woman, a druidess, does impress Maeve. Her first prediction is that the forthcoming struggle will end 'in peace', and this is where *The Death of Fionavar* opens.

The news is not all good, however. The druidess goes on to convey 'a vision of woe': the queen's beloved 15-year-old daughter, Fionavar, will die on the field of war. Maeve bans Fionavar from the battle front, but, having heard of her mother's most recent victory, Fionavar defies the old woman who has been charged with watching over her and rushes to the site of 'The Triumph of Maeve'. She is not mortally wounded in the expected way, as the fighting is over and the warriors have left the field. At the sight of carnage, however, she dies, in the words of the author's introduction, 'struck to the heart by the force of that new and terrible Imaginative Pity that has come into the world' (Gore-Booth, *Fionavar* 13). Pity or sympathy as a destructive, even violent power is a recurring theme in Gore-Booth's writing, as is her conviction that peace and freedom require struggle, even war. In her article, 'Sinn Fein rebellion', for *Socialist Review*, she argues that 'you cannot have peace without war' (qtd Tiernan 196), and in verse the same sentiment often appears, as in 'An Epitaph': 'Only through pain is perfect peace attained' (Gore-Booth, *Complete* 132). Peace serves multivalent purposes in Gore-Booth's work, including functioning as a marker of irony and contradiction, as is most wrenchingly the case in her short play written after the Rising, *The Sword of Justice* (1918).

In *The Death of Fionavar* the tragedy of her daughter's fate finally appears to convert Maeve to an ethic of peace, but this ironically bodes disaster. She divides her land and wealth equally among lords and lowly foot soldiers, claiming: 'All souls shall share alike and be content.' Contentment, however, is not the general reaction. Fergus objects: 'Great gifts befit great names and little men / Are grateful for little', while an unnamed warrior ominously predicts that 'The host will be rent / With the wrath of princes' (Gore-Booth, *Fionavar* 61). Maeve, adamant in her determination, is oblivious to warnings about the inevitable havoc withdrawal from her responsibilities will cause. She removes her crown, replacing it with a circlet of primroses, and turns her back on the world of male competition and violence, vowing to end her days on the banks of the Shannon in island seclusion and contemplation, the only real way to gain entry to Tirnanogue. However, her repeated entreaties to the body of Fionavar that she open the gates of Tirnanogue for her mother, while touching, may also hint at Maeve's hope to find a way into the land she still longs to subdue, another approach to the conquest that has eluded her. The play's conclusion is ambivalent at best. She exits the court in a kind of trance, leaving chaos and bloodshed in her wake. The harper Nera is the first to be killed as the queen drifts away. Maeve 'does not seem to hear' what Nera says to her about meeting 'again under the hazel boughs' (Gore-Booth, *Fionavar* 80), and the play concludes with these stage directions:

> *[A Warrior] stabs Nera as Maeve goes out. A warrior rushes forward to seize the fallen crown. Others try to hold him back. Another warrior snatches up the sword of Maeve— and the scene closes in confusion and wild disorder.* (Gore-Booth, *Fionavar* 81)

This scene suggests a military coup will take the place of Maeve's rule, allowing for reading her spiritual retreat as a self-centred and irresponsible move.

This play, like most of Gore-Booth's plays, uses Irish myth, but takes 'liberties' with them, as she says herself. Cathy Leeney and Emma Donoghue have both remarked on the significance of this choice of subject matter. Yeats liked to take credit for interesting the young poet in mythological subjects, but there is ample evidence that her interest in Irish legend predates any influence he might have exerted. Her plays rewrite and/or refocus Irish myth, replacing the chivalric code of male fraternity with a code of female solidarity. In these plays that centre on powerful goddesses, queens, and druidesses, it is female friendships and mother–daughter relationships that dominate. Female subjectivity and desire literally take centre stage. In Leeney's words, Gore-Booth 'places the female subject at the centre of the symbolic order, both linguistic and theatrical' (Leeney 86). What Donoghue has said of her poetry can be applied to the heroic dramas: 'she was inheriting traditions of gender polarity. For centuries male poets had cast themselves as suitors in relation to a feminine personification of nature . . . Eva lesbianised the couple' (Donoghue 18). Donoghue, speaking of the plays, goes on to say that 'What seems to have appealed to Gore-Booth about the women of Celtic legend was their independence and their focus on other women' (Donoghue 26). These cycles not only featured strong, aggressive women, but particularly queens and especially goddesses who had the power of metamorphosis, sometimes understood or represented by Gore-Booth as reincarnation, as in *The Buried Life of Deirdre*, other times as the movement between bodies, for example, the Mórrígan in her traditional form as a crow in *Unseen Kings*. The body is fluid and malleable for Gore-Booth, as we will see.

Gore-Booth was aesthetically and spiritually invested in the possibilities afforded by the idea of reincarnation, not only as a member of the Theosophical Society, but as a truly revolutionary feminist devoted to the disruption of not simply gender differences but the supposedly disinterested and inarguable foundation of those differences, biological sex itself. This element in Gore-Booth's philosophy surely influenced the decorations provided by Markievicz. The *New York Times Magazine* review describes the decorations as consisting of 'landscapes, flowers, cabalistic designs', while the *Manchester Guardian* notes 'gothic scrolls and flower patterns . . . breaking out into mystic symbolism and visionary scenes of the Celt' (qtd Tiernan 182). Gore-Booth's childhood interest in Irish myth and folklore developed into an interest in world myths, a central preoccupation of Theosophy. Markievicz, however, had no documented interest in Theosophy (though she did convert to Roman Catholicism, which may exert its own occult attractions).

Gore-Booth's letters to her sister were destroyed at Markievicz's death, and in Markievicz's letters there is no discussion of the collaboration on this play, so whose idea these designs were or what the discussions were about the use of them cannot be confirmed.[9] However, there is no denying that the design motif in general and in its details is cabalistic, esoteric, and hermetic, as is evident from the text's first illustration (repeated elsewhere in the play) (see Figure 6.1). This is also one of the few actual illustrations of an element of the play, namely, Maeve's discarded crown and robe, tossed across her throne. Most of the images do not refer to events in the text in any obvious way, but are nevertheless illuminating something at the heart of its message. To the left of the crown, in a direct line from it, are the intertwining snakes of the caduceus, a symbol from ancient Egypt and Greece, and this helixing dynamic shape recurs throughout the text's visual component, as in the facing pages in Figure 6.2, in which smoke, floating snakes, and thorns or brambles all gyrate across the margins, recalling Yeats's widening gyres as well as the drawings of atoms and chakras by Charles Leadbeater in his Theosophical publications from the first decade of the twentieth century, such as *Occult Chemistry* and *The Principles of Light and Colour*. The pentagram that decorates the caduceus-shaped vessel in Figure 6.2 is the shape surrounding a rose in

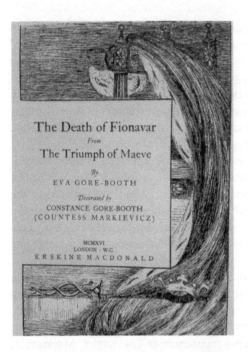

Figure 6.1: Title page of Eva Gore-Booth's
The Death of Fionavar.

Figure 6.2: Snakes of the caduceus, thorns
and brambles, and pentagram details from
Gore-Booth's *The Death of Fionavar.*

Figure 6.3: Pentagram and rose detail from Gore-Booth's *The Death of Fionavar*.

Figure 6.4: Winged ouroboros detail from Gore-Booth's *The Death of Fionavar.*

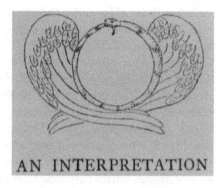

AN INTERPRETATION

the image at the end of Gore-Booth's introduction to the play explaining her method of mythical interpretation (see Figure 6.3), at the beginning of which is another drawing, that of a winged ouroboros (see Figure 6.4).

The emblem of the Theosophical Society, a Western mystical order founded in 1875 by mystic Helena Petrovna Blavatsky, was designed by Blavatsky, and is composed of an ankh, a hexagram, an ouroboros, a swastika, and the omkar symbol, many of which appear repeatedly in the visual scheme of *The Death of Fionavar*. Blavatsky's intent was to create an emblem that incorporated universal spiritual symbols, indicating the esoteric doctrines linking all world faiths. Another significant symbol in mysticism, including for orders like the Knights Templar, is the rose or the primrose. The primrose not only has esoteric significance, but is also associated with the world of the fairies. Primroses appear visually in the play (Figures 6.1 and 6.4 offer only a small sampling of the flower's many visual appearances), as well as textually. Blood-soaked primroses are the first shocking sight to greet Fionavar at the battlefield, for example, and Maeve renounces her leadership by exchanging a crown of gold for one of primroses. In discussing *Unseen Kings*, Leeney observes that text plays 'with the border separating spaces and identities showing them to be fluid and dissolving them. Poetic and symbolist language creates an atmosphere of indefiniteness that threatens polarities of the real and the unreal, peace and war, good and evil' (Leeney 86). It is this desire to undermine polarities that informs the decorative scheme of *The Death of Fionavar*, a connection that emerges from an understanding of Theosophy's specific significance for Gore-Booth, particularly when it comes to the transversal of heterogeneities and polarities.

Charles Leadbeater, along with Annie Besant (who identified herself as 'three quarters' Irish) inaugurated a neo-Theosophy early in the twentieth century that was much more engaged in social reform than the society had been. It became less of a secret club, and more public in its advocacies, including issues of feminism and animal rights. Dixon describes Gore-Booth's own Theosophy as an 'unorthodox Christian esotericism' (Dixon 190). A central appeal of Theosophy for Gore-Booth and other contemporary feminists is what outraged many others. One of the criticisms lodged against Theosophy in this fin-de-siècle period was that it promoted sexual deviance. According to Theosophy we all inhabited differently sexed bodies over the millennia, and could have been each other's daughters, sons, wives, and husbands. In her important foundational work, *The Secret Doctrine*, Blavatsky theorises that humanity will evolve to achieve spiritual androgyny resulting in the 'Divine Hermaphrodite' (Blavatsky 124–7). Theosophy prioritised a kind of immanentism that anticipated Bergson's creative evolution and even Gilles Deleuze's and Félix Guattari's rhizomes and various 'becomings' of others, which also recall Gore-Booth's 'Imaginative Pity'. Significantly for people like Gore-Booth, as Dixon points out, Theosophy undermined the prevailing inversion model of contemporary sexology which reasserted the primacy of the heterosexual impulse. But of course Gore-Booth had to further pervert the sexual perversions offered by Theosophy, which still assumed the polarities of the sexes, even insisting on them as necessary to the soul's development over the course of its various reincarnations, if only in order to ultimately transcend those differences.

Along with Roper and others, Gore-Booth, in this same revolutionary year of 1916, established an unusual and little-known publication, *Urania*, which used as one of its mottoes an aphorism sometimes attributed to Gore-Booth (though she borrowed it from Irish novelist Katherine Cecil Thurston's novel *Max*, about a cross-dressing woman): 'Sex is an accident.' Roper and Gore-Booth also worked as early editors of the journal, privately printed and circulated until 1940.[10] The journal explained its own oblique angle to prevailing norms of gender and sex:

Urania denotes the company of those who are firmly determined to ignore the dual organization of humanity in all its manifestations. They are convinced that this duality has resulted in the formation of two warped and imperfect types. They are further convinced that in order to get rid of this state of things no measures of 'emancipation' or 'equality' will suffice, which do not begin with a complete refusal to recognize or tolerate the duality itself. If the world is to see sweetness and independence combined in the same individual, all recognition of that duality must be given up . . . There are no 'men' or 'women' in Urania. [But they are like angels.][11]

The final line, in Greek in the original and also used as one of the journal's mottoes, along with the line preceding it, reference Matthew's Gospel that claims there is no marriage in heaven because there are no men or women there. The journal functioned largely as a kind of aggregator of other media from around the world. It culled and reprinted a number of stories of cross-dressing, mistaken sex, spontaneous sex change in humans and animals, same sex marriage, all demonstrating the unnaturalness of gender and sex. The journal also published contemporary original poems, including some by Gore-Booth, as well as retellings of myths and legends from around the world that corroborated the journal's stance on the radical indeterminacy of gender as something of a longer pedigree than Victorian separate-spheres ideology.

The journal suggested that reincarnation was a means to spiritual regrowth, a model of development that rendered physical sex and cultural gender irrelevant. Bodies themselves are mutable, sex an indeterminate fluid quality. And this in Gore-Booth's work is a matter of *aesthetic* as well as political importance, suggesting the necessarily incomplete nature of mimesis, a performance of the limits of representation and the determining powers of teleological narrative that has clear gender implications, as Leeney has cogently argued. The polarities conventionally understood to be operating in the construction of men and women were for Gore-Booth as immaterial as those limiting our understanding of the complex dynamic between war and peace.

Writing about blasted Dublin after the Rising, Gore-Booth likens 'Ireland the Unconquerable' to 'the human soul smiling through an agony of weakness at the secret of her enigmatic strength' (qtd Roper 44). For Gore-Booth weakness and strength, male and female, war and peace are not oppositional binaries, but processes to be negotiated, in both the past and the future, both of which exist in the present. Eva and Constance conceived of *The Death of Fionavar* believing one of them was soon to face execution. But, as the poem prefacing the play suggests, grief can be a source of the sublime. Theosophical principles of the unity of being and the persistence of life beyond our limited human temporality supported Gore-Booth's conviction that the bond between the sisters could not be broken, and her sister's contribution of 'cabalistic designs' to the text of the play can be read as a moving endorsement of that conviction. Certainly the visual and textual designs of *The Death of Fionavar* conspire to produce a picture of war that queers expected polarities, particularly those that obtain between politics and style, between love and war, and even between life and death.

Notes

1   The verb 'to queer' is used here in the sense of shifting perspectives from the normative. This sense of the verb derives from queer studies as it developed from the 1990s and is no longer necessarily only used in reference to sexual orientation or gender identity, though it remains anchored in a determination to oppose and defiantly deviate from the oppressive norms of heterosexist society:

> Queerness is sustained through its perpetual challenge to normalising mandates . . . Queer . . . can function in a number of ways: as a noun (naming something /someone), an adjective (describing something /someone), a verb (queering something /someone), an adverb (to do something queerly). Queer can be a political or ethical approach, an aesthetic quality, a mode of interpretation or way of seeing, a perspective or orientation, or a way of desiring, identifying, or disidentifying. (Taylor 14–15)

2   James Connolly writing for the *Irish Worker* in 1914, *Selected Writings* 26; Gore-Booth considered Connolly the 'most kindly and humane of men' (qtd Roper 44).

3   See Sonja Tiernan's magisterial *Eva Gore Booth: An Image of Such Politics* for more details about the sisters' lives. Most of the biographical material that follows is indebted to this biography as well as to Dermot James, *The Gore-Booths of Lissadell*.

4   For more about Esther Roper, see Lewis, *Eva Gore-Booth and Esther Roper*, the source for most of the details provided here regarding the couple's activities in Manchester.

5   From a letter to Margaret Wroe, dated November 1924. Quoted in *Poems of Eva Gore-Booth: Complete Edition* 87, italics in original.

6   According to Casement's biographer, Geoffrey De Parmiter, Gore Booth 'felt as if she had known Casement all her life' (Tiernan 187).

7   For example, Michel Foucault, in discussing the introduction of increasingly invasive technologies of policing desire in monasteries in the seventeenth century, argues that the 'scheme for transforming sex into discourse had been devised long before in an ascetic and monastic setting' (Foucault 20).

8   My thanks to Professor Tadhg Foley, who articulated this in the early stages of this project.

9   Few references to the drawings survive in Constance's letters. In a letter from Aylesbury Prison dated 8 August 1916 to Gore-Booth, always her 'Dearest Old Darling', Markievicz asks, 'When is your next book coming out, and the one with my pictures in it, if it ever does? They were very bad. I can do much better now. I was just beginning to get some feeling into my black and white when I left Ireland. I made quills out of rooks' feathers that I found in the garden' (*Prison Letters* 160). An undated fragment from around the same period, though obviously later,

refers to the published work: 'I love the book, it is a real joy. They have put the Rose in the triangle on its side, didn't I put it upright?' (*Prison Letters* 144).

10   For more about this publication, see Oram, 'Sexology and culture: "sex is an accident"' and 'Feminism, androgyny and love between women in *Urania*, 1916–1940'. See also Tiernan, '"Engagements dissolved": Eva Gore-Booth, *Urania* and the challenge to marriage'; 'The journal *Urania* (1916–1940): an alternative archive of radical gender masquerade'; and '"No measures of emancipation or equality will suffice": Eva Gore-Booth's radical feminism in the journal *Urania*'.

11   This passage is reproduced by both Oram and Tiernan in the articles cited above.

Works Cited

Blavatsky, Helena Petrovna. *The Secret Doctrine: The Synthesis of Science, Religion and Philosophy*. Cambridge: Cambridge University Press, 2011 edn, first published 1888.

Connolly, James. *Selected Writings*. Peter Beresford Ellis, ed. London and Chicago: Pluto Press, 1997.

Dixon, Joy. *Divine Feminine: Theosophy and Feminism in England*. Baltimore: Johns Hopkins Press, 2001.

Donoghue, Emma. '"How could I fear and hold thee by the hand': the poetry of Eva Gore-Booth'. Éibhear Walshe, ed. *Sex, Nation and Dissent in Irish Writing*. New York: St Martin's Press, 1997. 16–42.

Foucault, Michel. *The History of Sexuality: An Introduction*, vol. 1. Robert Hurley, trans. New York: Vintage, 1990.

Fox, Richard Michael. *Rebel Irish Women*. Dublin: Progress House, 1967.

Gore-Booth, Eva. *The Death of Fionavar from the Triumph of Maeve*. London: Erskine MacDonald Ltd., 1916.

—. *Triumph of Maeve*. Frederick S. Lapasardi, ed. *The Plays of Eva Gore-Booth*. San Francisco: EMText, 1991. 22–65.

—. *Poems*. London: Longmans, Green, and Co., 1898.

—. *Poems of Eva Gore-Booth: Complete Edition*. Esther Roper, ed. London: Longmans, Green, and Co., 1929.

—. *Unseen Kings*. London: Longmans, Green, and Co., 1904.

James, Dermot. *The Gore-Booths of Lissadell*. Dublin: Woodfield, 2004.

Leeney, Cathy. *Irish Women Playwrights, 1900–1939: Gender and Violence on Stage*. Bern: Peter Lang, 2010.

Lewis, Gifford. *Eva Gore-Booth and Esther Roper: A Biography*. London: Pandora Press, 1988.

McCormack, W. J. 'Irish gothic and after'. Seamus Deane, ed. *The Field Day Anthology of Irish Writing*, vol. 2. Dublin: Field Day Publications, 1991. 831–54.

New York Times Magazine 10 Sept. 1916: 2.

Oram, Alison. 'Feminism, androgyny and love between women in *Urania*, 1916–1940'. *Media History* 7:1 (June 2001): 57–70.

—. 'Sexology and culture: "sex is an accident"'. Lucy Bland and Laura Doan, eds. *Sexology in Culture: Labelling Bodies and Desires*. Cambridge: Polity, 1998: 214–30.

Roper, Esther, ed. *Prison Letters of Countess Markievicz (Constance Gore-Booth) and a Biographical Sketch*. London: Longmans, Green, and Co., 1934.

Taylor, Jodie. *Playing it Queer: Popular Music, Identity and Queer World Making*. Bern: Peter Lang, 2012.

Tiernan, Sonja. '"Engagements dissolved": Eva Gore-Booth, *Urania* and the challenge to marriage'. Mary McAuliffe and Sonja Tiernan, eds. *Tribades, Tommies and Transgressives: Histories of Sexualities*. Newcastle: Cambridge Scholars, 2008. 128–44.

—. *Eva Gore Booth: An Image of Such Politics*. Manchester: Manchester University Press, 2012.

—. 'The journal *Urania* (1916–1940): an alternative archive of radical gender masquerade'. Sharon Tighe-Mooney and Deirdre Quinn, eds. *Essays in Irish Literary Criticism: Themes of Gender, Sexuality, and Corporeality*. New York: Edwin Mellen, 2008. 55–69.

—. '"No measures of emancipation or equality will suffice": Eva Gore-Booth's radical feminism in the journal *Urania*'. Sarah O'Connor and Christopher Shephard, eds. *Women, Social and Cultural Changes in Twentieth-Century Ireland*. Newcastle: Cambridge Scholars, 2008. 166–82.

7

Agnes O'Farrelly's Politics
and Poetry, 1918–27

Ríona Nic Congáil

Agnes O'Farrelly/Úna Ní Fhaircheallaigh (1874–1951) was a prolific and influential participant in the cultural nationalist and women's rights movements of early twentieth century Ireland. In 1901, with the publication of *Grádh agus Crádh (Love and Anguish)*, she became the first published female Irish-language writer; later she would become a well respected Irish-language scholar, the leading female figure in the Gaelic League, a chief instigator of Cumann na mBan in 1914, and the president of the Camogie Association. It was not uncommon for an educated upper-middle-class woman, whatever her religious background, to be involved in literary circles and voluntary work of all kinds during the revivalist period. What set O'Farrelly apart from her female peers was her involvement in and command of the Irish language, which she acquired as a student at St Mary's University College, Dublin, and through lengthy visits to the Aran Islands every summer from 1898 to 1902.

Although O'Farrelly was much respected within the cultural nationalist and women's rights movements in the first decade of the twentieth century, during the following decade she became a marginalised and ridiculed figure because of her involvement in Cumann na mBan. O'Farrelly became increasingly disillusioned by the Irish political struggle, and withdrew from Cumann na mBan and the Gaelic League. Soon after her withdrawal from both organisations, the deaths in 1916 of two of her closest male friends, P. H. Pearse and Roger Casement, left her in a despondent state. O'Farrelly then turned to writing political and personal poetry. She published two poetry collections during her lifetime, *Out of the Depths* (1921) and *Áille an Domhain* (1927), the latter of which was the first Irish-language poetry collection to be pen-ned and published by a woman. This chapter will interrogate O'Farrelly's ideological persuasions and political background, while also providing an overview of gender, political, and linguistic tensions within Irish society during the first few decades of the twentieth century. It will conclude by analysing O'Farrelly's two collections of poetry, and will situate her poetry in terms of both post-classical Irish-language poetry and the work of the English Romantic poets.

O'FARRELLY'S LITERARY BACKGROUND

Agnes Farrelly (later O'Farrelly) was born in Raffoney in south-east Cavan, where her father was a prosperous Catholic landlord and farmer. Her local area was well known for its Anglo-Irish literary tradition: it was associated with Thomas Sheridan (1719–88), his son Richard Brinsley Sheridan (1751–1816), and Jonathan Swift (1667–1745). Another local resident, Charlotte Brooke (*c.*1740–93), had drawn much attention to the indigenous Gaelic literary heritage through the publication of *Reliques of Irish Poetry* in 1789. According to Mícheál Mac Craith, Brooke's work marked both the beginning of Anglo-Irish poetry and the transition of Irish-language poetry from manuscript to print (Mac Craith 271); through her work, too, Brooke created a precedent for future Irish women scholars. Even during her youth O'Farrelly was acutely aware of this local Anglo-Irish literary heritage – she referred to it in her earliest published correspondence in the *Weekly Freeman*'s children's column, the 'Irish Fireside Club', when she was 14 years of age (*Weekly Freeman* 13 Oct. 1888). By the age of 21, when she was the only female contributor to her local newspaper, the *Anglo-Celt*, she penned a series entitled 'Glimpses of Breffni and Meath', in which she continued to be an avid promoter of the work of the Sheridans and Brookes. But she had also begun by this time to display a keen interest, yet a limited knowledge, in what she termed 'the soft phrases of the Gael' (*Anglo-Celt* 29 Feb. 1896). Although the Irish language had been the spoken language among peasants in the local area during the lifetimes of the Sheridans and Brookes, there were few Irish speakers left during O'Farrelly's youth a century later. However, there still remained more native speakers of Irish in O'Farrelly's local area than anywhere else in East Cavan (Ó Duibhín 186–7).

Following her father's death in 1896, O'Farrelly received a substantial amount of money from his will, and used it to move to Dublin and enroll herself in St Mary's University College, Merrion Square. While there she was surrounded by the first generation of Catholic Irish women to receive university degrees, including Hanna Sheehy (later Sheehy-Skeffington), Máire Ní Chinnéide, and Mary Hayden (who taught history in the college) (Mac Curtain 71). Upon her arrival in St Mary's, O'Farrelly requested that the Irish language be taught as a university subject for women, which led to the Gaelic League vice-president Eoin MacNeill being enlisted as an Irish lecturer. O'Farrelly subsequently became the first woman to receive a BA and MA degree in the Irish language (and in later years, the first female lecturer and female professor of Irish), and she also became involved in every aspect of the Gaelic League. As the Gaelic League was the first adult organisation to welcome women on a par with men, it was an attractive organisation for O'Farrelly to join. O'Farrelly lobbied leading figures within the Gaelic League to further the organisation's commitment towards gender equality at every opportunity and she actively sought its support for her women's rights campaigns in university education. Simultaneously, and along with Mary Hayden, she sought support for the Irish language among her friends within the women's movement. Support was not always forthcoming, however: Hanna Sheehy-Skeffington was among the most notable figures within the women's movement to have little interest in the Irish language and Gaelic League (Sheehy-Skeffington Papers).

By the turn of the twentieth century, several of O'Farrelly's young and educated female contemporaries were engaging in the revivalist literary world. Many began their writing careers through the medium of English, but proceeded to embrace the Irish language to varying extents. Alice Milligan was coming to the fore, having co-edited *The Shan Van Vocht* from 1896–99 with Ethna Carbery. Mary E. L. Butler was hosting a children's column in a national newspaper and publishing short stories. Máire Ní Chillín was publishing folktales in the *United Irishman* – initially in English and later in Irish – and Norma Borthwick and Mairéad Ní Raghallaigh established The Irish Book Company in 1900, which became best known as the publisher of Peadar Ua Laoghaire's *Séadna* (1904). At the same time, the newly established Gaelic League Publications Committee was keen to create a literary corpus that would fill the void in Irish-language print literature, and as O'Farrelly was the most highly qualified woman in the Irish language, along with being an active promoter of the language, she was enthusiastic to write. She thereby became the Irish language's first published female writer. Having spent her summers among the women of Aran, O'Farrelly was very much aware of the rich literary tradition that had continued from generation to generation of women. This was an oral tradition, however, and when O'Farrelly set up a women's branch of the Gaelic League on Inis Meáin in 1899, few female native speakers of Irish were literate in their own language (Ní Fhaircheallaigh 79–81). As the island women became increasingly literate, O'Farrelly produced literature with them in mind as her readership: the aforementioned novella *Grádh agus Crádh* (1901); *An Cneamhaire* (1902), a story of love and emigration set on Inis Meáin; and a travelogue based on her experiences on the Aran Islands, *Smuainte Ar Árainn* (1902). Similar to many of her colleagues in the Gaelic League she wrote under several names: Agnes O'Farrelly, Úna Ní Fhaircheallaigh, and the pseudonym 'Uan Uladh' ('Lamb of Ulster'), the latter presumably chosen as a non-gendered play on 'Úna'. 'Uan' contrasted in this regard with some other prominent pseudonyms at the time, from the masculine 'Cú Uladh' ('Hound of Ulster') used by P. T. Mac Fhionnlaoich, to 'Plúirín Sneachta' ('Snowdrop') used by O'Farrelly's younger sister Lily.

O'Farrelly's early literary efforts received much praise from her peers, particularly given that she had been learning the Irish language for only five years, yet her adherence to 'foreign' and 'modern' narrative structures and plot devices irritated the critic Risteard de Hindeberg. Philip O'Leary has provided the most informative and insightful account of the tensions between what he terms the 'nativists' and 'progressives' within the Gaelic League: 'no single issue,' he argues, 'more sharply distinguishes progressivism from nativism than the eager openness to literary and intellectual innovations from the Continent' (O'Leary 52). O'Farrelly, like P. H. Pearse, Pádraic Ó Conaire, and other writers of the same generation, were 'progressives' in O'Leary's categorisation, as they embraced new ideas and literary forms from Europe. Their critics, most notably de Hindeberg, belonged to the 'nativist' school of thought, and espoused the indigenous Gaelic literary tradition.

Following on from her creative work O'Farrelly proceeded to edit *Leabhar an Athar Eoghan: The O'Growney Memorial Volume* (1904), a large-scale and expensively produced book showcasing the vast network and cohesion of the Gaelic League. By this stage, other writers including Máire Ní Chinnéide, P. H. Pearse, and W. P. Ryan were publishing their work. In the knowledge that more literature in Irish was becoming available to potential readers, O'Farrelly became less concerned with creating reading material in Irish herself. She moved her energies to the educational sphere, taking on the position of chief examiner in Celtic and answerable to the Board of Intermediate Education. Following the Irish Universities Act, 1908, O'Farrelly gained a lectureship in University College Dublin, alongside Douglas Hyde. She had just published her first work of scholarship, *Filidheacht Sheagháin Uí Neachtain: Cuid a hAon*, an edited collection of the poetry of Seán Ó Neachtain (*c.*1640–1729), which consisted of elegies and love poetry. As a Jacobite Ó Neachtain supported the political movement to return a Catholic monarch to the British throne (Pittock). From that point onwards, O'Farrelly dedicated much of her time to poetry and over the following 30 years she was to teach Irish-language poetry to generations of UCD students.

'NON-POLITICAL' POLITICS

Since the establishment of the Gaelic League in 1893, its constitution held a clause stating that 'The League shall be strictly non-political and non-sectarian' (Connradh na Gaedhilge). The clause had been inserted by the

League's founders so as to avoid the disunion and bitterness that they witnessed in the immediate aftermath of the Parnell split. Leading members, O'Farrelly and Hyde in particular, sought cohesion and unity through compromise within the League, and thus they attempted to suppress all questions and discussions relating to politics. Yet no clear definition as to what exactly was meant by the term 'politics' was offered publicly. As a result, members of the Gaelic League were free to interpret the term as they wished, and even those who were on the one hand trying to suppress the discussion of politics within the Gaelic League were themselves becoming increasingly embroiled in overtly political issues, such as education and gender equality. When the Irish Volunteers was established in November 1913 in response to the Ulster Volunteers' threat of resisting Home Rule, it was Eoin MacNeill, vice-president of the Gaelic League, who was credited with conceiving of such a defense force in his article 'The north began', published in *An Claidheamh Soluis* (Martin 24). However, it was the IRB that established the Irish Volunteers and used MacNeill's article and public persona, as a scholar and man of reason, as a front for their new organi-sation. As a respected public figure, O'Farrelly found herself in a similar position to MacNeill regarding Cumann na mBan. According to Jennie Wyse Power, O'Farrelly 'had shown special interest in the formation of a woman's organisation to assist the Irish Volunteers', as the Volunteers them-selves precluded female participation (Wyse Power 4). When Cumann na mBan was publicly inaugurated at Wynn's Hotel in April 1914, O'Farrelly was its chairperson.

O'Farrelly's speech at the inaugural meeting of Cumann na mBan indicated her view of the organisation's role within the nationalist movement at that time:

> We pledge ourselves here to-day to give this cause our support morally, financially and in every way we can. Let this be distinctly understood. We shall do ourselves the honour of helping to arm and equip our National Volunteers. Each rifle we put in their hands will represent to us a bolt fastened behind the door of some Irish home to keep out the hostile stranger. Each cartridge will be a watchdog to fight for the sanctity of the hearth. (*Derry Journal* 20 Apr. 1914)

O'Farrelly's address, subsequently condemned as 'conservative' among some scholars of women's history, was not characteristic of her (Sawyer 81). Since her student days, she had promoted the idea of women's full engage-ment in male-dominated affairs rather than merely 'helping' from the sideline. Her choice of vocabulary was most likely an attempt to forge unity among nationalist women of all types: to recruit ordinary women who worked in the domestic sphere and would not have been inclined to engage in such

organisations were it not that their own homes were in danger. As Senia
Pašeta clarifies helpfully, 'O'Farrelly's speech must be understood within
the context of the organisation's determination to avoid sectionalism at all
costs. As a Gaelic Leaguer and women's educational campaigner, O'Farrelly
knew better than most how important – and difficult – this was' (Pašeta 137).

Both O'Farrelly's inaugural speech and the apparently subordinate
position of Cumann na mBan vis-à-vis the Irish Volunteers were immediately condemned by Irish suffragists (*Irish Citizen* 2 May 1914). Hanna
Sheehy-Skeffington was most vocal in her criticism of Cumann na mBan,
claiming that 'Any society of women which proposes to act merely as an
"animated collecting box" for men cannot have the sympathy of any self-
respecting woman' (*Irish Independent* 6 May 1914). O'Farrelly believed that
the subordinate position of women in Irish society was caused by colonialism, a belief compounded by the work of several historians, including Eoin
MacNeill, who had studied the education, role and rights of women in
ancient Ireland and claimed 'free women' to be 'quite on a level with men'
(*Derry Journal* 7 June 1905). Thus, once Ireland retrieved its independence,
O'Farrelly trusted that 'the woman's question will solve itself' (*Irish Independent*
7 Nov. 1917). Of course, she was to become sorely disappointed in later
years, and in 1937 became one of the chief campaigners against the new
Constitution. In a letter to de Valera, dated 8 May 1937, she pleaded with
him as a fellow 'Gael' to rethink the subservient role attributed to women in
the draft Constitution ('Women and the 1937 Constitution').

While Cumann na mBan's provisional committee showed a united front
in the face of external criticism, it would prove more difficult to do so when
differences became visible within the organisation. From the outset, the
more militant women in Cumann na mBan were irritated by O'Farrelly's
stance. Áine Ní Rathaile (sister of The O'Rahilly, an influential member of
the IRB and Gaelic League) later stated, 'At the first meeting one of the
women present, Miss Agnes O'Farrelly, suggested that we should start making
puttees for the Volunteers. I was disgusted. I came away and told my sister-
in-law I was not going there again' (Ní Rathaile 1–2). To the likes of Ní
Rathaile and Kathleen Clarke, wife of IRB member Tom Clarke, O'Farrelly
not only represented conservatism, but initially hindered the military
advancement of the organisation (Pyle 145).

Following the split in the Volunteer movement in the autumn of 1914,
O'Farrelly continued to seek the compromise of a neutral stance in Cumann
na mBan in order to facilitate unity, just as she had done for many years in
the Gaelic League. Her stance received little support, however, and O'Farrelly
consequently resigned from Cumann na mBan (Wyse Power 5). Following
her resignation she became the subject of a smear campaign by members of

the most actively separatist branch of the Gaelic League – the Keating Branch – whose members published several newspaper articles in which they claimed that O'Farrelly's sympathies lay with Britain (Pyle 125). The Keating Branch featured many husbands of the more militant members of Cumann na mBan, and members of the Branch felt justified in sullying her reputation as they had been frustrated by O'Farrelly and Hyde's attempts to prevent the Gaelic League from becoming a militaristic organisation. Hyde was of course untouchable but O'Farrelly was not, and through this smear campaign, she became a public figure of some ridicule (*Sinn Féin* 19 Sept. 1914). Although O'Farrelly denied allegations of being pro-British, her reputation never fully recovered in nationalist Ireland. In 1915, when members of the Gaelic League voted to amend their organisation's constitution to include its espousal of a 'free' Irish nation, thereby becoming overtly political, both O'Farrelly and Hyde left the Gaelic League in disillusionment (*Irish Independent* 29 July 1915).

Over the following decade, both figures became less visible within the public sphere and the energies they had formerly dedicated to the Gaelic League were increasingly channeled into the Celtic Congress, which promoted scholarship and cultural connections among Celtic regions (Nic Congáil 351–76). However, O'Farrelly re-entered public life on occasion. In July 1916, when Roger Casement was sentenced to death for high treason, she joined his reprieve committee. Novelist Mary E. L. Butler, who also served on the committee, later stated that 'while differing strongly from the view held by Roger Casement with regard to the European War she [O'Farrelly] was to the last his loyal friend and none worked harder than she did to save him from the gallows' (qtd Ní Chinnéide 125). In early 1918, following the British army's heavy losses in the Great War, the conscription of Irishmen to the British army became more than an idle threat. O'Farrelly once more became involved in politics, as secretary of the organising committee of Lá na mBan (Women's Day), 9 June 1918, an occasion on which the nationalist women of Ireland were urged to voice their opposition to conscription (*The Leader* 8 June 1918). She aligned herself with former colleagues and Cumann na mBan organised many of the activities (*Freeman's Journal* 10 June 1918). In a letter to the editor of the *Irish Independent*, O'Farrelly urged women to sign the general anti-conscription pledge, and also the woman's pledge which 'ensures, in addition to the general resistance to conscription, that the women of the country will make it impossible to apply economic pressure to Ireland during the coming months' (*Irish Independent* 7 June 1918). The show of solidarity that ensued among Irishwomen was unprecedented. A contributor to *The Leader* commented that 'this women's day opens up boundless possibilities of national work for the women of Ireland. It was probably the most conscious national effort of Irishwomen so far recorded in Irish history, and it may well mark a new era in Irish national development' (*The Leader* 15 June 1918). Of course, as would be revealed the new era for Irishwomen would not materialise in the decades immediately after 1918.

POETRY AND PROPAGANDA

O'Farrelly was a lecturer in the Irish language in UCD at the same time as being a political campaigner. Her academic specialism was in post-classical Irish poetry, and she had edited a collection of the Jacobite Seán Ó Neachtain's poetry in 1908, which consisted of elegies and love poetry. O'Farrelly also taught the poetry of Aogán Ó Rathaille, and the work of both these poets influenced her own early poetry. Ó Neachtain's and Ó Rathaille's poetry conveyed a succinct political message during an age of transition (Mac Conmara; Ó Buachalla 201–10; 268–75). In the decade following 1916, poetry also became O'Farrelly's method of political engagement, a public political protest, reinitiating an age-old Gaelic tradition. No Irish-speaking woman had previously published political poetry, and apart from her gender, there was one fundamental difference between the poetry of Ó Neachtain and Ó Rathaille and that of O'Farrelly: she initially chose English as her medium of expression, thus blending the old with the new and embracing the language of the coloniser. This was not characteristic of O'Farrelly, as all of her earlier creative works, with the exception of one short story, were written in Irish in an effort to develop Irish-language literature and its readership. However, she chose to write her earliest poems in English for practical reasons: it secured her a wide readership, which Irish-language poetry could not achieve, and on this occasion, she chose to foreground her message rather than her preferred language. Furthermore, her earliest poems were aimed at English audiences and published in Manchester's *Labour Leader* and London's *Weekly Herald*, so as to garner support for the Irish situation among the English working class. In her earlier literary endeavours, she had often foregrounded a propagandist message rather than focusing primarily on aesthetics, and in this respect her poetry was no different.

O'Farrelly's first poetry collection, *Out of the Depths* (1921), provides a chronology of political events leading up to and during the War of Independence, along with personal snapshots written during major events of that war. O'Farrelly's first published poem 'Free!', written in December 1918, resembles the poetry of the Jacobite poets more closely than any of her later poetry, as she began by imitating the language, imagery and metre with which she was most familiar. It is an ironic poem, based on a statement made by Andrew Bonar Law 'that Ireland is now enjoying freedom', juxtaposing the suffering Irish with the comfortable English who care not for Ireland's predicament (O'Farrelly 9). In this poem, O'Farrelly invoked images of native Irish birds and animals in captivity as metaphors for Ireland's oppression: 'Yes! Free as is the captured lark / To beat his wings upon the bars / And sigh his quiv'ring soul away / That Heaven's space is not for him / Free as the deer in circling fence / Quick-sensing life with cramped limbs; / Or as the hound in kennel walls / Whilst stranger packs course mouthing by' (O'Farrelly 9).

O'Farrelly's political poetry consists of simple dichotomies. Ireland – represented as a feminine entity in keeping with the Irish-language poetry tradition – is portrayed in terms of past and present suffering, yet within her there is light, spirituality, purity, truth, hope and unity, all of which will enable her future salvation. She is an innocent victim of England's power and is struggling to embrace freedom. England therefore, as a dystopian state, is constantly juxtaposed with all the positive characteristics of Ireland: England's glory belongs to the past, she has sinned and continues to do so, she is represented by darkness, by un-Christian, dishonest actions, and her people are divided through her class system. The English aristocracy and politicians are constantly denounced throughout O'Farrelly's poetry as they represent pride, power and falseness of the soon-to-fracture empire. They misrepresent the beliefs of the ordinary English workers, whom she believed would follow the Russian example with a workers' revolution (O'Farrelly 11–12). Those poems aimed at English readers seek to persuade that the ordinary English person is being exploited to the same extent as the Irish peasant due to the British class system, and that working-class English people should therefore empathise with the Irish. While a strong sense of the injustices caused by the English emerges, O'Farrelly does not apportion blame in the case of destructive acts committed by the Irish themselves. For example, 'The Custom House', a vivid and immediate reaction composed by O'Farrelly in May 1921 as she watched the Custom House burn, makes no reference to the fact that it was the Irish themselves who caused the damage to their own historical records. Instead, she focuses on the historical importance and function of the building: 'Her youth knew Grattan's dream but proved it vain / And now she passes with her records dim / And all the trade she checked for England's gain / The past with all its glory and its sin / Thrust back into the void; insistent, grim' (O'Farrelly 25).

Unlike Alice Milligan, Ella Young and other contemporary poets whose poetry drew heavily on Irish mythology, O'Farrelly generally did not over exploit the mythological cycles of early Irish literature when she began to compose poetry. Her poetry was direct and accessible to the non-literary readers of newspapers at whom it was aimed. In 'Midsummer, 1921', however, she chose to embrace Irish mythology in a lament over the partition of

Ireland. This poem was published in the *Irish Independent* on 22 June 1921,
the date on which the Northern Ireland parliament first met. Her references
to Ulster's mythological figures and landscapes – from 'Cuchluain's Ulaidh'
to 'Dalriada's land', and 'Dún Severick where Maedhbh went ravaging' – in
the opening two stanzas serve to reflect the epic past: the rich literary heritage
of the Gael, which has now been divided in an unnatural manner. Similar to
Ó Rathaille and indeed the classical tradition which used pathetic fallacy as
a means of highlighting Ireland's anguish, O'Farrelly refers to 'Ruaidhrí's
Dark Wave' which 'shrieks out its cry of woe' (O'Farrelly 27). She alludes to
the myth of Lug's right hand and its ability to heal rifts, juxtaposing it with
the destructive division that England's 'royal hands' have imposed upon
Ireland. The Northern Ireland that she portrays in the second half of the
poem differs from the land of heroic myths in the first half. Northern Ireland
becomes synonymous with urbanisation and modern industry, with references such as 'proud town that builds stout ships of steel' and 'whirring
looms weave cloth of flaxen thread' (O'Farrelly 27–8). Weaving on a loom
is a central metaphor in *Out of the Depths*, something visible in a poem of
November 1921, 'The Weaver (At Downing Street)', the title a direct
reference to Lloyd George. For O'Farrelly, the weaver represents the person
with control over the way in which individual threads will be interwoven,
and the pattern that will be produced on a garment. Lloyd George, the weaver,
has the fate of the Irish in his hands, prompting O'Farrelly to question: 'Will
he weave us a garment of linen so white / Our wrongs will be hidden forever
from sight? / Or a raiment of two that must all come undone – / A shoddy old
clout that will rot in the sun!' (O'Farrelly 34–5).

The Irish Civil War, which began in late June 1922, prompted O'Farrelly
to write a different kind of poetry. Many components that were notably
absent from O'Farrelly's first collection – such as sentimentalism and representations of female and child suffering – appear within her Irish-language
poetry collection, *Áille an Domhain* (1927). Her shift to the Irish language
shows that she did not feel the same need to engage in strong propagandist
poetry after 1922, and it also reveals her wish to foster the development of
Irish-language poetry under the Irish Free State. She thus decided to foreground and explore language rather than continuing to engage in overt political
propaganda. A couple of the poems in this collection deal with repercussions
of the Civil War, and a poem of praise for Douglas Hyde and an elegy for
George Sigerson are also included, thus mirroring O'Farrelly's desire to
recreate the pre-colonial function of the *'file'* ('poet') who praised his patron
through verse. For the most part, *Áille an Domhain* consists of poetry in
homage to the Romantic movement, which reflects on the transience of life
and physical beauty, and celebrates the natural world. There is a strong

sense of the loneliness of the individual, an individual who has come to cherish the spiritual over the physical and is searching for spiritual fulfill-ment: 'Áilleacht shéimh do ghrádhas seal / Tumtha i maise bhí mo chroidhe / Líon mo shúil le deise cruth / 'S m'anam lom ar easbuidh bídh' (Uan Uladh 5).

O'Farrelly's Irish-language poetry and indeed her scholarship in the Irish language received scant attention at the time of their publication, and have been the subject of little analysis to this day. This lack of attention contrasted with vocal responses to her early creative work, whether it was liked or loathed by her fellow revivalists. Two clear reasons exist for the silence on her later work in the Irish language: first, the Gaelic League had become less focused on the Irish language and more focused on politics, which led to less of an impetus to analyse new literature; second, scholarship and poetry were not accessible to general readers to the same extent as prose. It is unfortunate for O'Farrelly's reputation that the most often cited reference to her ability as a scholar is a statement by UCD student Brian Ó Nualláin (Myles na gCopaleen) that 'It was a shock to find that Duggie Hyde spoke atrocious Irish, as also did Agnes O'Farrelly (though the two hearts were of gold)' (O'Nolan 194). Of course, Ó Nualláin *was* a satirist, and it was highly unlikely that Hyde and O'Farrelly would have been appointed as professors of Irish without a strong command of the spoken language, along with the written language. O'Farrelly's English-language poetry like-wise received scant attention among critics and general readers in the 1920s. However, the private correspondence between some of O'Farrelly's peers reveals that her English-language poetry was the subject of some quiet ridicule (Fischer and Dillon 57). Aesthetic merit was not O'Farrelly's priority in her English-language poetry: she had a political message that she wanted to transmit in each of her poems, and she used simple language, basic rhymes and hyperbole on occasion to convey her messages. Her later Irish-language poetry reveals more craftsmanship and as her purpose became less political, aesthetics became increasingly important.

In her poetry, O'Farrelly seeks a compromise: between two traditions and between two languages. This makes her more difficult to study: English-language critics have limited access to her writings, and so find it easier to exclude her from references to revivalist prose and poetry (for example, there is no mention of O'Farrelly in Lucy Collins, *Poetry by Women in Ireland: A Critical Anthology 1870–1970* (2012) nor Justin Quinn, *The Cambridge Introduction to Modern Irish Poetry, 1800–2000* (2008)), although her peers such as Alice Milligan and Douglas Hyde are mentioned. Irish-language critics, meanwhile, do not engage with her writings because her work does not fit seamlessly within the Gaelic tradition. The in-betweener status of the bilingual writer in twen-tieth-century Ireland is perhaps best summed up by Alan Titley, who states

that 'the bilingual writer in Ireland runs the danger of being treated with sus-
picion by both traditions without gaining the entire respect of either' (Titley 21).

Regardless of the aesthetic merits or demerits of her poetry, it remains
a fact that O'Farrelly was the first woman to publish a collection of Irish-
language poetry. Whether one can claim her to be a founding mother of
twentieth-century poetry in Irish is more of a vexed question. Such a claim
would entail a retrospective repositioning of her poetry within the canon,
which is complicated by the fact that the foremost female contemporary
poets in the Irish language are unaware of her poetic precedent (although
they are very much aware that Irish-speaking women traditionally engaged
in oral literature, and that women were often the subject of poetry rather than
the composers). Nuala Ní Dhomhnaill best articulates how late twentieth-
century female Irish-language poets felt about their literary foremothers and
the patriarchal structures that excluded them from literary history:

> The fact that the few women poets in the tradition appear as distant ghostly islands
> in a great sea of indifference and a fog of unknowing bothers me, not just in itself
> but also because I know in my heart and soul that it is not the whole picture, nor
> the true picture, but very much the result of the vagaries of canon making. *What is
> going in, and what is being left out.* (Ní Dhomhnaill 107)

O'Farrelly may have played a fundamental role in ensuring that future
female Irish-language poets would have easier access to higher education,
but her poetry did not appear to have any direct influence on future women's
poetry in Irish. In her poetry, as in her cultural and political work, O'Farrelly
followed man-made structures that were already in place, working within
the system as a woman rather than being more radical by challenging the
poetic structures themselves. It took a later generation of feminist poets,
including Ní Dhomhnaill, to subvert the structure of Gaelic poetry.

CONCLUSION

It appears that Agnes O'Farrelly was the only woman to publish Irish-
language poetry in the first half of the twentieth century, yet her poetry was
never critically examined, nor even taken seriously. It was only when Máire
Mhac an tSaoi – daughter of Seán MacEntee, a founding member of Fianna
Fáil, and of Margaret Browne, also a lecturer in Irish-language poetry in
UCD during O'Farrelly's time – published her first collection of poetry in
the 1950s that critical attention began to be paid to a woman writing poetry
in the Irish language. During the revivalist period there were several Irish-

language women writers who wrote prose and drama for adults and children alike, but by the 1930s and 1940s, with regressive legislation being introduced by the Irish government regarding women in public life, the writings of these women disappeared from the public consciousness. They were replaced by Peig Sayers and her biography, both of which would go on to become representative of all Irish-speaking women in the late nineteenth and early twentieth centuries. Peig Sayers was illiterate, impoverished, Irish-speaking, Catholic, and lived to serve the needs of her husband and children. As such, she was disempowered and in no way threatening to the status quo. She therefore represented the role for women envisaged in the 1937 Constitution: homemakers, but not educated public figures. This conception excluded women like O'Farrelly. Of course, Sayers's autobiography was facilitated and edited by Máire Ní Chinnéide, one of O'Farrelly's educated peers, but her role in the production of *Peig* received scant attention in the years following the book's publication.

As a result of her immersion in Gaelic League ideology, O'Farrelly always sought to espouse compromise in her public life. However, because of her efforts to seek compromise in Cumann na mBan in 1914, a year of heightened tensions, she fell foul of two powerful political camps: militant nationalists and militant suffragists. Although she would work with both again in the years to come, her reputation never completely recovered. The majority of historians who have studied this period in Irish history provide a narrative that is sympathetic to either the militant nationalist or militant suffragist cause. Within their narratives, O'Farrelly's clouded reputation is perpetuated, without the provision of any analysis of her stance, and thus her importance within the nationalist and feminist movement can easily be dismissed. With the exception of Senia Pašeta's recent work on Irish nationalist women's history, few publications take a more open approach to O'Farrelly and Irish women's history more generally during the revivalist period. O'Farrelly's reputation to this day is revelatory of dominant strands of thought within historical and literary scholarship since the foundation of the Irish Free State, and is indicative of the need to supplement these narratives with a view that refuses to pathologise figures of compromise. Only then will many currently hidden contributors to Irish public life finally get their day in the sun.

Works Cited

Brooke, Charlotte. *Charlotte Brooke's Reliques of Irish Poetry.* Lesa Ní Mhunghaile, ed.Dublin: Irish Manuscripts Commission, 2009.

Collins, Lucy, ed. *Poetry by Women in Ireland: A Critical Anthology 1870–1970.* Liverpool: Liverpool University Press, 2012.

Connradh na Gaedhilge. *The Gaelic League*. Dublin, 1896.

Fischer, Joachim and John Dillon, eds. *The Correspondence of Myles Dillon, 1922–1925: Irish-German Relations and Celtic Studies*. Dublin: Four Courts Press, 1999.

Mac Conmara, Dáibhí, ed. *Aogán Ó Rathaille: Dánta*. Baile Átha Cliath: Aquila, 1968.

Mac Craith, Mícheál. 'Charlotte Brooke: a romantic metaphysical?'. *Études Celtiques* 29 (1992): 271–84.

Mac Curtain, Margaret. *Ariadne's Thread: Writing Women into Irish History*. Galway: Arlen House, 2008.

Martin, F. X., ed. *The Irish Volunteers, 1913–1915: Recollections and Documents*. Dublin: James Duffy & Co., 1963.

Ní Chinnéide, Máiréad. *Máire de Buitléir: Bean Athbheochana*. Baile Átha Cliath: Comhar, 1993.

Ní Dhomhnaill, Nuala. 'The hidden Ireland: women's inheritance'. Theo Dorgan, ed. *Irish Poetry since Kavanagh*. Dublin: Four Courts Press, 1996. 106–15.

Ní Fhaircheallaigh, Úna. *Smaointe ar Árainn /Thoughts on Aran*. Ríona Nic Congáil, ed. Gaillimh: Arlen House, 2010.

Ní Rathaile, Áine. WS 333, Bureau of Military History.

Nic Congáil, Ríona. *Úna Ní Fhaircheallaigh agus an Fhís Útóipeach Ghaelach*. Gaillimh: Arlen House, 2010.

Ó Buachalla, Breandán. *Aisling Ghéar: Na Stíobhartaigh agus an tAos Léinn, 1603–1788*. Baile Átha Cliath: An Clóchomhar, 1996.

Ó Duibhín, Ciarán. 'Cainnteoirí dúchais na Gaeilge in Oirthear Uladh'. Fionntán de Brún agus Séamus Mac Mathúna, eds. *Éigse Loch Lao I: Teanga agus Litríocht na Gaeilge i gCúige Uladh sa Naoú hAois Déag*. Béal Feirste: Ollscoil Uladh, 2012. 185–99.

O'Farrelly, Agnes. *Out of the Depths*. Dublin: Talbot Press, 1921.

O'Leary, Philip. *The Prose Literature of the Gaelic Revival, 1881–1921: Ideology and Innovation*. University Park: The Pennsylvania State University Press, 2005 edn, first published 1994.

Ó Neachtain, Seághan. *Filidheacht Sheagháin Uí Neachtain: Cuid a hAon*. Úna Ní Fhaircheallaigh, ed. Baile Átha Cliath: Connradh na Gaedhilge, 1908, reprinted in 1911.

O'Nolan, Brian. 'The last of the old physics (1930–1939) II'. James Meenan, ed. *Centenary History of the Literary and Historical Society of UCD 1855–1955*. Dublin: A&A Farmar, 2005. 194–8.

Pašeta, Senia. *Irish Nationalist Women, 1900–1918*. Cambridge: Cambridge University Press, 2013.

Pittock, Murray G. H. *Poetry and Jacobite Politics in Eighteenth-Century Britain and Ireland*. Cambridge: Cambridge University Press, 1994.

Pyle, Hilary. *Cesca's Diary, 1913–1916: Where Art and Nationalism Met*. Dublin: Woodfield Press, 2005.

Quinn, Justin. *The Cambridge Introduction to Modern Irish Poetry, 1800–2000*. Cambridge: Cambridge University Press, 2008.

Sawyer, Roger. *'We Are but Women': Women in Ireland's History*. New York: Routledge, 1993.

Sheehy-Skeffington Papers, Manuscript 41,177/37, National Library of Ireland.

Titley, Alan. 'Introduction'. Dermot Bolger, ed. *The Bright Wave/An Tonn Gheal*. Dublin: Raven Arts Press, 1991. 12–22.

Uan Uladh (Úna Ní Fhaircheallaigh). *Áille an Domhain*. Baile Átha Cliath: Brún agus Ó Nóláin, 1927.

'Women and the 1937 Constitution', File S9880, National Archives of Ireland.

Wyse Power, Jennie (Siobhan Bean an Padhraigh). 'Cumann an mBan: its inception and its work'. *Leabhar na mBan*. Dublin: Cumann na mBan, 1919. 4–7.

8

Uncomfortable Bodies in Women's Accounts of 1916

Lucy McDiarmid

The dead-horse-centered, GPO-centered 1916 is vivid and compelling, but there is more to the Rising than the traditional story. Recent scholarly work has brought different narratives to light.[1] The women's witness statements in the Bureau of Military History as well as women's diaries and memoirs of 1916 are a rich source of detailed and alternative versions of the Easter Rising. One recurrent topic in these accounts, sometimes emphasised and sometimes treated as a detour from the main narrative, is the uncomfortable body. Few histories of 1916 have yet focused on toilets, nakedness, prostitutes, or sexual harassment, topics that might be considered marginal, irrelevant, or inappropriate, but so many of the stories and 'asides' in the women's accounts cover these subjects that they constitute an important part of their experience of the Rising.

The women authors of the witness statements were primarily members of Cumann na mBan, the militant women's nationalist organisation founded in 1914 to 'advance the cause of Irish liberty', or of the Irish Citizen Army, the workers' paramilitary organisation founded in 1913 by James Connolly, James Larkin, and Jack White after the violence directed against protesters during the strike and lockout. Some of the women were members of both. The history of Cumann na mBan 'was to be rewritten many times over the years' (Pašeta 132), but it is generally agreed that among its unofficial founders were Jennie Wyse Power and Mary Colum.[2] Among its first 'provisional committee members' were also Louise Gavan Duffy and Nancy O'Rahilly. Agnes O'Farrelly was its first president. The Irish Citizen Army included both men and women among its members. According to Helena Molony, the Abbey Theatre actress and activist in the causes of feminism, nationalism, and labour, 'the women in the Citizen Army were not first-aiders, but did military work, except where it suited them to be first-aiders. Even before the Russian Army had women soldiers, the Citizen Army had them' (Molony 39).

The women who recorded the episodes discussed in this chapter were, then, committed activists who had chosen to be 'out' (a term whose usage in this context was new at the time of the 1916 Rising) in a revolution.[3] They tend to situate what there is of body-narratives in semi-public zones, places where lower-rank male officials, Irish or English, were in charge. Although the leaders of the Rising and the communal life of the garrisons feature in all their accounts, the stories that focus on the body take place slightly behind the scenes, often in sites where strangers are in intimate – too intimate – contact, in situations of unwanted closeness. Central to almost all of these accounts, at their heart, is a concept the women never name but often describe, a discomfort, a sense of impropriety, even, on occasion, taboo. More important than wounds or fatigue or hunger, somatic issues more obviously critical in war narratives, is the feeling that a physical boundary has been violated, and that something very 'wrong' has happened, 'wrong' in a deeper way than the merely physical.

Episodes relating to the sexualising and de-sexualising of bodies are the most prominent. Notable among these is one told by Brigid Foley, a Dubliner who had been active in the Gaelic League since the age of 15.[4] She was a member of Cumann na mBan, and during the Rising she worked at two outposts of the GPO garrison, carrying dispatches and doing whatever work was needed. She was arrested the week following the surrender during a raid on her house and was taken to a temporary women's prison at Ship Street Barracks, at the western end of Dublin Castle. Later she and other women were moved to Richmond Barracks and finally to Kilmainham. This anecdote is from the part of her narrative that takes place in Kilmainham. Of the women imprisoned there, she writes:

> They were all marvellous. We sang all the national songs through the night, although the soldiers tried to shut us up. The prison was filthy as it had not been used for 16 years. There were no chairs, or forms or tables. We had to sit on the dirty floors with our backs against the dirty walls. We got skilly in bowls that night; this was a sort of watery porridge. We got the same in the morning. We had no appetite for our skilly that day as we heard the shots that killed our leaders. The military sergeant did not leave us in any doubt. He came in and told us with great satisfaction that 'four more were gone today'.
>
> When we wanted to go to the lavatory we had to knock at the door and two soldiers with fixed bayonets brought us to the lavatory which was a dry closet that had no door. The soldiers stood jeering at whatever girl was in the closet, with the

result that for the eleven days I was in Kilmainham I never went to the lavatory and on my transfer to Mountjoy I had to be treated at once and for a long time after by Dr. Cook, the prison doctor. This horrible experience had a permanent effect on my constitution. (Foley 14)

Foley is not attacked by a weapon or touched by anyone, but she is injured, and the injury 'had a permanent effect on my constitution'. She is injured by the soldiers' gaze and by their words; that is the 'horrible experience'. Hers is a narrative of the body, but no body parts are mentioned: they don't need to be. The attack is psychological, not physical, and it is a complete humiliation. Because Kilmainham is 'filthy' and the closet is 'dry', the lavatory must already be disgusting, but in addition it 'had no door'. The boundary that is violated here is visual: an adult woman requires privacy on the toilet, certainly privacy from men. (As Aunt Lydia says in Margaret Atwood's *The Handmaid's Tale* (1985), 'To be seen . . . is to be penetrated' (Atwood 38).) By not only gazing but jeering, the soldiers call attention to the violation: they insist on it; they make it impossible for Foley to ignore the fact that she is being viewed.

The gaze and the jeering are culturally complex: they express anger and contempt, the contempt of the victor for the defeated, the imperial ruler for the colonial subject, and the male for the female. Any one of these relationships would explain the jeering, but the Irish women are the locus of all the despised categories. As Mary Douglas writes: 'The body is a model which can stand for any bounded system . . . the body is a symbol of society . . . the powers and dangers credited to social structure [are] reproduced in small on the human body' (Douglas 115). The Kilmainham soldiers take out on the women what they feel as British about Irish. Modestly, Foley never mentions the way she helped the other women there, but Marie Perolz praises Foley in her account: 'At Kilmainham I was very depressed when I knew the men were being executed. I could neither eat nor sleep. Only for Brighid Foley I would have died. She kept up my courage and tried to force me to eat' (Perolz 11).[5]

The national component of the humiliation is clear because the same treatment was given to men just after the surrender, when the Volunteers (and a few women) were lying on the grass in front of the Rotunda. As Eamon Dore tells it, Captain Perceval Lea Wilson got Tom Clarke, Sean MacDermott, and Ned Daly to the front of the building, and 'stripped all three to the skin in the presence of us and, being broad daylight, in the presence of nurses looking out of windows' (Dore 20). And in the words of Volunteer Joe Sweeney, Lea Wilson 'made all sorts of disparaging remarks about him' – i.e. he was jeering (qtd Griffith and O'Grady 7). (In 1920 Lea Wilson was assassinated by Irish soldiers.)

In its emphasis on violation of a visual boundary and on the sexualising of women in captivity, Foley's story about the lavatory in Kilmainham is central to the argument about 'uncomfortable bodies' in unwanted intimacy as it occurs in semi-public spaces during the Rising. Other episodes from the women's memoirs repeat those elements in her narrative. Visual boundaries work both ways: the women themselves are uneasy about seeing men's naked-ness. Catherine Byrne was (she claims) the first member of Cumann na mBan in the GPO; she jumped through a window – a closed window – on the side of the building when she was not allowed in the front.[6] She was 20 years old and had a First Aid certificate; on the first day of the Rising she dressed several wounds, and this is her description of one of them:

> I gave First Aid to other wounded Volunteers. Before I had time to have any food myself I was told by a Volunteer that one of the guard in the storey above had been wounded. and required first aid. When I went up to the guardroom I found the wounded man and in the presence of Father Flanagan, who was uncovering the soldier's wound which was near the groin (the bullet had entered there and come out through the back) I applied a large bandage, really a belly-band, and tied it at the side in an effort to stop the bleeding. There was not much blood, as the bleeding was internal. The soldier was taken immediately to hospital where I heard afterwards he died. (Byrne 4)

Byrne's witness statement, which is dated 1950, appears to have been written by herself, not given orally in an interview with the Bureau of Military History as some of the others were. There is a detailed, carefully made table of contents with chapter titles like 'How I came to be first Cumann na mBan member in G.P.O.' and 'I give First Aid and prepare food for the Volunteers'. Most of the other statements are not divided into chapters as hers is. And so the structure of the operative sentence is interesting: before Byrne uses the words 'uncovering' and 'groin', she writes the phrase 'in the presence of Father Flanagan'. Syntactically, the priest comes between the very young woman and the wounded man's naked body. Before she indicates that she has looked at his naked groin area, she makes it clear that she was in the presence of a priest: he de-sexualised the occasion.

Of course there is a potential contact taboo here as well as a visual one, because Byrne has to touch the man's body in intimate places and applies a bandage. The same concern about a woman's treating of a wound near the sexual parts of a man's body occurs in Áine Heron's witness statement. Her family on both sides 'had all been Fenians', and, as she says about the Rising, 'it was what I had been looking forward to always and I wanted to be in it, though the time was not really opportune for me as I expected a baby – my third – in August.' (Heron 4)[7] She was 'in it', one of about three pregnant women (on record) active in the Rising.[8] She did first aid work mostly at the Four Courts garrison, but on the Monday of Easter Week she and another woman set up a temporary medical centre in a shop on Church Street. As Heron writes:

> It may have been Monday evening we had our first casualty. Someone came along and asked were there any Cumann na mBan here? We asked what the wound was and got the reply, 'A deep cut in the thigh'. Miss Hayes suggested that as I was a married woman I should take it on. It was Eddie Morkan who had cut himself with his sheath knife when jumping over a barricade. I dressed the wound and Eddie told me afterwards that the dressing lasted for three weeks and was finally taken off in Knutsford Gaol. (Heron 4)

The salient line – 'as I was a married woman' – is a minor point in the passage, but it forms an important element in women's narratives of the body in 1916 because it doesn't exist in isolation. In the previous episode, it was the priest who de-sexualised the man's wound and sanctioned the sight and touch of a 20-year-old woman. Here it is not the celibate asexuality of the priest but the marital, maternal sexuality of Áine Heron. 'Miss' Hayes, unmarried and therefore innocent of the naked adult male body, should not dress a wound in the thigh – or so Miss Hayes herself thinks, and Heron accepts the taboo and mentions it in her statement. She then shifts the emphasis to Eddie Morkan's gratitude about what a good job she did.

In the context of these two statements, it is worth looking at what the English writer Vera Brittain says on the same subject in *Testament of Youth*. In this classic First World War memoir, published in 1933, Brittain writes about her experiences during the war in which her beloved brother Edward, her fiancé, and several close friends were all killed. As the war began, she was studying English literature at Somerville College Oxford, but in 1915 she began working in a hospital in Devonshire taking care of wounded soldiers.

> Throughout my two decades of life, I had never looked upon the nude body of an adult male; I had never even seen a naked boy-child since the nursery days when, at the age of four or five, I used to share my evening baths with Edward. I had therefore expected, when I first started nursing, to be overcome with nervousness and embarrassment, but, to my infinite relief, I was conscious of neither. Towards the men I came to feel an almost adoring gratitude for their simple and natural acceptance of my ministrations. Short of actually going to bed with them, there was hardly an intimate service that I did not perform for one or another in the course of four years, and I still have reason to be thankful for the knowledge of masculine functioning which the care of them gave me, and for my early release

from the sex-inhibitions that even today – thanks to the Victo'
up to 1914 dictated that a young woman should know nothing
and their clothes until marriage pitchforked her into an ir
and highly disconcerting intimacy – beset many of my fem..
both married and single. (Brittain 165–6)

At age 20, Brittain is the same age as Catherine Byrne ('in the presence of
Father Flanagan') and other women active in 1916. What is interesting here
is that Brittain confronts directly and explicitly her innocence of 'the nude
body of an adult male'. The subject of the paragraph is not her first aid work
but her 'early release' from Victorian 'sex-inhibitions'. The word 'pitchforked'
shows the shock and power of the force that transforms an innocent virgin
into 'a married woman', to use Áine Heron's phrase. All the pressures of
society, custom, 'Victorian tradition' go into that verb, 'pitchforked', an agency
stronger than the woman's own in determining the way she encounters
heterosexual intimacy.

Vera Brittain is of course writing her own 'testament'. Her subject is her
own political/spiritual/psychological development, a kind of 'Bildungsroman',
not an official statement of political work for a 'Bureau of Military History'
accounting for her national service during the war. Given the generic convention in which she is writing, she has the luxury of constructing her
subjectivity out of her own unofficial home-front experiences. The 1916
women are more concerned to construct themselves as part of a collective,
as Cumann na mBan, or Citizen Army, or a descendant of Fenians. And the
sources that are witness statements from the Bureau of Military History are
aware of their context, a state archive created 'to assemble and co-ordinate
material to form the basis for the compilation of the history of the movement
for Independence' (1913–21) (report of the Director, 1957, qtd 'Bureau').
All of the accounts appear motivated by an interest in showing what work
they did, how in a very practical way they contributed to 'the movement for
Independence'. Their externality and the emphasis on material detail make
even these distinctly gendered episodes emphasise their identity as part of
the larger 'history of the movement for Independence'.

The de-sexualising of the body by priests also enters the narrative when
the women are left without the protection of the Volunteers. Brigid Foley
writes about a night when she was the only woman in Kilmainham; all the
others were released, but a detective told her she was 'wanted', so she had to
stay. She writes:

I spent that night by myself in Kilmainham – in a different cell – so terrified that I
remained on my knees behind the cell door all night. I should mention that the

soldiers often were drunk and two of the Church St. priests thought it advisable one night to stay in the prison all night for the protection of the girls. (Foley 15)

She doesn't say if any priests were there the night she was alone; presumably they were not, and that's why she was on her knees the whole time. In a similar episode, Brigid Lyons remained in the Four Courts garrison after the men were arrested; she was told by both Ned Daly and a British officer to stay, along with some of the other Cumann na mBan 'girls'.[9] She writes:

> We slept again in the judges' ermine, with a big guard outside the door. We had chocolate and cream crackers before we went to sleep. One of the Church St. priests, Fr. Columbus, stayed in the room with us till morning by way of protection. We were only allowed to the bathroom in twos and threes under escort. Two were allowed to the kitchen to make tea, also under escort. (Lyons 6)

It is the 'Church St. priests' who 'protect' the women in both accounts, and here also the vulnerability of women going to the bathroom forms part of the narrative. Having been jeered at in the lavatory, Foley was 'terrified' at being the only woman jailed in Kilmainham. Lyons's account is more matter of fact, but then, she had not been harassed. The presence of the priest is one more interesting detail, like the chocolate and the ermine and the escort to the bathroom. The emphasis is equally on all these details.

In one episode, the idea but not the fact of sexual harassment is exploited as a defense strategy. Helena Molony, 33 at the time of the Rising, tells the story of what happened at the Citizen Army outpost at City Hall as the British army captured it:

> the troops poured up the stairs and came in to where the girls were. It would never occur to them, of course, that they were women soldiers. Actually, the women in the Citizen Army were not first-aiders, but did military work, except where it suited them to be first-aiders. Even before the Russian Army had women soldiers, the Citizen Army had them. The British officers thought these girls had been taken prisoner by the rebels. They asked them: 'Did they do anything to you? Were they kind to you? how many are up here?' Jinny Shanahan – quick enough –answered: 'No, they did not do anything to us. There are hundreds upstairs – big guns and everything'. She invented such a story that they thought there was a garrison up on the roof, with the result that they did delay, and took precautions. It was not until the girls were brought out for safety and, apparently, when they were bringing down some of the men, that one of the lads said: 'Hullo, Jinny, are you all right'.
>
> The officer looked at her, angry at the way he was fooled by this girl. I think that is important, because that may have delayed them, by some hours, from getting to the men on the roof. It was very natural for the British officer to take her

story, and to think there were hundreds of men along the roofs of the City Hall and Dame Street, as she told them. I would not blame him for being taken in, when she said: 'There are hundreds of them with big guns.' I thought that was something for which Napoleon would have decorated her. (Molony 39–40)

Here, each band of men suspects the other of sexual harassment, but no one has been harassed. As Molony suggests, their first thought on seeing women is of captivity and sexual vulnerability; they can't imagine the women as part of the military. These officers are obviously of a higher class than the guards at Kilmainham. In this comic version of the usual situation, both sets of soldiers function as the priests do in the previous episodes, protecting the women from the sexual advances of the other soldiers.

As this anecdote and the others suggest, most women's accounts of 1916, whether in witness statements, diaries, or memoirs, do not focus on interiority, like Vera Brittain's 'testament'. Nor are they like captivity narratives, which Elaine Showalter has called 'the first literary form dominated by women's experience' (Showalter 35). The Irish women's captivity is brief, it is collectively experienced, and – as they present it – it forms part of a longer national experience of revolution and resistance.[10] However, their representations of imprisonment do, in Showalter's words, testify to 'women's courage, resourcefulness and strength' (Showalter 35). The collective nature of those qualities, the way they are always distributed among women rather than attributed to a single hardy soul, is shown most dramatically in accounts of the temporary captivity many of them shared. As Molony's narrative and many others make clear, the British military was not prepared for women rebels and had no site ready to imprison them in. Starting with the Citizen Army women arrested Monday from the City Hall garrison and continuing through the week after the surrender, the military stashed the women they wanted to lock up in a dirty, unused back room in the Ship Street Barracks, and it was one of those semi-public zones in which unwanted intimacies took place.

Brigid Foley, ever sensitive to the unhygienic, says it was 'a terrible place; there were no sanitary arrangements. A sergeant came with a bucket which he placed behind the door. We became infested with fleas and lice' (Foley 13). This space recurs in many women's memoirs as a site of discomfort; but all the accounts show that the discomfort inflicted by the all-male British military generates a temporary sisterhood among the women, even among those who are strangers. And so another kind of body-narrative emerges in Ship Street Barracks, one of deliberate proximity rather than violation of boundaries, and one of voluntary rather than unwanted intimacies. Within the male, military zone, the women create a small zone of feminist comfort.

This narrative is most visible in the cameo appearances of a prostitute in the accounts of Dr Kathleen Lynn, Brigid Foley, and Kathleen Clarke.[11]

Only in Lynn's account is the woman called a prostitute. Here is Lynn's diary for the night of Saturday/Sunday 29/30 April, which Lynn spent in Ship Street:

> 29th April. Sat night - Sun. mg. Terribly excited drunken prostitute brought in, nearly mad, her brother shot Tues & she had gone to see body. We couldn't quiet her. Two soldiers came in, one held revolver to her head, other twisted her wrists, Emer jumped up, told him to stop & had revolver turned on her. They were brutal. D. G. they left I gave poor soul morphia [?] hypo. She lay down & slept beside me.

> 30th April . . . . poor prostitute woman got out, with notes for E. Young & L. S. She was very grateful – I had long chat with her – [12]

Two nights later, 2 May, Lynn is no longer there, nor is the prostitute, but she returns. Here Brigid Foley takes up the tale:

> During the night a variety of people – not all of them Sinn Feiners – were brought in. There was an awful din. One woman especially was making a row. When I asked her why she was there she said she had run after one of the Volunteers with a loaf of bread and a soldier had hashed it out of her hand. She lifted a stone and threw it at the soldiers who arrested her. I told her that one of our friends – Mrs. Clarke – was very ill and asked her to shut up and give her a chance to rest. She replied that if she made enough row and we objected, they would let her go. She told the policeman that she had left a young baby at home and wanted to feed it. She was let out. (Foley 13)

And here is Clarke's account of the same episode. Marie Perolz and Brigid Foley are brought in, and

> there was a commotion outside the door. It was banged open, and a woman with four soldiers tumbled in. She was holding them, two with each hand, and yelling, 'What did ye do with my dear, darling Doctor Lynn? Where is she?'
> She was a big, powerful woman, and held the four soldiers apparently without much trouble; they were small and young. They were struggling to get free. In the struggle, her shawl fell off. To my horror her back was completely naked; the soldiers had torn every stitch of clothing off her in their struggles with her before they reached Ship Street. I picked up the shawl, put it around her, and whispered to her to let the soldiers go. In her surprise at my action, she let two of the soldiers go, but, looking at me suspiciously, she retained her hold on the other two. Then Miss Perolz took a hand, and persuaded her to let the other two go.
> She and Miss Perolz sat down in a corner and had a heart-to-heart talk. She told Miss Perolz that her brother had been out in the Rising, got wounded during the week and managed to get home. In the street where she lived were also many

of those we called 'Separation Allowance women' . . . some of them informed on her brother. When the British soldiers came to arrest him he made an attempt to escape and was shot dead. She became abusive to the soldiers and they arrested her. That was how she had been in Ship Street with Dr Kathleen Lynn, and other women prisoners who were there. She had been released before Dr Lynn and the others were moved elsewhere.

That day, she told Miss Perolz, a British officer was passing down her street with a squad of soldiers and she recognized him as the man who had shot her brother. She caught up a brick and flung it at him, and that was how she came to be arrested a second time. While she was telling her story to Miss Perolz, she would look across at me every now and then, and whisper to Miss Perolz, 'Are you sure she is a Sinn Feiner? Are you sure she is not one of them wans in the pay of the British?' It took some time for Miss Perolz to convince her I was all right, and could be trusted. Then she announced that she would be out of there in an hour. She asked us to keep quiet. (Clarke 89)

The distressed woman bangs on the door and yells that that her 'babby' will die if she cannot get home. She confides in the other women 'He's weaned long ago', to make it clear she is acting. The sergeant finally lets her out. Clarke writes: 'The memory of her tragic story remained with us' (Clarke 90).

This episode makes visible the non-judgemental, protective, maternal impulse of four women (Lynn, Clarke, Perolz, and Foley) towards a less privileged woman. Lynn has given her morphine and let the woman sleep beside her; hence she is 'my dear, darling Doctor Lynn'. Clarke covers her nakedness, and Perolz was soothing her and Foley listening to her. The same physical intimacy obtains in the sleeping arrangements for women who remain; they sleep in close proximity to keep one another warm, even though in this case they don't know one another well.

The floor was the only place to lie on, and the only coverings we could find were a couple of old blankets. Both blankets and floor were filthy. We laid one blanket on the floor and used the other to cover us, and by lying very close together it barely covered us. (Clarke 91)

The women get many bodily comforts from one another: morphine, warmth, and, in one episode, an education in self-defense. When Clarke is brought into the barracks, she recognises a 'young girl' (her words) who is a member of Cumann na mBan, but they do not acknowledge one another till the soldiers have gone. Later in the evening,

three or four young British soldiers came into the room . . . The girl was sitting on a bench, reading, with her elbows on her knees, when one of the soldiers sat down beside her, flung his arms around her and attempted to kiss her.

She stood up without saying a word, boxed him thoroughly, resumed her seat and continued reading. I felt extremely proud of that girl; at the time I could have hugged her. From the way she tackled the young man I think she must have had boxing lessons. He was quite defeated, and made no further attempt to molest her. I only wish I could remember her name; she was a girl anyone would be proud of. (Clarke 90)

Here national politics and gender politics overlap entirely in the sexual harassment of a rebel. The harassment adds an element of gender to the political alliance that already exists among the women, and of course it also increases the emotional intensity of the moment. Clarke feels what a later generation might call 'feminist solidarity'. Her word 'defeated' implies there is at least one space in which Irish can defeat English.

Figure 8.1: Photo of Kathleen Clarke from 1924 in Limerick lace with a Claddagh brooch. Reproduced by kind permission, John J. Burns Library, Boston College.

Soon Clarke, too, is harassed:

Some time after this episode I was sitting on a bench, completely absorbed in my thoughts and fears for my husband and brother, and in a dim way hearing Miss Perolz and Miss Foley arguing with the soldiers. Then Miss Perolz asked me something about my children, and the next thing I knew I was being chucked under the chin by one of the soldiers, saying, 'Surely this kid is not old enough to have children!'

I was unable to box like the girl, though speechless with indignation, but under my gaze that man slunk away; that was murder in it. (Clarke 90–1)

Under these unpleasant circumstances, Clarke takes the girl as her role model, copying her fierceness even though she puts it into her face rather than her fists. There is 'murder' in her 'gaze': the belligerent response is somatic in its form of expression, and it works in the physical realm: the man 'slunk' away. The war between the sexes in Ship Street Barracks replicates, overlaps with, and repeats the struggle of the Rising – but with a better outcome. The national struggle has (temporarily) been lost, but the women's struggle has (temporarily) been won.

In one unusual case, the proximity of uncomfortable bodies, male and female together, causes a fit of laughing that is both hysterical and comforting. The anecdote comes from the witness statement of Aoife de Burca, a professional nurse who was working in the GPO. Her account was written in July 1916, when all the details were fresh in her mind. At one point she describes the evacuation of the GPO at seven in the evening on Friday 28 April. She has left the building in a small group of nine wounded men, three of them on stretchers, two doctors, a few nurses, and eight Volunteers. As they reach the Coliseum, 'bullets began falling like rain . . . it seemed as if bombs were being thrown by the dozen about us and we expected every moment would be our last.'

Suddenly Captain Doyle rushed in, ordering lights to be extinguished (we had two candles), and everyone to lie flat on the floor; we did so, every man and woman of us, heads and heels all huddled together in the most bewildering confusion, for the space was small for such a number. It was pitch dark. One man began to light a cigarette and the Captain ordered him to put it out at once. Another young chap was standing beside me, not thinking there was another inch of ground to be found, and I gave him a chuck, saying to him to lie down somehow or another as I felt every minute a bullet would send him toppling over. The girl that was nearest to me was trying to prepare for death, and I thought I would do likewise. I tried to make an Act of fervent Contrition, but the situation was bordering on the comical as well as tragedy, so I burst out laughing instead. Another girl did likewise, and very soon we were all at it. I remember one wounded Volunteer saying 'That's right, let's keep our spirits up though we are facing death.' Anyway, that laugh did us good and I recollect wishing not to die so that I could relate it all some day. (de Burca 20–1).

In her First World War memoir *The Forbidden Zone*, Mary Borden says that as a nurse, she felt 'it was my business to create a counter-wave of life' (Borden 94–5), and so Aoife de Burca's laugh does here, not from duty but from impulse, quite spontaneously. The inappropriate but unavoidable touching of male and female bodies, 'heads and heels all huddled together in the most bewildering confusion', with an Act of Contrition in the midst of all that, triggers a series of emotions: first a laugh in the midst of the uncomfortable intimacy, expressing embarrassment and anxiety at the same time, then an epidemic of laughing, as the mixed emotions of the first laugh spread to everyone lying on the floor; then a feeling of gratitude as the wounded man praises the group for keeping 'our spirits up'. Like the women in Ship Street Barracks who create a zone of feminist intimacy within a hostile male zone, so too does this little group escaping from the burning GPO creates a zone of rebel intimacy and emotional comfort within a war zone.

Women's accounts of the Rising are useful texts in which to study how Irish women write about the body in war. The one woman wounded fighting in the Rising, Margaret Skinnider, says nothing about her physical pain; she cries because the people treating her have to destroy her Volunteer uniform, and because now she cannot 'bomb the Hotel Shelbourne' (Skinnider 40). In their authorial voices, the 1916 women (unlike Vera Brittain) do not generally philosophise about the body. In their detailed accounts of involvement, they construct themselves as soldiers and citizens, engaged in the practical work of revolution. Their interest in the external – the missing lavatory door, the heads and heels, the girl who boxed the soldier, the poor woman with nothing under her shawl – has left idiosyncratic vignettes that convey the life of the body with vitality and eloquence, though such was never their object.

Notes

1 See for instance Taillon; McCarthy; Ryan; Ryan and Ward; Pašeta; McCoole, *Easter Widows* and Morrison.

2 See Pašeta, Ch. 7 for a detailed history of the founding of Cumann na mBan and debates about its relation to the Volunteers. See also McCarthy.

3 For comments on the term 'out', see Humphreys, May 1916. There are also witness statements by a number of women who were not 'out' but witnessed important political moments or episodes in the period 1913–23.

4 Many of the women's names pose special problems: some of them married and wrote narratives of the Rising under a name different from the one they used in 1916. Others

Gaelicised their names and over the years used both Irish and English versions. In most cases, the English version of the name has been used. For ease of reference, the women referred to here who were married at the time of the Rising will be referred to by their married names (e.g. Kathleen Clarke), and those who then were single will be referred to by their maiden names (e.g. Catherine Byrne). Brigid Foley's first name is spelled different ways in different documents, and her signature in the witness statement is hard to read. I have settled on 'Brigid' because that is what most scholars use.

5   Marie Perolz (1874–1950) was a member of Cumann na mBan and the Irish Citizen Army. During Holy Week, she delivered dispatches to Waterford, and during Easter Week she was sent to Cork and Kerry with messages. She was active during the War of Independence and later involved with the Irish Women Workers Union. In 1919, she married James Flanagan.

6   Catherine Byrne (1896–1971) was born in Dublin, the daughter of a coach trimmer. She was a member of Cumann na mBan and was stationed in the GPO during the Rising, giving first aid and delivering dispatches to other garrisons.

7   Áine Heron (1884–1952) was married to Thomas Heron, a general labourer. She performed first aid work at several garrisons and after the Rising was active in the National Aid Association. She was a member of the Cumann na mBan executive committee in 1922.

8   The others were Una Brennan and Phyllis Morkan. See McDiarmid 75.

9   Brigid Lyons Thornton (1896–1987) was born in Co. Roscommon and trained as a medical doctor at UCG. She was a member of Cumann na mBan and travelled to Dublin with her uncle, Frank McGuinness, to participate in the Rising. Later, among many jobs in public health, she worked as a child welfare pediatrician for Dublin Corporation.

10   On the issue of the activist Irish women's collectively defined identity, see Steele.

11   Kathleen Lynn (1874–1955) was born in Mayo and trained as a medical doctor. A member of the Irish Citizen Army, she served as medical officer in the City Hall garrison during the Rising. Later she served as vice-president of the Sinn Féin executive and was active in the suffrage and labour movements. Kathleen Clarke (1878–1972) was born into a Fenian family in Limerick City. In 1901 she married the Fenian activist Tom Clarke, one of the 14 men executed in Dublin after the Rising. She was a member of Cumann na mBan and later became the first woman lord mayor of Dublin (1939–41).

12   All quotations from Kathleen Lynn's diaries are taken from ACC/1990/1, KL/1, Royal College of Physicians.

Works Cited

Atwood, Margaret. *The Handmaid's Tale*. New York: Everyman's Library, 2006 edn, first published 1983.

Borden, Mary. *The Forbidden Zone*. London: Heinemann, 1929.

Brittain, Vera. *Testament of Youth: An Autobiographical Study of the Years 1900–1925*. London: Penguin Books, 1993 edn, first published 1933.

'The Bureau of Military History (1913–1921)'. Military Archives. Available at: militaryarchives.ie/collections/online-collections/bureau-of-military-history-1913-1921 (Accessed 7 Nov. 2015).

Byrne, Catherine. See Rooney, Catherine (née Bryne).

Clarke, Kathleen. *Revolutionary Woman*. Helen Litton, ed. Dublin: O'Brien Press, 1991.

de Burca, Aoife. WS 359, Bureau of Military History.

Dore, Eamon. WS 153, Bureau of Military History.

Douglas, Mary. *Purity and Danger: An Analysis of the Concepts of Pollution and Taboo*. Abingdon, Oxon: Routledge, 1984.

Foley, Brigid. See Martin, Brigid (née Foley).

Griffith, K. and T. O'Grady. *Curious Journey: An Oral History of Ireland's Unfinished Revolution*. Cork: Mercier Press, 1998.

Heron, Áine. WS 293, Bureau of Military History.

Humphreys, Nell. UCDA P 106, Papers of Sighle Humphreys.

Lynn, Kathleen. 1916–55. ACC/1990/1, kl/1, Holograph diary. Royal College of Physicians.

Lyons, Brigid. See Thornton, Brigid (née Lyons).

Martin, Brigid. WS 398, Bureau of Military History.

McCarthy, Cal. *Cumann na mBan and the Irish Revolution*. Cork: Collins Press, 2007.

McCoole, Sinéad. *Easter Widows: Seven Irish Women Who Lived in the Shadow of the 1916 Rising*. Dublin: Doubleday Ireland, 2014.

—. *No Ordinary Women: Irish Female Activists in the Revolutionary Years 1900–1923*. Dublin: O'Brien Press, 2004.

McDiarmid, Lucy. *At Home in the Revolution: What Women Said and Did in 1916*. Dublin: Royal Irish Academy, 2015.

McGarry, Fearghal. *The Rising: Ireland, Easter 1916*. Oxford: Oxford University Press, 2010.

Molony, Helena. WS 391, Bureau of Military History.

Morrison, Eve. 'The Bureau of Military History and female republican activism, 1913–1923'. Maryann Valiulis, ed. *Gender and Power in Irish History*. Dublin and Portland: Irish Academic Press, 2009. 59–83.

Pašeta, Senia. *Irish Nationalist Women, 1900–1918*. Cambridge: Cambridge University Press, 2013.

Perolz, Marie. WS 246, Bureau of Military History.

Rooney, Catherine. WS 648, Bureau of Military History.

Ryan, Annie. *Witnesses: Inside the Easter Rising*. Dublin: Liberties Press, 2005.

Ryan, Louise and Margaret Ward, eds. *Irish Women and Nationalism: Soldiers, New Women and Wicked Hags*. Dublin and Portland: Irish Academic Press, 2004.

Showalter, Elaine. 'Dark places'. *New York Times, Sunday Book Review* 6 June 2013: 35.

Skinnider, Margaret. *Doing My Bit for Ireland*. New York: The Century Company, 1917.

Steele, Karen. 'When female activists say "I": veiled rebels and the counter-history of Irish independence'. Gillian McIntosh and Diane Urquhart, eds. *Irish Women at War: The Twentieth Century*. Dublin and Portland: Irish Academic Press, 2010. 51–69.

Taillon, Ruth. *When History Was Made: The Women of 1916*. Belfast: Beyond the Pale, 1996.

Thornton, Brigid. WS 259, Bureau of Military History.

9

'If No One Wanted to Remember'

Margaret Kelly and the Lost Battalion

Jody Allen Randolph

Sheltered behind high convent walls, four girls looked out across Dublin Bay to the city. Having no home to go to, they had remained in the convent for the Easter holiday. Their mother had died when the eldest was seven, and the youngest a year old. Their father, whose work as a ship captain sent him to sea for weeks at a time, found places for them in the Dominican convent in Kingstown where they passed their girlhoods. As one sister would recall in an unpublished memoir, the younger girls were already asleep in their narrow iron beds, the high white bed curtains pulled tightly around them, when a noise awakened them. From the tall windows overlooking the bay, they saw the sky erupting in 'flaming pink'. Only Peggie, the eldest, knew for certain what was happening. 'It's a rebellion,' she explained to her sisters, 'against England . . . their leader is Patrick Pearse' (Coughlan).

At 13, encouraged by the nuns, Peggie was already becoming a writer. What she witnessed that week would go into her writing, into her war stories and into her novel. Within a few years she would leave the convent and join Cumann na mBan, the influential women's Republican organisation formed in 1914, working first in an office and then as a courier, moving messages and arms around the city (Andrea Doyle). A few years later, she would be a headlined author on the covers of literary magazines and journals. In 1924 her novel set during the Rising would win a prestigious Tailteann Games prize for fiction. A few decades later, she would slip into the silences of family and a shifting national retrospect.

In the years immediately following the Rising, Peggie Kelly had become an ardent believer in the national, feminist and socialist movements in Ireland. She joined the national struggle first as an activist, and then as a militant. After the signing of the Treaty in 1921, and with the establishment of Saorstát Éireann, women like Peggie Kelly were eventually sidelined by a state set on distancing itself from the uncompromising vision of its first militants. Like many others, her contribution was not defined or recorded. Her name does not appear in the lists of Dublin members of Cumann na mBan. Nor does it appear in the ambitious two-volume corrective to *The Field Day Anthology of Irish Writing* that focused exclusively on women's writing. In the story of Irish literature of the 1920s and 1930s she is not even a footnote. Her life as a woman coming of age at the end of empire – both participating in war and registering its effects in her fiction – would be forgotten if not for one small biographical detail: her youngest sister's youngest daughter had become a poet.

With her focus on women writers in a national tradition, Eavan Boland is the sort of niece one would expect Peggie Kelly to have. However, Boland never met her aunt and knew very little about her. She had heard her aunt's name mentioned once in childhood, and then never again.[1] She did not know her Aunt Peggie had written war stories set during the War of Independence, or a novel set in 1916. She certainly did not know that she had had an aunt, much less two, active in Cumann na mBan. But this chapter is not about Eavan Boland. It is about women like her aunt who contributed to radical change in Ireland but were excluded from the record of that change, so excluded that retrieving their narrative can only happen when someone stumbles over an unexplained detail and unravels a forgotten history.

For me that detail arrived on a claim made in 1922 against the new Free State on behalf of the Kelly sisters, recently orphaned by a shipwreck that took their father's life. At work on a biographical chapter on Boland's work, I was tracking the story of her grandfather's shipwreck and drowning off the coast of France in March 1922. The claim provided two addresses for his elder daughters Margaret and Winefred: 56 Hill Street, Glasgow and 15 Marino Crescent, Clontarf. An internet search revealed that the Irish writer Bram Stoker had grown up in the Clontarf house years before the Kelly sisters arrived. What the search did not reveal, however, what might easily have remained in the shadows Peggie Kelly's life had been consigned to, was that 15 Marino Crescent was Harry Boland's family home.

In the years between 1915 and 1922 Harry Boland played a pivotal role in Irish events. Joining the Irish Republican Brotherhood in 1904 and the Volunteers in 1913, he was sentenced to death for his role in the GPO in the 1916 Rising, a sentence later commuted to ten years penal servitude (Fitzgerald 45). Released early, he was elected as a Sinn Féin candidate in the general election of 1918 but refused to take his seat in Westminster. The following year he joined the First Dáil, established after a landmark election. In September 1919 the British government declared this Dáil illegal. In 1921 the Dáil declared war on Britain and the War of Independence ensued. When the country plunged into civil war with the signing of the Treaty in December 1921 and the subsequent shelling of the Four Courts in June 1922, Harry

Boland was among the first leaders to be killed, shot by Free State soldiers three weeks before his friend Michael Collins was killed by IRA soldiers. Cumann na mBan turned out in force to Boland's funeral at Glasnevin (McCarthy 212).

At the time of Harry Boland's funeral, Cumann na mBan had been in existence for eight years. An all-women paramilitary organisation, it was founded in response to the formation of the Volunteers. Members drilled with the Volunteers and were trained in first aid and signalling. A key part of their training was the use and upkeep of revolvers and rifles (Matthews, *Renegades* 251). In 1916 Cumann na mBan joined the Volunteers and the Irish Citizen Army in the GPO. After the executions that followed, enrolment grew sharply as a new nationalism swept the country and a generation was reshaped by the Rising. During the War of Independence Cumann na mBan 'shared the risks with the men of violence, death, arrest and imprisonment', as historian Mary McAuliffe points out: 'they participated in gun running, message carrying, running safe houses; they were the ones who faced constant raids on their homes by Black and Tans/Auxiliaries and they were often violently mistreated. They more than answered the call to arms and, in return, demanded a full role in the anticipated Irish republic' (McAuliffe 6).

When Peggie Kelly and her sister Winnie left the convent in 1919, events suggest they were drawn into the national movement and radicalised. By day, they worked shifts in a hidden office, typing documents, cleaning and transporting guns, and carrying dispatches from rooms where Maude Gonne and Constance Markievicz came and went. By night, from their lodgings in Harry Boland's family home, they almost certainly worked as couriers (McQuaile). In the story told by Peggie's daughters and Winnie's son, the Black and Tans found the sisters burning documents in an open fire when they raided the house, most likely in the spring of 1921. Within hours two Special Branch detectives visited them from Dublin Castle (Andrea Doyle). Fearing arrest, they fled on the mail boat to Glasgow where they found work as typists, where Peggie worked on her novel, and where they learned of their father's fatal shipwreck at the end of March 1922 ('Wreck of Dublin Steamer').

But on 27 April 1916, where this story begins, their father was very much alive in his bunk in a German prisoner of war camp outside Berlin, where he and his crew had been held captive for nearly two years.[2] In an unlucky circumstance, his ship had arrived in Hamburg just as England declared war on Germany in August 1914. The girls who lost their mother five years earlier were now cut off from their father. Back in Dublin Captain Kelly's daughters watched thousands of Sherwood Foresters march past the convent gate after disembarking at Kingstown Harbour (Andrea Doyle). 'All day long, from Dun Laoghaire into Dublin, went the rumble of artillery, and the tramp of marching feet', Peggie would later recall in her novel *Noreen*, 'through Monkstown and Blackrock they went, sweating, singing, regiment after regiment–khaki-clad hordes' (O'Driscoll, *Noreen* 318). What they witnessed that week would be used again as Peggie took imaginative possession of the Rising, restaging it in print in her novel and short stories.

If Peggie Kelly's work is not mentioned in scholarship on Irish women writers of the 1920s and 1930s, this may be partly due to a single circumstance: she wrote under a male pseudonym. Her fiction and journalism were published under the name Garrett O'Driscoll. Yet by 1929, when her novel *Noreen* was finally published in London, her gender had become an open secret in the Irish press, with some reviewers using 'she' and others using 'he' to describe her.[3] By publishing under this pseudonym, Peggie Kelly might have hoped to find readers she might not under a feminine name. But perhaps a more compelling reason is that she started to publish her fiction in the early 1920s, at a time when not just discretion but safety required separating her writing life from her revolutionary one.

In fact, Peggie Kelly had pressing reasons for discretion. By the time Garrett O'Driscoll's first war story was published in November 1922, Free State forces had already arrested and interned 40 members of Cumann nBan in Mountjoy Gaol (Matthews, *Dissidents* 58). Four months later, the Free State government outlawed the organisation, declaring it a threat to the stability of the new state. By the following November, an additional 645 suspected members had been interned in Kilmainham Gaol, Mountjoy Gaol and The North Dublin Union (Matthews, *Dissidents* 117). Years later during her annual tea with her former comrades, Peggie Kelly would comment that she escaped arrest only because she had had the brains to outthink it. Looking around the table, she realised every woman present had been jailed (Andrea Doyle).

What Peggie Kelly needed to protect we will never fully know. She exercised a level of discretion common among republican women both during the conflict and afterwards. Consequently few accounts of her involvement survive and these are mere fragments. In one account she and her sister Winnie, both in Cumann na mBan, are harbouring Joe McGrath, a Dublin Brigade Volunteer on the run.[4] When the Black and Tans raid the house, the sisters tuck him beneath the dining table under a long tablecloth and carry on coolly with their dinner (Lydon). In another account Kelly is on the tram at Westmoreland Street when both ends of the street are suddenly closed by Auxiliaries. As the Tram is searched, a man seated beside her silently passes a revolver, which she slips down the front her blouse (Andrea Doyle). A third fragment finds the sisters with Oscar Traynor, brigadier of the Dublin Brigade, who for a time resided in the same house, but the story of what the women did for him is lost (McQuaile 2014).[5] Another lost story, one nobody remembers Peggie Kelly telling, is what happened when the sisters returned from Glasgow following their father's death on 24 March 1922. Insurance claims find them back at 15 Marino Crescent, which suggests they were living there when the Civil War started and when Harry Boland was killed in Skerries on 1 August 1922. The sisters were still living in the Boland's house in 1924 when Garrett O'Driscoll won the Tailteann Games prize. However many of the events and circumstances may have been lost through Peggie herself: she would tell her daughter that she knew a great deal, that she had been trusted at high levels, but that she would go to her grave with those secrets, and she did.

How Peggie Kelly came to be trusted at such a young age is unclear. How she and her sister were recruited to the national movement is impossible to document. One common route into the movement was the Gaelic League, or Conradh na Gaeilge, in whose classes both girls enrolled after leaving the convent. Young women without a mother, and a father away at sea, they would have been attractive as couriers, having no one to insist on their safety, no one to ask where they had been. As Peggie would later recall, they took terrible risks, risks that put their lives in jeopardy, risks she would not romanticise by recounting to her own daughters (Andrea Doyle).

For two motherless girls still in their teens, the revolutionary years brought opportunity as well as risk. The romance of risk was accompanied by the risk of romance. In her book *At Home in the Revolution*, Lucy McDiarmid describes how 'the intimate proximity of young men and young women working together unchaperoned for a lofty ideal meant that the possibility of attraction was ever-present, an attraction licensed and encouraged by shared revolutionary goals' (McDiarmid 75). But if detail is missing from this phase of her life, an extraordinary document by the young Peggie Kelly leads, if not to evidence, then to powerful and justifiable speculation. The document is in the form of a poem, framed as an address to a dead IRA rebel.

Written in 1922 after the signing of the Treaty, on the threshold of the Civil War, the poem is called simply 'A Ballad of Twenty-Two'. At first glance, it is written in the style of the patriotic songs and in the old ballad cadences familiar to nationalist poetry in Ireland. But there is an edge and accuracy to the poem that lifts it out of the category: a perfect melody and an off-kilter grief. In the third last stanza it continues its address to a dead fighter, a soldier-victim of the national struggle:

Were we prodigal of laughter,
     Rebel O? –
In the face of the hereafter
     Rebel O?

Of the faith that did not falter,
Love that named the world its altar,
Singing hope that dared the halter
   Rebel O?
   (O'Driscoll, 'A Ballad of Twenty-Two')

The lines are not abstract nor do they seem ideological as so many of the ballads of the time do. On the contrary, they are clearly personal. They suggest a shared world, a shared commitment and – with the erotic shimmer on the world 'altar' – perhaps a shared love.

The poem is dedicated to Liam Mellows. And it is with him, the extremist and iconic representative of uncompromising republicanism, that the speculation begins and ends. Mellows, born in England in 1895, grew up in Wexford. Just seven years older than Peggie, he was a member of the Irish Republican Brotherhood and a leading figure in both the Rising and the War of Independence. On meeting him James Connolly told his daughter, Nora, 'I have met a real man' ('James Connolly'). His eloquence and oratory – sometimes high-flown – can be glimpsed in his last letter to his mother, written hours before his execution at the hands of the Free State in 1922: 'Though unworthy of the greatest honour that can be paid to an Irish man or woman, I go to join Tone and Emmet and the Fenians' (Coogan 33).

How likely is it that Mellows knew Peggie? On paper at least, more than likely. He knew and worked with Harry Boland, was in the United States with him in 1919, and came back to Ireland where it is more likely than not that he visited the Clontarf house. He was also a close friend of Andy Doyle whom Peggie would later marry (Andrea Doyle). Andy occupied the cell next to him on the morning of his execution and mourned his loss (McQuaile 2013). Added to this is the fact, provided by Peggie's daughter, that a large photograph of Mellows hung in their home throughout her childhood.

But off paper, the evidence remains slight. Was there a romance, a relationship of some sort? There are no letters, no written records. And yet the poem remains a haunting text, a surprising and wrenching account of love and betrayal, confident in tone and intimate in address, and dedicated to Mellows. All by itself it breaks a silence in which too many women in the national struggle of that time remain shrouded. It evokes the passion, the purpose shared in common, the equal participation in a rare moment of Irish history. Yet like so much about women's lives at that time, it remains a question, not an answer.

To be hidden by your side,
   Rebel O:

In my youthood, in my pride,
    Rebel O:
For the laid are the unlying,
The unsaddened, the unsighing,
And the dead are the undying
    Rebel O:

Were we foolish with our youth
    Rebel O?
Were we foolish with our truth
    Rebel O?
Too, too easily believing? –
Over-young and undeceiving? –
Too, too readily-achieving
    Rebel O?
    (O'Driscoll, 'A Ballad of Twenty-Two')

In many revolutionary romances, Lucy McDiarmid argues, 'it was their common project that brought them together' (McDiarmid 75). 'A Ballad of Twenty-Two' clearly points to a common project. It clearly mourns for the loss of someone who shared and inspired it: the mysterious 'Rebel O' of the refrain. But none of this points clearly enough to a connection between Peggie Kelly and Liam Mellows for guesswork to proceed to biography. Yet even in the shadow world of guesses there is enough energy and power in the lines to remind us of how insular and energetic a culture was bred by the national struggle. The poem testifies to its time, and lacking other details, that has to be enough.

While their respective relationships with Mellows may have brought them together more closely after the Civil War, what first connected Peggie Kelly and Andy Doyle was undoubtedly their role as trusted messengers for the Bolands during the War of Independence. An officer in the Dublin Brigade, Andy described to his former commanding officer, Ernie O'Malley, how he carried messages between Boland's household at 15 Marino Crescent and Michael Collins in several locations around the city (Andrew Doyle, Interview). On one such errand, he must have met the Kelly sisters. He struck up a relationship with Winnie first, before falling in love with her older sister (McQuaile 2013). That Andy worked in the National Library, where he kept a gun carefully hidden, surely caught the bookish Peggie's attention (Andrea Doyle). A lone image survives of their courtship: they would meet after work on St Stephen's Green where watching trees in different weathers brought them relief from wartime realities (McQuaile 2014). Such happiness must have been interrupted by long separations: first when Peggie was on the run, then when Andy was, and finally when he was imprisoned by the Free State army for his role in the Four Courts at the start of the Civil War.

When his daughters asked what he did during the War of Independence, Andy told them he was in charge of 'transport'. In one story he is commandeering automobiles from the Kildare Club and in another he is giving de Valera driving lessons on Rathgar Road. In a third story, trapped when the Auxiliaries block off both ends of D'Olier Street, he drops a revolver into a street grate. To be caught with a gun meant risking being put up against a wall and shot. Asked by his youngest daughter had he ever shot anyone, he told her it was a question she must never ask (Andrea Doyle). According to witness statements in the Bureau of Military History archives, Oscar Traynor promoted Andy Doyle to adjutant of the Second Battalion, Dublin Brigade the week of Bloody Sunday, November 1920 (Colley 56). Andy had joined the Volunteers in 1918 at 17 years old and, according to a family story, was active in the burning of the Custom House in May 1921 (McQuaile 2013). After escaping from the Four Courts on 5 July 1922, he was picked up by Free State forces a week later and imprisoned at Mountjoy Gaol with his friend Liam Mellows (Andrew Doyle, Prison). Devastated by Mellows's execution in December 1922, he kept for the rest of his life the book Mellows was reading when he was taken out to be shot (Andrea Doyle).[6] When the Civil War ended in July 1923, Andy was moved to Newbridge Internment Camp, where, like many republican prisoners, his health was affected by beatings and hunger strikes. He remained in Newbridge until his release in 1924.

The story of their courtship during wartime when both Andy and Peggie risked arrest and imprisonment, violence and death, is not one they shared with their daughters. That war changed the rules and realities of courtship is borne out in recent studies of the revolutionary generation. 'The revolutionaries were part of a generation that explored forms of liberation other than the political and national', Roy Foster argues in *Vivid Faces*, 'and one of these was the drama of loving.' McDiarmid points out 'flirtation and courtship continued with difficulty or were thwarted, registering the instability and uncertainty of a time when it was not clear what rituals of any kind were going to obtain' (McDiarmid 91).

While Peggie Kelly and Andy Doyle left no account of the uncertainties of being young revolutionaries in love, Garrett O'Driscoll did. The poem dedicated to Mellows, 'A Ballad of Twenty-Two', with its searing questions, is just one instance. Another is 'A Flippant Young Man' (1922), a love story with strong autobiographical elements, in which a motherless young woman, Mabel, tends to a wounded Volunteer on the run with whom she falls in love. The Volunteer asks her to memorise the face of the officer who tracks him to her home and threatens to burn it down. He also gives her an important document to deliver, which she hides in her hair. There are hints that Mabel has performed such patriotic duties before, that she has taken risks both in war and in romance. After heading into business in Dublin at 17, she explains, she angered her aunt with rumours of her activities: 'I used to go out to Benediction that never saw a chapel,' she explains, 'and I used to do hours of overtime that never saw an office' (O'Driscoll, 'A Flippant Young Man' 169).

The pseudonym that concealed **Peggie Kelly's** identity during war and its perilous aftermath freed Garrett O'Driscoll to explore her wartime experiences under the subterfuge of fiction. In a series of war stories she published between 1922 and 1926, young activists work together in situations of flirtation and love, danger and death. At the centre of these stories are the female comrades of Volunteers on the job, on the run, on the mend, living and hiding and loving and dying for Ireland. In most of Garrett O'Driscoll's war stories love plots are intertwined with war plots. New couplings are often challenged by violent injury or thwarted by death. An early short story, 'The Lacklander', describes Cumann na mBan members attached to a Volunteer unit in 'two dull rooms at the heart of the city that saw many stirring things'. Flirtations and romantic feelings develop between the young women who roll bandages and clean guns and the men who come and go from a back room 'whence filtered strange, abominable smells, and where mild explosions had once or twice occurred'. At the end of the story, the narrator is the only one left of her original unit. Thinly fictionalised in her description of the 'two dingy rooms' is the experience of a young woman working at the centre of the conflict who 'saw faces come and go and return; and other faces go and never return' (O'Driscoll, 'The Lacklander' 1–2).

The stories she wrote during the War of Independence and Civil War may comprise Garrett O'Driscoll's most compelling work, but they were not what made her name as a writer. Her 1924 novel *Noreen* set the stage for a much more acclaimed debut. 'Famous names, attached to good stories', reads the headline attached to her name on the cover of a 1925 issue of *Green and Gold Magazine*. Earlier that year, the magazine had featured a cover cameo devoted to her work. A year after she won the Tailteann Games prize, her new status as the author of *Noreen* was advertising her stories.

In *Noreen* Garrett O'Driscoll depicts a secure childhood that Peggie Kelly did not have – on a family farm at the edge of a small village, with holidays presided over by a doting mother and stern father. Instead of three sisters, the main character Noreen Donegan has three older brothers. The narrative follows their growth from childhood to adulthood in the twilight of empire. A study of a revolutionary generation in pre-revolutionary times, the novel locates the big issues – history, myth, language – within the lives and the minds of ordinary children in a small family. It is this portrait of ordinary family life that drew praise from the Tailteann Games prize judges, Compton Mackenzie and James Stephens. Mackenzie singled out O'Driscoll's family portrait for particular praise as 'one of the most tender pictures of childhood I have ever seen' ('A Tailteann prize novel' 4).[7]

Structured into four 'books', the first and longest book is set in the fictional farming village of Ballygrath. It is dedicated to 'The Chief', Eamon de Valera, one of the key figures of the revolution who was, when the novel was finished, still interned by Free State forces in Arbour Hill Prison. Dublin and Glasgow are the settings of the second book, which invokes a symbol of republican sacrifice in its title – 'The Book of the Lily'. O'Driscoll attaches the significance of the lily not to the young men who will die for Ireland but to a young woman, Lila, who befriends them.[8]

If an Irish rural childhood at the turn of the century is the novel's foreground, the background is one of suppressed unrest. A small portrait, crumbling with age, of the 1798 leader Robert Emmet hangs in Noreen's bedroom on the family farm. Her eldest brother Con looks at it daily, musing 'Isn't it queer how they have forgotten him?' (O'Driscoll, *Noreen* 125). Con writes poems and stories about Ireland but hides them in the bottom of a press. He confides in Noreen that he hears 'dead men's voices in the wind: Wolfe Tone's, Lord Fitzgerald's, Owen Roe O'Neill's, and Hugh Roe O'Donnell's, and Sarsfield's and hundreds of others' (O'Driscoll, *Noreen* 47). A Fenian grandfather – a reputed member of an illegal secret organisation and convicted felon – is seldom mentioned (O'Driscoll, *Noreen* 59).

But the brother who teaches Noreen the names of Irish heroes also teaches her Irish. 'Don't say "thanks",' he corrects her, 'say, "*mait agath*"' (O'Driscoll, *Noreen* 74). Their education at home conflicts with their education at the village school, where the schoolmaster speaks rapturously of Walter Raleigh, Sir Philip Sidney, General Wolf and other heroes of 'old England'. When Noreen's middle brother, the quiet, serious Michael, asks what of 'old Ireland', he is accused of 'inciting his class-mates to insubordination' (O'Driscoll, *Noreen* 56–7). In the public meeting that follows, the schoolmaster resigns. His replacement starts a debating society, inserting young Michael as president (O'Driscoll, *Noreen* 76–8). Their first debate, 'Is Irish a dead language?' fails miserably (O'Driscoll, *Noreen* 85–8).

If an outdated Victorian authority was thrown off in the classroom, it was also under pressure at home. The brilliant, brooding eldest son, Con, chafes under his father's patriarchal authority, refusing to bend. After heading to Dublin to study medicine, he severs ties with his father's unjust rule. At the heart of their conflict is Con's desire to think things through for himself rather than acquiescing in blind obedience to his father's views on justice, religion, the contours of the nation, the existence of God.

While the first half of the novel depicts rural life at the end of empire, the second half follows the Donegans as they sell the farm and move to the city.

In Dublin Michael becomes a 'newspaper man' and soon starts a social club where a new type of socialising between men and women takes place. 'It's all about Gaelic, and Gaelic music and singing', Noreen explains to Lila, 'one man that comes is an expert on round towers and another is an expert on the harp, and Michael writes articles in Gaelic for his paper' (O'Driscoll, *Noreen* 203).

Now the complications of romance take the foreground as personal resonances of a troubled history emerge. Noreen falls in love with Lila's half-brother Kenn, but her marriage is blocked by her brother. Not only is Kenn English, but he is also a soldier in the British army while Noreen's brothers are in the Volunteers. When Michael asks Noreen to give Kenn up, she realises she has 'failed her part in the bargain of comradeship' (O'Driscoll, *Noreen* 311).

Five months after giving up marriage for Ireland, Noreen awakens to her brothers buttoning their green Volunteer uniforms. In the days preceding, she watched British regiments arrive in Kingstown, 'thousands of them singing' as they hauled their big guns into the city (O'Driscoll, *Noreen* 321). She asks her brothers, with hesitation, if she was right not to marry Kenn, followed by a hint that Kenn has recently visited her in his British army uniform. Towards the end of the novel when Noreen visits her brother's grave in the village they left as children, it is hard not to imagine Peggie Kelly visiting another farming village for the memorial service in which her father's name was added to her mother's gravestone in Termonfeckin: 'Death around her, and about her, and before her and behind her' (O'Driscoll, *Noreen* 277).

Peggie Kelly started writing this novel during the War of Independence, when she and others worked 'tirelessly for the lads', taking the reins of revolution from an older generation (O'Driscoll, 'Lacklander' 2). She saw many of them die for a new Ireland shaped by their own youthful hopes. She worked on the novel while on the run in Glasgow, with the deaths of the Civil War, including Harry Boland and Liam Mellows, before her. She finished her novel after the Civil War drew to a close in April 1923, while her future husband was still interned by Free State forces. Shadowing her life in words, her fiction mines both personal and national grief, and the poignant rooms where one blurred into the other.

Garrett O'Driscoll was just 22 when her novel won a prize in the first Tailteann Literary Competitions in 1924. Although her father had drowned less than two years earlier, when her award was announced from the stage of the Abbey Theatre, it must have seemed that the shadows were clearing. 'Out of a period of terror of strained hearts and tragic incident we are reverting to normality', explained W. B. Yeats at the Tailteann Games opening banquet (Walsh 403). The Aonach Tailteann Committee had hoped to divert attention away from Ireland's recent carnage and to consolidate the young state in the eyes of the world by reviving an ancient Irish festival as a mass sporting and cultural event on par with the Olympic Games. 'The sense that this was a great national cultural occasion was underlined by the awards given for drama, poetry, prose, short stories and novels', Paul Rouse observes in *Sport and Ireland* (Rouse 251). The new state intended to create an international spectacle of the games, explains Paige Reynolds, and the literary prize-giving ceremony was no exception (Reynolds 184).

The awards ceremony was held in the Abbey Theatre with a full house of distinguished visitors. Most had been invited by Yeats in his capacity as the chairman of the Aonach Tailteann Distinguished Visitors Committee. Awarded the Nobel Prize for Literature the previous year, Yeats now took the stage to introduce the literary awards evening. As part of the awards evening, not one but three of the Abbey's early plays were staged: Yeats's *Kathleen ni Houlihan*, Synge's *Riders to the Sea*, and Lady Gregory's *The Workhouse Ward* ('Tailteann literary awards' 7).

During the second interval the literary prizes for English-language literature were announced from the stage. Journalist David Sears took the gold prize for his novel *Children of Thor* which 'told the story of a very terrible time–the time of the "Black and Tans" in this country'. Compton Mackenzie explained that Sears's 'was not really a very well written book but it had life and would remain as a record of the time with which it dealt' ('Tailteann literary awards' 7). When Mackenzie announced the silver-prize winner, however, he singled O'Driscoll out for praise: 'Mr. O'Driscoll's *Noreen*, for which second prize was awarded, was a very beautiful book containing one of the most tender pictures of childhood he had ever seen', reported the *Irish Times* ('Tailteann literary awards' 7). The ironies of the evening could not have been lost on Peggie Kelly. The previous year, as the Civil War ground down to a close without a negotiated solution, the Abbey Theatre had been ceded to the Free State by Yeats and Lady Gregory. Garrett O'Driscoll, an anti-Treaty republican and a member of a banned organisation, was one of the first women writers honoured by the Free State, had they but known it, for a book that, as Mackenzie described it, 'had been written less for the author than for Ireland'.

But even with these events detailed and noted, questions must remain about the remarkable early experience of Peggie Kelly. Some of these questions are about transmission. How for instance did a woman writer who inscribed female characters into revolutionary events in her fiction – something the new literature often overlooked – become erased from the national canon? How did a recognised young novelist whose voice was heard even through the acoustics of the new state fade so quickly from public memory?

There may be some clues in a short story Garrett O'Driscoll published in the mid-1930s, 'Lavender in God's Garden'. It provides glimpses of the new state in which Peggie Kelly married, had children, and continued to live after the excitement of the national struggle. In the story, the parent-less heroine feels she has only two options on the death of her grandfather: the home or the convent, marriage or a nunnery. When breaking off her engagement to enter a convent feels like the greater freedom, it is clear we are in a new fictive space: a hinterland of constraint and limited choice that is far from the Ireland Peggie Kelly hoped for a decade earlier.

In addition to this, the first decade of the new state was often inhos-pitable to those who had envisioned it. Women's rights, workers' rights, the 'equal rights and equal opportunities' of the Proclamation seemed to fall far short of being priorities (O'Connor 11). At their annual convention in October 1921 Cumann na mBan restated their primary aim: 'to follow the policy of the Republican Proclamation by seeing that women take up their proper position in the life of the nation' (Clonan). In February 1923, in a foreshadowing of the conservative decades that would follow, Cardinal Logue issued a strongly worded pastoral letter denouncing young women and girls involved in dissident activities ('The voice of the church').

There were other warning signs. The first film censorship act was passed five months later, in July 1923. In 1929 the Censorship of Publications Act was passed, following the appointment of the strangely named Committee of Evil Literature in 1926. Within a few years, many of the journals Garrett O'Driscoll headlined in had closed or gone out of business. As Gerardine Meaney observes of this period, 'the heady mix of movements which had seemed to offer revolutionary change dissolved into an intense and claustro-phobic conservatism' (Meaney 976). In the 1930s, this conservatism would bring new legislation limiting women's employment outside the home after marriage (1932, 1934) and banning contraceptives (1934). A new constitution in 1937 would ban divorce and provide alarmingly restrictive language about Irish women's place in the home. Writing to de Valera on 25 May 1937, Garrett O'Driscoll joined many women writers of her generation in register-ing her 'utmost dismay' at how the constitution, then in draft form, introduced 'legislation to discriminate' against 'certain classes of citizens and especially against women'. [9] In a rare occurrence, she signed both her married name and her nom de plume, bringing together her identities as private citizen and public writer to protest the ominous direction the new state was taking.

While the degree to which women were prevented taking up 'their proper place in the life of the nation' in the decades following independence helps explain the disappearance from public memory of visible women writers like Peggie Kelly, it is not the only factor. Perhaps the clearest suggestion to why women like Peggie Kelly were eventually overlooked is found in an essay by Garrett O'Driscoll, 'Those of the lost battalion', published in 1934 on the twelfth anniversary of the bombardment of the Four Courts. The essay describes how republican revolutionaries who fought for freedom from British rule and helped shape 'a newer, swifter more Gaelicized Ireland' were eventually marginalised by the new state.

> They stood in all seasons, in all weathers, at those same draughty street-corners when a 'job' was on, their pockets snagging with revolvers and Mills bombs; waited patiently perhaps for hours on end, till the 'job' came by. They took off their shoes and crept by their parents' doors on their way to bed at 4 a.m., morning after morning, then rose again at eight. They were always at hand, always in touch, when there was work to be done. They were the generous flowing blood, the aching bone, the straining muscle of the Fight. (O'Driscoll, 'Lost battalion' 8)

In the new Ireland they fought for and lost, the article suggested, these men had lost their opportunities and their context. Unemployed or, more likely, unemployable in the Free State, they continued on until 'the river they had dredged with unremitting, indomitable, routine heroism, under fire, rose and bore them inshore and kept them there' (O'Driscoll, 'Lost battalion'8).

The essay is both eloquent and incomplete. Strangely enough, missing from her account of the rank-and-file routine heroism that provided the backbone of the revolutionary years are the hidden histories of her Cumann na mBan comrades. By the end of the 1920s Peggie Kelly had also lost her context, both as a writer and as a revolutionary. In her introduction to Sinéad McCoole's *No Ordinary Women*, historian Margaret Ward explains:

> For those who had rejected the Treaty and found themselves on the losing side in the ensuing Civil War, it was not a welcoming state. In the atmosphere of bitterness following the republican defeat women were condemned by the victorious Free State as 'furies' and blamed for setting brother upon brother. It is hardly surprising that too few felt their lives would be interesting to future generations. Most appear to have kept silent about their past life . . . Those who had children were unlikely to have had their papers kept by family members, who seem not to have grasped the importance of their mother's contribution. (McCoole 13)

It is plain enough now that the Ireland Peggie Kelly and Garrett O'Driscoll hoped for did not happen and was not handed on. Instead, what was inherited was silence: the gradual disappearance of a national conversation in which the new Ireland could be discussed on those terms. In her 2014 volume *A Woman without a Country*, Eavan Boland weighs these silences as they became a shaping force in the early life of her mother Frances Kelly (sister of Peggie), born in 1908, and the early death of her grandmother Marianne Kelly (mother of Peggie) in 1909.[10]

If no one in my family ever spoke of it . . .
If no one wanted to remember . . .
If no one ever mentioned how a woman was,
what she did,
what she never did again,
when she lived in a dying Empire.

(Boland, Woman without 29)

What troubled Boland was not whether her grandmother's short life had included her country, 'but whether that country had included her' (Boland, *Woman without* 38). A hundred years on, even in the midst of current centenary celebrations, that question remains. The motherless girls who watched the Rising from their convent window remained outsiders: women for whom the story of Irish history was their story, but who nevertheless could neither create nor control the emergence of a nation in which, to paraphrase Adrienne Rich, their 'names did not appear' (Rich 24).

Notes

1   Boland was told only that her aunt had written 'a book that won a prize judged by Compton Mackenzie.' Personal interview, 14 Sept. 2015.

2   Captain James Kelly and the crew of the *SS City of Berlin* spent all four years of the war in Ruhleben prisoner of war camp. They were released shortly after the armistice in 1918.

3   Garrett O'Driscoll's continuing intention to be identified as a male writer is evident in a letter to the *Irish Press* 29 Jan. 1934, in which her good friend Rosamond Jacob congratulates Garrett O'Driscoll for 'his splendid article on cruelty to animals in Ireland'.

4   Like Harry Boland, Joe McGrath was imprisoned for his role in the 1916 Rising, was elected in the 1918 general elections as a Sinn Féin TD and sat in the First Dáil. Travelling as part of Michael Collin's staff to the Anglo-Irish Treaty negotiations in London in 1921, he served as minister for labour in the Second Dáil. After resigning in 1924, he went on to found the Irish Hospital Sweepstakes where he employed Winnie Kelly and many other republican women.

5   Oscar Traynor was imprisoned for his role in the 1916 Rising and went on to become a brigadier in the Dublin Brigade in the War of Independence. He later served as minister of defence, among other cabinet positions.

6   Family members do not recall the title of the book, which is now lost.

7   A reviewer for the *Irish Independent* praises the book on similar terms, but faults it both for a story that is 'dull enough' and 'a marked weakness in the dialogue' ('A Tailteann prize novel' 4).

8   'The Book of the Lily' is dedicated to 'Jenny M. of Scotstoun'. That Kelly protected Jenny M.'s surname in addition to her own suggests the possibility that she too was a member of Cumann na mBan.

9   I am grateful to Deirdre Brady for directing me to the Department of the Taoiseach file S9880 at the National Archives in which this letter is stored.

10   Frances Kelly (1908–2002) was Peggie Kelly's (1902–69) youngest sister, the youngest of the girls at the convent window. She was eight years old in April 1916. After leaving the convent in 1924, she lived in the Boland's house at 15 Marino Crescent with Peggie. Poet Marianne Kelly (1877–1909) was their mother.

Works Cited

Boland, Eavan. *A Woman without a Country*. Manchester: Carcanet, 2014.

—. Personal interview. 14 Sept. 2015.

Doyle, Andrea. Personal interview. 17 Oct. 2014.

Doyle, Andrew. Prison number 10669. Prisoner's Location Book, Civil War Internment Collection, Military Archives, Cathal Brugha Barracks, Rathmines.

—. Interview with Ernie O'Malley, UCD Archives. UCDA 17b/95 [pp 4–16, 24–5], 101 [pp 1–38] and 105 [pp 81–94]. 1948–49.

Clonan, Tom. 'The forgotten role of women insurgents in the 1916 Rising'. *Irish Times* 20 Mar. 2006.

Colley, Harry. WS 1687, Bureau of Military History.

Coogan, Tim Pat. *The IRA*. New York: Palgrave Macmillan, 2002.

Coughlan, Aileen. 'The Brass Trumpet'. Unpublished radio script *n.d.* Aileen Coughlan private papers.

Fitzgerald, David. *Harry Boland's Irish Revolution*. Cork: Cork University Press, 2003.

Foster, Roy. *Vivid Faces: The Revolutionary Generation in Ireland 1890–1923*. London: Allen Lane, 2014.

Jacob, Rosamond. 'Letter'. *Irish Press* 29 Jan. 1934: 6.

'James Connolly at Constance Markievicz's residence'. Irish War of Independence Figures: Liam Mellows. Irish Volunteers Commemorative Organization. 7 Apr. 2012.

Lydon Hegarty, Deirdre. Personal interview. 19 May 2015.

Matthews, Ann. *Dissidents: Irish Republican Women: 1923–1941*. Cork: Mercier Press, 2012.

—. *Renegades: Irish Republican Women: 1900–1922*. Cork: Mercier Press, 2010.

McAuliffe, Mary. 'Centenary year of the formation of Cumann na mBan memorial speech – Glasnevin Cemetery'. Decade of Centenaries. 2 Apr. 2014.

McCarthy, Cal. *Cumann na mBan and the Irish Revolution*, second edn. Cork: Collins Press, 2007.

McCoole, Sinéad. *No Ordinary Women: Irish Female Activists in the Revolutionary Years, 1920–1923*. Dublin: O'Brien Press, 2003.

McDiarmid, Lucy. *At Home in the Revolution: What Women Said and Did in 1916*. Dublin: Royal Irish Academy, 2015.

McQuaile, Colm. Personal interview. 6 Jan. 2013.

—. Personal interview. 11 Oct. 2014.

Meaney, Gerardine. 'Identity and opposition: women's writing, 1890–1960'. *The Field Day Anthology of Irish Writing: Irish Women's Writing and Traditions*, vol. 5. Cork: Cork University Press, 2002. 976–80.

O'Connor, John. *The 1916 Proclamation*. Dublin: Anvil, 1999.

O'Driscoll, Garrett. 'A Flippant Young Man'. *Green and Gold Magazine* 2:8 (Sept. –Nov. 1922): 167–76.

—. 'Lavender in God's Garden'. *Catholic World* 134 (Feb. 1932): 676–82.

—. *Noreen*. London: George Roberts, 1929.

—. 'The Lacklander'. *Green and Gold Magazine* 5:18 (Mar. – May 1925): 1–11.

—. 'Those of the lost battalion'. *Irish Press* 2 July 1934: 8.

—. 'A Ballad of Twenty-Two'. Unpublished poem *n.d.* Aileen Coughlan private papers.

Reynolds, Paige. *Modernism, Drama, and the Audience for Irish Spectacle*. Cambridge: Cambridge University Press, 2007.

Rich, Adrienne. *Diving into the Wreck: Poems 1971–72*. New York: Norton, 1973.

Rouse, Paul. *Sport and Ireland: A History*. Oxford: Oxford University Press, 2015.

'Tailteann literary awards: Irish plays at the Abbey: distinguished visitors present'. *Irish Times* 9 Aug. 1924: 7.

'A Tailteann prize novel'. *Irish Independent* 6 Jan. 1930: 4.

'The voice of the church: a word to women who foment strife'. *Freemans Journal* 12 Feb. 1923: 5.

Walsh, J. J. *Recollections of a Rebel*. Tralee: Kerryman Ltd., 1944.

Ward, Margaret. *Unmanageable Revolutionaries: Women and Irish Nationalism*. Dingle: Bandon, 1983.

'Wreck of Dublin steamer: Drogheda captain lost'. *Drogheda Argus* 8 Apr. 1922.

10

Writing the Rising

Lia Mills on *Fallen* (2014)

I used to love the story of the Easter Rising. Growing up, I had a romantic notion of it that sat comfortably with the soft-focus nationalism that – in fairness to my younger self – was fed to us pretty relentlessly every step of the way through our formative years in the Ireland I grew up in. The mythology of Irish nationalism is thrilling – rebellion, dissent, fiery speeches delivered across the open mouths of graves or from the dock. The story of the Rising, in particular, has the makings of good fiction: characters who seem larger than life; loyalty and betrayal, courage and danger; the highest of high stakes; impossible odds; crushing defeat turned to triumph in the end. In the convent schools I went to we were particularly primed to respond to the notion of sacrifice and here was that same principle transferred to politics – but I was too far gone on the language and imagery of both to notice the overlap.

The one detail that jarred with me, even then, was the received notion that Dubliners were hostile to our heroes when they were rounded up after the surrender and taken off to jail. After all, Dublin is where the main action of the Rising happened. Dublin paid the price, and there's is posterity, giving out because some Dubliners – but by no means all – were angry.

So far as I knew, none of my relatives had any direct connection with the Rising – although I do come from the kind of family where total strangers turn out to be first cousins, and solitary (so far as we believed) ancestors are later revealed to have had a clatter of siblings, half-siblings and step-siblings we just did not know about. My parents were of that 'whatever you say, say nothing' generation.

But one day, sitting in my car at the bottom of Dominick Street (in Dublin) waiting for the lights to change, I realised that I was looking more or less directly at the place where my mother was born – over the shop on Parnell

Street – in a rotten building, demolished long ago to make way for the Ilac Centre. It seemed to me that the shopfronts, apartments, fast food joints and hotels around me sank into the pavement while the walls of an older city – crumbling, sooty and rotting at the seams – rose to reclaim their rightful place.

The lights changed. I drove away, but the atmosphere of that older street stayed with me. Something profound in my sense of who I was had changed. There were personal reasons for that which are irrelevant here; what matters in relation to *Fallen* is that I suddenly understood that my family had everything to do with the Rising, because they lived through it. My mother was a toddler there, in the middle of the looting and the fires, with the British army camped outside the door, martial law, food shortages. What's more, my father was within three months of being born, over on Merrion Row. If you draw a rough circle around the area of most intense fighting during the Rising, they were each living on the circumference of that circle, enclosing an area of roughly four square miles. It must have been terrifying. For the first time, I wondered what that might have been like.

The question stayed with me until I reached a point where I knew I would have to write my way through to an answer. I knew something about the literary, cultural and social history of the time because back in the last century I had a teaching and research fellowship at University College Dublin and my research project was to rediscover forgotten Irish women writers (1885–1915). I had unfinished business with those women, a PhD I had walked away from. Many of the writers I had studied and read, thought about and written about, were cultural and/or political activists. I thought the main character in the novel I wanted to write would be such a woman: dynamic, intelligent, committed and in-the-know. It was an exciting time in Ireland – on the brink of change, opening to a future that was full of possibility. Women were winning the right to a university education and would soon win the right to vote; pride in a specifically Irish culture was manifest in a thriving arts scene and in small, home-grown industries; public and private arguments about nationhood and our future relations with Britain were lively, fraught, often ugly – but Ireland was at least a place where ideas of citizenship and the ideals of a genuine republic were being formed and discussed, and the concept of equality was at the heart of it.

What I knew of the Rising suggested a perfect structure for a novel, starting on Easter Sunday 1916 and ending the following Sunday. It seemed to come from a child's primer on plotting: normal world, disruption, escalation, complication, annihilation, a new world emerging from the ruins of the old. I began my research by reading contemporaneous accounts of the Rising and later historical accounts, along with the memoirs of some participants and witnesses.

Here's an irony: I came to women's studies with the zeal and elation of discovery. Of course there were women writers in Ireland for as long as there had been writing in Ireland – why wouldn't there be? Of course there were women activists and thinkers and campaigners for this issue and that – why wouldn't there be? It was all there to be rediscovered, excavated and told. But the magnetic/centripetal force of the Rising narrative as it came down to us was so strong that it seemed to draw all those other stories into it, to bend their shapes to its overwhelming energy. Everything was shaped, coloured and lit by its relation to a nationalist agenda, an agenda that blinkered me even as I was looking at previously forgotten participants in our national drama. That atmosphere was so pervasive that it choked the story I tried to tell from the outset. I had fallen, yet again, for a dominant, nation-directed narrative. I had allowed it to obscure the complexities of a real and multi-dimensional world, failed to notice the erasures and silences between the lines.

I didn't understand what was wrong, at first. I couldn't find the sweet spot that would let me in to the imaginative space a novel-in-progress needs to occupy. I could make shapes on the edge of the story all I liked but every word that came out of my characters' mouths was wooden and second-hand and politically correct, as though lifted from some pamphlet or other. My characters were not characters at all but cardboard cut-outs, like the paper dolls Alanna plays with in the novel. It was a nightmare. Every time I told someone I was writing a novel about the Rising it felt like a lie.

A residency in the Centre Culturel Irlandais in Paris changed everything. I arrived near the end of August, a day or two after the anniversary of the liberation of Paris in 1944. Everywhere I went, literally everywhere, on street corners and city walls as well as on monuments, there were plaques and fresh flowers commemorating *x*, who was executed here, *y* who was lifted there, or *z* battle. Traces of Europe's wars were visible everywhere on the continent, but in the Ireland of 2009, instead of remembrance we had a willed and collective amnesia. The irony was that in our rush to establish ourselves as a plucky, defiant and ultimately successfully *rebellious* nation, we had committed the most pro-establishment and conformist of crimes: we had accepted the official version of events without question or challenge. Without asking whose interests that version might serve.

I had brought a recently acquired copy of Tom and Mary Kettle's *The Ways of War*[2] with me. The coincidence of reading Mary Sheehy Kettle's introductory essay there, in Paris, surrounded by reminders of war, was extraordinary. Every raw, angry, grief-stricken word was a revelation. She opened an entire alternative Irish universe in my mind and brought it vividly to life: outward looking, progressive, optimistic (possibly naive) with a passionate commitment to parliamentary democracy, the world of constitutional nationalism that Tom Kettle represented before he became something of a poster boy for the British army, going around the country exhorting patriotic Irishmen to join up and fight. Mary Kettle believed that time would vindicate her husband, but it is painfully clear from her account that he knew better.

In the *médiathèque* of the CCI I went on to read about the Great War, and the part that Irish soldiers played in it, what happened to them during and after it. Reading their stories – those who went because soldiering was the only way they could feed their starving families and those who sincerely believed that fighting would help to bring about Irish independence – I felt angry on their behalf. After the Rising – you could even say because of it – they were betrayed by absolutely everyone: the army they fought in, the British government, our own eventual government. After a few years they became one more uncomfortable truth that could not be talked about.

I spent time hanging out in graveyards reading memorials and thinking about those forgotten soldiers.[3] Every second museum I visited in Paris revealed new aspects of the Great War, the appalling extent of our wilful amnesia, in Ireland; the depth of our (public) silence and how smoothly and comprehensively our national creation myth had obscured the possibility of any other reading.

I only came to understand what my problem had been as I began to solve it. The women I had studied back in the last century are not fictions. They resisted my attempt to fictionalise them, other than in passing reference or in casual walk-on parts such as the appearance of Mary Hayden close to the beginning of the novel. Katie, the main character in *Fallen*, is something of a hybrid. She has an undergraduate education but is still limited by the expectations of her family's class and politics. She is clued-in enough to know who the various factions are but not enough to expect the Rising when it begins. (Few people were, including many who fought in it.) Like her brother Liam (and like Tom Kettle, who taught Liam economics) she is a constitutional nationalist but unlike them she does not agree with the war, or that Liam should join the British army to fight in it. She is the kind of character who, in other circumstances, might well have found her way inside a garrison to stand with the rebels but Liam's death entangles her loyalties and makes that impossible.

Maybe, too, I had needed to get out of Ireland to break the deadlock in my mind. In Paris I began to think about the Rising in a wider European context, both the international influences that motivated some of the participants and the effect of perceptions of the Rising on the later experience of Irish soldiers. After Paris, I went to the Imperial War Museum in London to read those soldiers' letters, among other things. Later, Vera Brittain's extraordinary letters and memoir, followed by the memoirs of other participants, yielded more understanding of the tragic waste and futility of war.

Along with the anger that began in the CCI, I felt shame – for having been so compliant in the erasure of those other stories, the silence that largely, in 2009, surrounded the experience of Irish soldiers[4] – and, yes, a kind of grief that spilled over into the narrative. I gave that grief to Katie instead of the knowing, politically right-on position I had assigned to her in earlier drafts.

I was shocked when I learned the extent of the violence of the Rising – the damage to the city, the number of casualties. At a recent count[5] 485 people were killed, almost 1,500 were severely wounded and 100,000 people had to go on relief, having lost everything in the fires. If Dubliners were angry at the time – and there is evidence to show that many were in sympathy with and supported the insurgents – they had every right to be. The anger did not last long. Public sympathy swung around fast enough, with the executions. But I did wonder why people – politicians in particular – persisted in referring to the 16 men who were executed as though theirs were the only lives lost, when in fact more citizens of Dublin were killed than rebels, soldiers and police put together. I wondered why I never heard a word about the number of citizens of Dublin city who risked their own lives to help total strangers who were stranded or injured. When we were taught about the Rising in school, it was all about the rights and wrongs of it, whether you were for or against, right or wrong; whether you won or lost. There was praise and there was blame, but no suggestion that there were other choices to be made.

The most basic research uncovered the facts of the Rising. They challenged any tendency to view it as an uncontested and marvellous event that led unerringly to (partial) independence. They certainly dispelled any lingering whiff of romance. They were never exactly lied about or covered up – they didn't need to be. It was a literal case of 'don't mention the war'. And that shocked me too. How gullible and uncritical I had been in this instance, where I had no problem challenging and opposing other aspects of our national ideologies and hierarchies – the Rising turned out to have occupied a sort of blind spot in my psyche.

The only thing I could honestly do, then, was to try to set aside all my previous notions of the period and go into my novel blind, using the question the city itself had seeded in me as a guide: what would it be like to live through that violent week, if you did not know who was behind it, what was happening, how long it would go on or what would happen next? I knew there were many very brilliant and fascinating women alive and working in various fields at the time. I knew they had participated in the Rising, but I left them to history. They knew too much. Maybe I knew too much about them, too, and that's what got in my way. To write one of them at that time would have felt like writing-by-numbers, or to an agenda. As Sam Goldwyn once said, 'If you have a message, send a telegram.'

I'd be lying if I said I didn't have moments of unease about all this, but I was used to that unease. Every book I have written has caused me to wonder if perhaps, this time, I will really have to leave the country, for one reason or another. So much so that it has almost become my measure of whether a piece of writing is becoming a book – as *Fallen* did, against the odds and against all my own blindnesses, assumptions and preconceptions.

Notes

1   Parts of this introduction have been adapted from a piece first published in the *Irish Times* (online) 5 June 2014. Available at: irishtimes.com/culture/books/the-story-behind-fallen-my-take-on-the-rising-1.1818865 (Accessed 13 Nov. 2015).

2   Published posthumously in 1917. Tom Kettle was killed at the Somme on 9 September 1916, four months after the murder of his brother-in-law Francis Sheehy-Skeffington by a British officer during the Rising and the execution of his friend and former colleague Tom McDonagh, one of the signatories of the Proclamation of Independence.

3   I am indebted to Gail Ritchie, fellow resident at the CCI, who shared a lot of those graveyard walks and conversations.

4   Notable exceptions are Frank McGuinness's play *Behold the Sons of Ulster, Marching towards the Somme* and Sebastian Barry's novel *A Long, Long Way.*

5   '1916 necrology 485' Glasnevin Trust. Available at: glasnevintrust.ie/visit-glasnevin/news/1916-list/ (Accessed 13 Nov. 2015). I had previously put this number at 447.

11

Extract from *Fallen*

THURSDAY 27 APRIL 1916

Katie has met a woman called Vivienne at the Royal City of Dublin Hospital, Baggot Street. Up from the country for the Spring Show, Vivienne has volunteered her car as a makeshift ambulance but she doesn't know her way around the city. Katie goes with her as a guide.

When we'd unloaded our cargo of woman and boxes at the back door of the hospital, Vivienne asked me to direct her to Butt Bridge, where there was a clearing station. I wondered what time it was, but all the clocks we passed had stopped. The light was fading, but whether it was night falling or the pall of smoke dragging a premature blanket up over the city, I couldn't say. There was a lot of military traffic. Vivienne's painted red crosses got us by.

'I'm going out to France myself,' Vivienne was saying. 'With the ambulance corps. I'm due to leave next week.' She slowed for a last turn. We both said *Oh!* at the same time. In front of us, on the far side of the river – my side of the river – the city was ablaze.

The flames made a weird kind of light, bright and dark at once. A horde of fiery ghosts, thousands of slaughtered soldiers from the Front, come home to vent their fury. They thrashed their limbs about, struggled with the window-frames, strained to break free, fell back and shoved fiery fists across the streets to rattle the roofs with flaming fingers, their breath black with rage. The river was oily and orange, its surface a canvas of wavering, hot colours. My throat burned. My skin and eyes were dry, inflammable as paper.

We got permission at the checkpoint and drove along the quays to Butt Bridge. A gunboat was moored on the seaward side, towering over a barge. At the clearing station, people sat or lay on the pavement, waiting to be taken to hospital. A doctor moved among them, deciding who had most need and where best to send them. Eventually he came to inspect the back seat of Vivienne's car. He looked us over too. 'Can you handle this?' he asked, indicating a pallid man in a torn shirt who lay on a plank with his knees bent, a hand cupped over his right eye.

'What's wrong with him?'

'His eye. Move your hand, there, and show them.'

The man lifted his hand. A piece of metal jutted from his eye. There was a dark ooze running down his face. I felt sick.

'Can you take him to the Eye and Ear?'

Vivienne looked at me.

'Yes,' I said, meaning I knew where it was.

'He needs extreme care,' the doctor said. 'You'll have to drive slowly. And keep him calm.' Two privates lifted the plank and stowed the man across Vivienne's back seat. The plank snagged on the leather. It barely fit inside the width of the car.

Aside to us, the doctor said the man would likely lose the eye in any case. He said to keep him calm. I sat in beside Vivienne, but looked back over the seat at the man. Imagine losing an eye. Imagine being sighted one minute, blind the next.

Vivienne leaned over the steering wheel to see her way. A fraction of moon gave occasional light, shifting through cloud or smoke as we drove away from the checkpoint. I had to switch between telling her where to turn and talking any old rubbish to the groaning man. About the weather. About my daft brother running away with a theatre troupe like a 12-year-old following a circus. I quickly ran out of things to say.

The moon came and went, what there was of one, through drifts of cloud. We made our slow and careful way. No one shot at us. At Adelaide Road, our charge was carried off on his plank.

'Your seat's destroyed,' I said to Vivienne, but she didn't seem to care.

'Come on,' she said. 'There's more where he came from.'

It was easy to talk in the car, both of us looking out of the window at the road. Vivienne told me she had eight younger brothers and sisters, as well as two older brothers.

'Who'll mind your younger brothers and sisters when you're gone to France?'

She laughed. 'My older brothers have wives now. The farm is theirs, and all that goes with it. It's their turn. This is my chance, and I'm taking it.'

When we got back to the clearing station, we saw hundreds of people moving slowly through Beresford Place on the far side of the river. They emerged from a dense, reddish fog carrying bundles and bags and babies.

'Not that them poor souls ever had much,' a woman said, 'but what there was is gone up in flames. Them boys in the Post Office have a lot to answer for.'

A heavy rumbling, like a train loose on the road, made us look round. The most peculiar vehicle I'd ever seen approached the bridge. A vast metal cylinder was mounted longways on a lorry driven by a soldier. There were slits, like in a pillar box, cut into its sides. We watched it huff and grumble along. The engine strained under the weight, reminding me of the time Liam mistook a lorry for a shell and thought his time had come. 'What on earth—' I said.

Vivienne snorted. 'It's like some class of a siege engine, delivering boiling oil.'

When the strange vehicle had passed, we were directed to a place where we could stop the car. We reported our success with the eye man to the doctor in charge, who was less impressed than he might have been and assigned us to take three women and a man to Paddy Dun's. We installed them in the back of the car, with much wincing and adjustment of injured limbs, a wrist here, an elbow there, and set off again. One of the women had a shattered shoulder. Tears poured down her face with every jolt.

When we got to the hospital, one of the women shook my hand, declared that mine was cold and gave me her cardigan, saying, I'd have more need of it now she was going inside. 'And nothing, not hell nor high water, will get me out again before daylight.'

We made several more journeys that night. I told Vivienne about Liam, and about Eva. She told me she'd had a sweetheart but he was killed in training for the army. His unit was sent to mend a wall on a local estate and the wall fell on him and crushed him. It was pointless, she said. And that, as much as anything, had decided her on going out with the ambulance corps.

I wanted to say something about Hubie, but I was afraid that if I started to talk about him I wouldn't be able to stop. Instead I told her I might go to London to learn about antiques and fine art, come back to work in a shop.

'What's stopping you?'

'Good question.' I was an adult, after all. Thousands of people, millions, made their way through life alone. Why did I need my parents' approval?

Vivienne mistook my silence. 'Are you tired? I am. But let's keep going as long as we can.'

I'd stopped noticing corners and low-hanging railway bridges by then. Anyone could have shot at us, at any time, but no one did. Less was said as the night wore on. Less needed to be said. There was a fog in my mind that matched the smoky, acrid air. I lost track of time, but hours must have passed before the engine stuttered and we coasted to a stop on a side street off Great Brunswick Street.

'That's it,' Vivienne said. 'We've no more petrol.' Some soldiers pushed the car into a yard, said it could take its chances there for the night. They told us to go on up to Holles Street, where there was a waiting room set up for volunteers like us, with blankets on the floor for us to sleep on.

The waning moon took a knife to the sky, spilled a weird light through the smoky air as we made our way along. Was it my imagination that the walls of the houses we passed were warm, that they breathed sulphur? Ahead of us, at the mouth of a lane, were three soldiers. One of them had a corporal's chevrons on his sleeve. They were looking our way. A fox in a moonlit garden is one thing; in a kitchen seeking eggs it's another. I wished I'd Liam's coat to pull around me.

'Well,' the fat soldier drawled. 'Well, well. What have we here?'

Their eyes were hard and flat. I pulled myself up straight and tried to walk past, but he lowered his rifle and stopped me. Vivienne stood a little behind me. She was so small, almost like a child.

'Let us through.' I hated that my voice was uneven.

The fat soldier planted himself in front of me, so close the buttons of his uniform grazed the front of my dress, his face pushed towards mine. I could smell him. Sweat and the rotten breath of teeth unwashed for days, a stink of tobacco.

Cold stirred in a place so deep inside me I couldn't name it. Everything inside me slowed. I'd a sensation of creepy-crawlies tracking across my skin, through the fine hairs on my neck and down my goose-fleshed arms. This was my city. They'd no business here, telling me where I could or couldn't go.

Fatty bumped himself against me. 'Give me a fucken reason.' His voice slimed into my ear. 'Just one.'

Liam's voice bid me go easy, but words flooded out of me in a low torrent. 'My brother fought and died in your army. If he was here now, he'd soon sort you out. Have you nothing better to do than harass women on the streets?' The strangest thing happened then. I felt Liam leap to surround me, like a cloak, his hand at my mouth. *Say no more.*

The fat soldier bounced his bulk against me again, almost gently. 'And have your lot nothing better to do than stab us in the back?' He stood back and lifted his rifle to my breast. 'If this was a bayonet,' he growled. 'I'd rip your traitorous, bitching guts out and spread them for the dogs.'

I couldn't speak through Liam's restraining fingers, or the hammer of my heart.

'Steady, Phil.' The Corporal gripped his arm and pulled it back. The other soldier shouldered his rifle and slipped away, eyes averted. The Corporal spoke rapidly into Fatty's ear. 'Save your bullets for them that needs 'em.'

Fatty bristled and glared, but he lowered the gun.

'Come on.' The Corporal's voice was clipped. He stamped along beside us, a tense escort, leaving his horrible friend behind. When we reached the back door to the hospital, Vivienne thanked him. I said I'd go on back to Percy Place.

'There's a curfew,' the Corporal said.

'I have a permit.' I showed him the paper I'd taken from Con's car. While he scanned it, I told Vivienne she could come with me if she liked. I wasn't sorry when she said no, she couldn't walk another step, she'd stay in the waiting room. She said she'd keep me a spot, in case I was turned back.

The Corporal sighed. 'Considering what happened earlier,' he said, 'I'll walk with you.'

We didn't speak on the way.

There was a checkpoint at the bridge. Yesterday's slaughterhouse. No, it was past midnight, that carnage was two days ago. 'Let her pass,' the Corporal said.

'You live here?' the sentry asked. 'One of your neighbours got himself shot this afternoon. Watching. What do you all think this is, sport?'

A chill ran through me. 'Who? Which house?'

'Go on before I change my mind,' the Corporal said. 'Stay off the streets from now on, or you'll get what's coming.'

From *Fallen* by Lia Mills (Dublin & London: Penguin Ireland, 2014. 254–9).

Index